D0918524

RAHEEM "MEGA RAN" JARBO

DREAM MASTER
A MEMOIR

FROM THE STOOP TO THE STAGE TO THE STARS

authorHOUSE®

AuthorHouse™
1663 Liberty Drive
Bloomington, IN 47403
www.authorhouse.com
Phone: 833-262-8899

© 2021 Raheem "Mega Ran" Jarbo. All rights reserved.

No part of this book may be reproduced, stored in a retrieval system, or transmitted by any means without the written permission of the author.

Published by AuthorHouse 12/11/2020

ISBN: 978-1-6655-0995-4 (sc)
ISBN: 978-1-6655-0993-0 (hc)
ISBN: 978-1-6655-0994-7 (e)

Library of Congress Control Number: 2020924097

Print information available on the last page.

Any people depicted in stock imagery provided by Getty Images are models, and such images are being used for illustrative purposes only. Certain stock imagery © Getty Images.

This book is printed on acid-free paper.

Because of the dynamic nature of the Internet, any web addresses or links contained in this book may have changed since publication and may no longer be valid. The views expressed in this work are solely those of the author and do not necessarily reflect the views of the publisher, and the publisher hereby disclaims any responsibility for them.

THIS BOOK IS DEDICATED TO EVERYONE WHO EVER PUSHED ME TO BE BETTER THAN I EVER THOUGHT I COULD BE. MY MOTHER, DORIS. MY DAD, EDWARD (RIP). MY WIFE, RACHEL. MY BABYSITTERS, MS. GERTRUDE (RIP). MS. EVELYN (RIP). MY KINDERGARTEN TEACHER, MS. GREENWALD. MY 4TH GRADE TEACHER, MRS. GRAHAM. MY 6TH GRADE TEACHER, MRS. SMITH. MY ALGEBRA TEACHER, MR. HARMON. MY 7TH GRADE ENGLISH TEACHER, MR. Z. MY HIGH SCHOOL ENGLISH TEACHER, MRS. DIXON. MY FRIENDS, PRODUCERS, COLLABORATORS, TOURMATES, MENTORS, AND ANYONE WHOEVER TRUSTED ME.

EVERYONE ON THE 6500 BLOCK OF WOODSTOCK STREET. DR. SAM RICHARDS. ALL OF THE GAMES, MUSIC AND EXPERIENCES THAT HAVE HELPED TO SHAPE ME.

TO MY FRIENDS, MY FAMILY, AND EVERY SUPPORTER IN EVERY CITY ALL OVER THE WORLD. THANK YOU ALL, SO MUCH. I HOPE YOU ARE ENTERTAINED AND ENLIGHTENED BY THESE WORDS... AND MOST IMPORTANTLY, I HOPE THIS BOOK EMPOWERS YOU TO TELL YOUR OWN STORY.

PUSH

I was the man of the house at 12
Contemplating ways to make it up out this hell
Survive and maybe write a book all about the tale
Cause momma said with just a smidgen of doubt, you fail
So since then I hit the block with no ounce to sell
Cause I knew she wasn't bailing me out the jail
If i got caught, so I fought for the heart
To take part in an art that would likely
Tear my soul apart, so
Call me conscious cause I don't spit nonsense
I just give em options, diversify the topics
Knock it if you must, you wouldn't be the first one
I'm certain, got thick skin so it don't hurt none
If I was cursing and blurting stupidity
It'd only make the situation worsen
My people are thirsting, while demons are lurking
It's bout time somebody pulled back the curtain
So I gotta

Push, like a mother giving birth when it hurts, gotta
Push when the scene look the worst I'm the first one to
Push for Dr. King and Push for Malcolm
Push the powers that be and change the outcome
Push like a mother giving birth when it hurts, gotta
Push when the scene looks the worst, I'm the first one to
Push for Peltier; push for Lumuumba
Push for the babies. Push for the future.

MEGA RAN'S MUSIC CATALOG REFERENCED IN THIS BOOK

- *THE CALL* (2006, RAHM NATION RECORDINGS)
- *MEGA RAN* (2007, NO LABEL)
- *THE 8TH DAY* (2008, NO LABEL)
- *MEGA RAN 9* (2009, RANDOMBEATS MUSIC)
- *FOREVER FAMICOM* (2010, NEOSONIC PRODUCTIONS)
- *BLACK MATERIA* (2011, RANDOMBEATS MUSIC)
- *MEGA RAN 10* (2011, RANDOMBEATS MUSIC)
- *LANGUAGE ARTS (VOL. 1-3)* (2012, RANDOMBEATS MUSIC)
- *CASTLEVANIA: THE NOCTURNAL CANTATA* (2013, RANDOMBEATS MUSIC)
- *BLUR BOMBER* (2013, RANDOMBEATS MUSIC)
- *THE CALL: 8 BIT ANNIVERSARY EDITION* (2014, RANDOMBEATS MUSIC)
- *SOUL VEGGIES* (2015, BRICK RECORDS)
- *EMERALD KNIGHTS* (2015 RANDOMBEATS/RESPECT THE UNDERGROUND)
- *RNDM* (2015, RANDOMBEATS MUSIC)
- *EXTRA CREDIT* (2017 RANDOMBEATS MUSIC)
- *EMERALD KNIGHTS 2* (2018 RANDOMBEATS/RESPECT THE UNDERGROUND)
- *THE VISITOR* (2018, SOULSPAZM RECORDS)
- *AGES, VOL. 1* (2019, RANDOMBEATS MUSIC)
- *2 HANDS UP* (2020, NEASTRA MUSIC)

FOREWORD

We ain't givin' up,
'Cause we ain't get enough,
So, go on get 'em up.
Don't look down.

—"Lookin Up," *Mega Ran 10* (2012)

Hello! It's your boy, Austin Creed; you may know me as Xavier Woods, ⅓ of the New Day, a gamer, a WWE Superstar, and a lover of fine things. You're about to read a book about one of the most talented humans ever to walk this earth. He is someone that I am lucky to call a friend. He is not afraid to chase his dreams. And most importantly, he is someone who can make you want to do the same.

When I met Raheem, I feel like I forced him to be my friend. That sounds ridiculous but I knew that he loved what I loved, and that if we met, I knew we'd hit it off. One day, I was searching the WWE database for theme music to use. At one point I came across his song "Lookin' Up." The lyrics hit me:

But eventually, I decided to be true to me,
Probably the best decision that I had ever made.
Now every September 3 is like July 4.
We up in magazines, we headline tours.
I never could've dreamt this back in '94.
Got here in five years, just imagine five more.

It was bright, it was smart, it was motivational. On top of that, the beat slapped. I couldn't stop listening to it, so I looked around on the internet to see if he had any other songs. What I found blew my mind. I found albums performed by a man who was living the same struggle as me.

Living life as a Black nerd and being able to put those feelings to a beat eloquently was so impressive to me. So much of hip-hop was about cars, money, women, etc., and I felt a disconnect. I liked listening to it, but I never thought hip-hop would be relatable to me, subject-matter wise. This was different. Mega Ran was different. Raheem had been through all the same things that I had. Going to school and being expected to be a certain way because of the color of your skin was something that we shared. That's why his music spoke to me. I had never experienced anything like that before. So, I somehow creepily found his booking email and shot him a message asking if I could use one of his songs as my theme music.

Working as an indie wrestler can be tough. I've bounced around to several different promotions, wrestling for ten people to wrestling for one hundred thousand. I've heard every empty promise, every bold-faced lie and had been "on the verge" of "making it big" more times than I can count. In my journey, I learned that being an entertainer is the same, no matter where you go. From wrestlers to actors to singers, we have all experienced the same bumps and bruises along the way. That's what drew me to Raheem.

I pushed and pushed to create something out of nothing, and it worked better than I ever could have imagined it with The New Day. Raheem has done the same in his transformation into Mega Ran. Taking the road less traveled. Sticking to your guns. Betting on yourself and your ability. No matter what the world threw at Mega Ran, he threw it right back. Harder, faster, and stronger... just like the Mega Man character he got his name and inspiration from. I came for the music but stayed for the story and motivation.

From there, I just badgered him through emails and texts, then later hanging out at show, into being my friend. Since then, I've seen him bounce around the world on international tours making his presence known. I've seen Mega Ran make you feel good about yourself and makes you want to be even better than you currently are. Going and seeing him perform live is truly an experience. I've never seen a musician who has such a real connection with his fans. Everyone in the crowd knows what it's like to feel how he describes feeling in his songs. It's an amazing thing to see.

Congratulations on obtaining this book.

Enjoy the wild ride on which you are about to embark.
Keep It Tight.

Austin Creed, aka Xavier Woods

Austin is a WWE Superstar, YouTube host and member of the team "The New Day," nine-time WWE Tag Team Champions and holder of the WWE record for longest tag team title reign at 483 days.

PROLOGUE

It is a peculiar sensation, this double-consciousness, this sense of always looking at one's self through the eyes of others. One ever feels his twoness-an American, a Negro; two souls, two thoughts, two unreconciled strivings; two warring ideals in one dark body, whose dogged strength alone keeps it from being torn asunder.

—W.E.B. Du Bois, *The Souls of Black Folk* (1903)

Philadelphia, PA, December 18, 1996

My middle school teacher, my high school teachers, my college advisor, and my mother told me that as a Black man I'd have to work harder, smarter, and be better than my White counterparts to make it in this world. I never wanted to believe it, but the past forty years have proved to me they were most certainly correct.

There's an invisible competition in the heads of most marginalized people in this country... we all feel it. It's like everyone lines up on the starting block of a big race, but our legs are tied together by rope, while the other runners have jetpacks strapped to their backs. While obviously not true in reality, it sure feels that way at times. We have to tell ourselves this while visualizing the struggle – it's the carrot that motivates us to be better than our perceived best. Everyone has obstacles that can hold them back from greatness – it's what you do when facing those obstacles that shows what you're truly made of. The true legends turn tragedy into triumph.

Pleasing God. Pleasing parents. Pleasing the world. In that holy trinity of life goals, pleasing one's self isn't afforded much room. Though

I had a hard time focusing when younger, high on my list of priorities was being the best person I could for my mother, who worked her hardest to keep me on the straight and narrow, and getting a well-paying job that could help support myself and a family. But somewhere along this path, music entered my life and really managed to complicate things even further.

Halfway through my second year of college I still didn't have a clue what I wanted to do for a living. I was in the midst of changing majors for the second of three times: from pre-dentistry to journalism, then later to African-American Studies and English. After squeaking by my first semester with C's, I anticipated time at home with friends and family. My best friend Chuck, later known as JonBap, and I watched wrestling tapes, played video games, and wrote rap songs during the winter vacation.

I brought my Sega Genesis home for break. I jammed and slammed all over Chuck in *NBA Live '97*, and then switched gears to writing hip-hop songs. We named our rap group Double Impact, based on the ridiculous Jean-Claude Van Damme movie of the same name. One memorable night, things flowed so well with our exercises in rhyme that we wrote three new songs. We stayed awake well past midnight listening to new music by 2Pac, Mobb Deep, and other favorite hip-hop artists.

Things were perfect.

Earlier that night, my uncle, Bobby Lee Durham, stopped by our house and asked if I wanted to ride with him down South. Now, down South for us was Rock Hill, South Carolina, where all my family was born and raised. Uncle Bobby was my favorite uncle, and he had a signature style all his own, defined by his hearty laugh, million-dollar smile, the Jheri curl he rocked as long as I could remember, and the smelly cigars he puffed on that billowed smoke like an overworked steam engine. Uncle Bobby lived out in the sticks, and didn't come by often, so I cherished every moment we had together.

Every year during the holidays, we took a trip to Rock Hill and spent time with the family; that year was no different. Uncle Bobby loved Cadillac's, and that year's trip to South Carolina was the perfect time to road test his brand new, shiny 1996 Seville. I would never have imagined passing up an opportunity to ride with my favorite uncle in a brand-new car to a much warmer South Carolina.

Yet, to my surprise, I heard myself say, "No thanks, Unc'. I'm gonna stay here."

My reply stunned Mom and Uncle Bobby, who asked again if I wanted to go.

"Naw, I'm good," I said. "Thanks, though."

The inspiration was flowing. I told myself that I'd see him when he got back.

Uncle Bobby exhaled a cloud of cigar smoke (in the house, which Mom hated), shrugged, and said, "All right, see ya later. Be good."

Chuck and I resumed our hip-hop sessions while Uncle Bobby, my Aunt Liz, and my cousin Adrienne hopped in the Caddy and rode off to Rock Hill for Christmas fun, time with family, and food. Uncle Bobby had worked as a trucker for Consolidated Freightways for over twenty years, so he'd meandered up and down every road of the United States more times than he could count. We used to joke that he could make that trip with his eyes closed, so I felt he didn't need an extra driver – a convincing argument for staying home in what was one of my most productive vacations ever. Chuck and I were in the zone, writing Double Impact rap songs until the wee hours of the morning.

Around 3 a.m. the next morning, a panicked banging on my door woke me, and I knew something was wrong. The culprit was my older cousin Vince, who as far as I could recall, had never come to our home before. Vince wasn't Uncle Bobby's son, but he lived closest to the city so we were the first family members he could reach. Mom was at work, so I had to endure hearing the worst news imaginable for a nineteen-year-old while alone.

"Hey, Ra.... Um…. Uncle Bobby got shot.... He's gone... he's gone, cuz."

Vince proceeded to weave the dark tale while I listened in rapt disbelief. On his way back to Philly, Uncle Bobby had stopped at an unassuming rest stop in Dale City, Virginia around midnight. Uncle Bobby made his way to the men's room alone. Then, three gunshots shattered the still night air. Aunt Liz and Adrienne saw two males running to their cars. They traced the men's path back to a disgusting bathroom stall to find my favorite uncle bleeding to death, robbed of one hundred and fifty dollars. He had defensive gunshot wounds to his head, chest, and hands. My aunt and cousin witnessed his last breath and then drove his Cadillac back to Philly, weeping into the night's wind.

Uncle Bobby was gone.

The three gunmen, Andre V. Carter, Michael T. Baggett, and Khalif Rodriguez, were kids my age. To this day, I can't understand the reason they gave for the murder of my uncle. They weren't broke, and they weren't desperate – they were from typical, middle-class families. Their ages weren't the only things we had in common. The three boys were also aspiring rap artists. However, whereas Chuck and I just listened to the gritty street opera of Mobb Deep or 2Pac lyrics, those kids dreamed of living them.

Andre, Michael, and Khalif were convinced that the only way to make it in the rap game was to appear "real". They thought the only way to get a reputation was to do real things. They believed if you rapped about drugs, guns, and women, then you had to live that life. In their eyes, the worst thing you could ever be called was fake. While other f-words are usually fair game in hip-hop, this f-word is what every rap artist desperately strives to avoid.

The boys thought that to appear real they had "to catch a body" as their seven-page testimony read. It didn't matter who, it didn't matter when, and it didn't matter why. They had to shoot someone in cold blood and live to write a rap about it. That's what hip-hop was to them – Real and Cold. So, when Andre, Michael, and Khalif trailed Uncle Bobby down I-95, it wasn't personal in their eyes. It was just business. Uncle Bobby's murder was another sad case of someone being in the "wrong place at the wrong time."

Vince accepted the unenviable task of driving all over Philadelphia at 3 a.m. to break the news of Uncle Bobby's tragic death to each family member. He left ten minutes after his staccato hammering at the door. I was home alone, attempting to process the worst thing I'd encountered in my young life.

As a nineteen-year-old college student whose mind was usually only on my next meal or next party, I went through every emotion imaginable. I felt hurt, sadness, and then overwhelming guilt. The first two passed, but the monstrous guilt I felt for not accompanying Uncle Bobby that night never left. It still hasn't.

I should have been there, I thought. That truth ricocheted in my head as I tossed and turned in bed, crying through the night. I replayed a fictional series of events in my head. In each, I walked to the men's stalls with my uncle that fateful night, and they always played out three different ways.

FLASH The gunmen saw Uncle Bobby and me enter the restroom, but moved on.

FLASH The gunmen enter the restroom, and we take them down, *Rush Hour* style.

FLASH The gunmen shoot Uncle Bobby then turn and shoot me. We both die.

Because I regretted joining him on the trip, of all these scenes, the one with my death is the one I revisit most.

Michael and Khalif both conspired against and told on Andre under oath, who they claimed was so proud of his actions that he'd put that night's events in a rap song. The deadpan lyrics offered in eulogy to my uncle by his killer read:

> Three to your head,
> *Bang bang bang*, he's dead.

On top of being a heartless, cold-blooded killer, Andre really needed to step up his rap game.

As angry, hurt, and sad as I was, I realized those kids had only performed what they thought was expected of them, based on the lives they saw depicted on camera, heard on cassette, or experienced in life. I started thinking that as pretentious and corny as it sounded, artists, especially established ones, have a huge responsibility when they get behind that microphone and must understand the true power of words. As rappers, we speak to an audience who may not be getting "proper home training," as Mom succinctly puts it. The Bible even states, "Death and life are in the power of the tongue."

But music is only half the story. Tupac Shakur may have been known as a thug or a rapper, but before that, he was a poet. He attended the best performing arts school in Baltimore and achieved high marks. The late Albert Johnson, known as "Prodigy" of the rap group Mobb Deep, is the great-great-grandson of the founder of Morehouse College, one of the oldest Historically Black Colleges in US history. Neither of these gentlemen have mentioned those facts in their bodies of work.

KRS One said, "All I really have is hip-hop, and a Glock / The results are obvious if I'm confined to my block." That sounded like Andre, Michael, and Khalif to a tee. I didn't know them at all, but I could guess what their home life looked like. I could picture their surroundings. And they didn't look very different from mine. What was the difference? What sent me off to college and them to jail?

Jack Nicholson's character in *The Departed* said, "I don't want to be a product of my environment. I want my environment to be a product of me." That line stuck with me big time. Just because I grew up among violence, drugs, and drama didn't mean that had to be my life. I recognized that I had the power to write a different story.

In *The Souls of Black Folk* DuBois cites the example of the Black artisan as, conflicted between producing goods and art that reflect the unique perspective and life experience, and goods that are marketable and acceptable to a broader population they are engaged in a battle of double aims. Music is a product. By working to create what is the best expression of himself, he will be deemed unsuccessful, and by creating what makes him successful he fails to express himself and, in some ways, may appear to be rejecting his true self. Musicians want to give you the real, but Black people are often afraid of revealing their entire self to the audience for fear of judgment. Therefore, we repress. We cover up. We close off sections of our life or personality that may be considered "too Black." We let people touch our hair. We change our tone and accent. We shrug off racist remarks. We smile when we don't feel like smiling."

I wish I could blame Uncle Bobby's murder for my lack of focus in college and the tough time I had in academia, but the truth is that I was already on a rocky path before I got the news. Freedom had turned this once phenomenal student into a lazy bum. Shaken, I had to somehow return to campus a week later and continue my journey.

Uncle Bobby's death motivated me to take everything more seriously, from school to music, and I entered the next semester recharged and refocused. I didn't pull a 4.0 GPA, and I didn't attain instant stardom, but I'd say the next twelve years were extremely transformative.

Welcome to the world of Raheem Jameel Jarbo, also known as Random, and later known as Mega Ran. Dream Master. Hey Hey, Alright.

CHAPTER ONE

LATCHKEY

You better come straight home,
Anybody knocks on the door, just say no,
Keep the living room straight and don't touch that stove,
And don't let anybody tell you we broke.

—"Latchkey," *Ages, Vol. 1* (2019)

I CALL THIS BOOK "DREAM MASTER" in reference to two seminal pieces of pop culture media that were influential to my upbringing. First, "A Nightmare on Elm Street 4: The Dream Master" which was released in 1988. I don't know much about this movie, except that it was on the TV during a sleepover at my cousin David's house, and he let me watch it despite my mother's strict instructions not to. I stayed up all night after, and never watched another horror movie. Freddy Krueger, the antagonist of the film, haunts teenagers as they sleep, attacking them in their dreams fueled by their fear. Kristen, the lead character, is able to manipulate the items, places and even people that appear in her dreams, and uses this gift to defeat the evil Freddy... or so we thought. Though scared to death, I was intrigued with the idea that she had the power to control her own dreams. What would I dream about if I could control them?

Two years later, Capcom released a game for the Nintendo Entertainment System (NES) called "Little Nemo, The Dream Master." This cute but difficult platformer chronicled the adventures of a little boy who had the most outrageously vivid dreams. While Kristen's included a burnt-up dude with a striped sweater, Nemo's dreams were usually of far off, colorful lands with giant bees, bugs, and animals that Nemo could control after giving them candy. The game was alright, but it really rekindled my thoughts on the power of one's imagination. This is why I say that video games saved my life. More on that later.

Remember the show "Dream On?" For the one year that we had premium cable when I was growing up, the short-lived HBO series was my favorite thing on TV. In the show, Martin Tupper, a 30 something divorcee, spent so much time in front of the TV as a child that every moment of his adult life reminded him of an old black-and-white program. I'm like that with video games. I can connect every major moment of my life to a video game console and what I was playing on it at the time. It all began in 1983, with the Christmas gift of the millennium, the Atari 2600. Sure, I'd gotten a ton of G.I. Joes, He-Man, and Captain Power action figures, but that Atari got the most play that year. Pac-Man, Yars' Revenge, and Pitfall took up my entire life at that point. Games were there even when friends or my parents weren't.

Orcs and Men. Capulets and Montagues. 50 Cent and Ja Rule. Mom and Dad. Warring together, even though separated. Beefing until the end of time. And because of this, my family history is a cloudy, murky tale of lies, omission, and deception. I'm honestly too afraid to find out the whole story, for fear it may be worse than I expect.

I know a man named Eddie who is my father. However, we don't have the same last name. My mother doesn't even have her given name, yet as far as I know, she'd never been married. Confused yet? If so, it's okay. I've lived with that uncertainty as long as I can remember. I will probably need Henry Louis Gates or ancestry.com to help a brother out.

I've retrieved pieces of the story at different times from my mother, depending on her mood. My name, Raheem Jameel Jarbo, is Arabic. *Raheem* means compassionate, and *Jameel* means handsome. Great choices. As far as I know, my last name, Jarbo, is of African descent, though I've met some people in my travels with the name and they were European. From what I've gathered from bits and pieces of overheard conversations, the man who married my mother, Moses Jarbo, is from Liberia. When I searched for him online, I found a man who was the president of a liberation outfit in that country.

I'd also overheard that he was always traveling to Africa on missions for the Peace Corps. That's all I know. When I try to find out more, I get a headache. I've never met Moses, who I call my African Father. Even if he didn't raise me, I feel like he had a huge influence on who I am, or at least who I think I am. My name is a huge part of my identity, though it's been one I wasn't always proud of. Raheem Jameel Jarbo. What a mouthful. No one could pronounce it correctly, and they still can't. If I get called "Ryan" one more time… anyways.

My father Eddie, is a hard-working Black man with more sob stories than a season of *Iyanla: Fix My Life*. He and Mom met sometimes in 1973 in a bar in Philadelphia, most likely to a thumping disco beat coming out of the jukebox. They maintained a healthy relationship until one hiccup occurred: Me, born on September 3, 1977. They never got married, and their relationship ended not long after then, if not well before that.

Mom was determined to raise me on her own, with no help from a man she considered to be a reckless, egotistical drunk. I have no memories or photos of him holding me as a child. She ensured he was nowhere around during the most formative years of my life. I don't recall him being there, so that's true. The reason why is the only thing up for debate. I don't know if he chose to neglect me, or if my mother pushed him away, or there's a third side to the story that I'll never get. Regardless, I maintained my love for Pop, because it was easier than harboring hatred.

One time when I was about six, I was outdoors playing when my father happened to be in the neighborhood and decided to stop by the block to say hi to me. I was elated. Before then my father was sort of a myth. I brought him up in conversations when other kids talked about their dads to fit in, but they'd never seen him. My jubilation stopped suddenly when my mother cursed at him loudly, in front of everyone outside, and embarrassed him. She specifically told him to never visit, and so he listened. For a time.

He initially promised weekly visits, but Pop would come by every few months and pick me up from my after-school babysitter. We spent our time together shopping or eating out at a nice restaurant. He went out of his way to ensure that our day was infinitely better than an average day with mom.

But when I think about the moments we had, they always seemed to be in direct and blatant opposition to my mother's orders and requests. There's the time he bought me *Contra* for the Nintendo Entertainment System for Christmas in 1988. *Contra* was a game Mom had said I couldn't own because it was too violent. In 1993 he took me to the Mummers Parade when Mom had said going downtown was too dangerous. Then there was the time he gave me a beer when I was underage, which was also against Mom's wishes. I didn't realize it then, but he used our moments to challenge me and to ensure that we had the best day ever.

As I grew older, I began reaching out and attempting to strengthen our relationship. I would visit him once a week at his home, a tattered one-bedroom apartment in North Philly, above a vintage TV shop that somehow is still in business. On one visit, my dad told me that although he wished things had worked out with him and my mother, he didn't like how she tried to control him. She didn't want him going to bars even though they had met at a bar. He implied that my mother turned him away from his fatherly duties by being cold and mean to him. As was the case with my mother, I got small chunks of the story each time I hung out with him, which meant I was somewhere in the middle of her side, his side, and the truth.

Dad's tendency to break promises and make excuses led to an inconsistent and unsteady relationship. Nowadays we still chat occasionally, and I do appreciate him trying to maintain contact at this stage of my life despite what we've been through. As a kid I defended him to the death, whenever Mom slyly insulted him. "That sounds like something your old dumb daddy would've said," she'd mention whenever I said or did something that reminded her of him.

Although Mom and Pop didn't get along, I never saw violence in the home. I only recall seeing them disagree once in front of me. Of all things, it was about barbershops. My mother would take me to the barber college down the street for a free haircut from a student on

Tuesdays, and my father didn't think they did a good job. He wanted me to go to a "real" barbershop to properly absorb the culture and not look like they put a bowl over my head before they cut me. I didn't know what he meant, but I found out soon enough.

In the movie *Barbershop*, the old head Eddie, played by Cedric The Entertainer, describes the relationship between the African-American community and the barbershop better and more succinctly than I ever could when he says, "Is this a barbershop? I mean, if we can't talk straight in a barbershop, then where can we talk straight? The place where a Black man means something! Cornerstone of the neighborhood! Our own country club."

After Mom and Dad's disagreement, from about age ten and on, Mom would let me walk with friends from the neighborhood to the barbershop a block away called The Total Look. The shop contained the typical fare you'd expect at a barbershop in an African-American neighborhood—loud-mouthed, wise-cracking barbers, tons of foul language, and the occasional street entrepreneur walking in to sell customers bootleg cassette tapes, watches, shoes, or even hot dinner plates. The fried fish was off the chain. In the back of the shop sat a dusty Ms. Pac-Man machine that just might claim responsibility for my relationship with video games today. While I waited on my traditional cut (a Hustler, the Philadelphia name for an even low fade; in New York they called it a Caesar), I'd usually spend my spare time thumbing through *Jet* magazines, or pumping quarters into Ms. Pac-Man. I'd set a new high score every two weeks, just to watch it get wiped when Mr. Kenny, the shop owner, cut the power at the end of each workday. Mr. Kenny was a nice man, soft spoken, very deliberate in action and he didn't waste words or electricity. While the rest of his barbers were boisterous jokesters, he'd just listen and give others looks as sharp as his clippers.

I recall one conversation when Mike, my barber, explained to the other barbers (with the kids listening) that it was important to make a bunch of babies while you're young, rather than waiting until you were older.

"If you're twenty-one when you have a kid," Mike explained, "by the time you're thirty, you can still hang out, and your kid is old enough to stay home by himself. Shoot, my son can wash his butt, wash the dishes, do laundry, and tuck himself in while I'm at the club gettin' faded." Dad Goals, I guess.

Later, I heard Mike went to prison for defaulting on child support payments. That was news I picked up at the shop. Many barbers in the city enjoyed the job for the hours. No work on Mondays? Perfect. No credit check? Sweet. There was also the fact that most income made at the shop was in cash, and off the books. As long as a barber kept the shop owner paid every week for his chair space, he was free and clear. Unfortunately, Mike found out the hard way that hiding funds from the government (and your child's mother) can come back to haunt you. He did a year in jail and didn't return to the shop after.

Vic was the new guy who took over Mike's chair. As you may know from the *Barbershop* movie, being a new guy in the chair meant no customers. You had to earn your reputation in the shop. Vic never had a wait, and I saw that his own hair was kept well, so I decided to give him a chance. He was just as sharp as Mike, with none of the problematic opinions or deadbeat dad tendencies. I'd go to the shop every other Saturday for my Hustler and Ms. Pac Man, until one fall morning when walking by the shop to go to school, we saw broken glass and yellow police tape. Later that night, the Action News telecast reported an unidentified burglar had broken into the shop by removing the air conditioner unit above the door and climbing in. He planned to take the barber's equipment, and whatever was left behind, probably to sell for drug money.

Without knowing it, the thief tripped a silent alarm, which prompted Mr. Kenny to roll up strapped. When he arrived to confront the burglar, Mr. Kenny shot him as he tried to flee, killing him. Mr. Kenny then called the police as the man took his final breath. I watched the story on the 6:00 news, stunned.

Kenny was sentenced to two years in prison for the murder and possession of an unregistered handgun, but the shop remained open and still does to this day. My mother demanded I find a new barbershop in the area. Luckily, barbershops were like liquor stores in my hood – you couldn't throw a rock without hitting one.

For the next few years, I got my haircut at Mac's, run by Mr. MacDonald, a wise old gentleman who played jazz music while cutting hair and kept his shop completely quiet and drama-free. Not even a block away, Mac's shop was the opposite of the raucous atmosphere at The Total Look. No Ms. Pac Man machine, not even Galaga. It was safe, but safe isn't fun. The most action-packed moment I had there was when I asked Mr. Mac to give me three parts on the side of my head; I thought he was going to have a heart attack when he asked, "Boy, have you lost your cotton-pickin' mind?"

I eventually returned to The Total Look once I got to a point when my mother didn't ask where my haircuts came from anymore. It was just too much fun being there, getting the straight talk from brothers who had been around the longest. We learned who was cheating on whom, who sold drugs, and even learned who was planning to take over the shop from Mr. Kenny. This treasonous takeover talk got back to the management however, and shortly thereafter, The Total Look was closed again for several years. I had to get my haircuts from Vic at his home for a while until a new shop opened.

Barbershops combined so much of what I grew up to love and appreciate – community, video games, new music, and camaraderie. As an only child, it was (and remains) one of the best ways to have a conversation with another adult about life, no matter how silly or insignificant. I appreciate the barbershop – that culture is still a huge part of who I am, and it always will remind me of my father. I still go to the barbershop as often as I can today, and though my barber may be slow, or get distracted easily, he's still my barber, and that special barber-client privilege makes it extra special.

I was like most of the kids I encountered growing up. Most of us were raised by single mothers. Mom worked in a factory setting at Honeywell for a long time. Honeywell manufactured parts for thermostats as well as aerospace systems and commercial products. It sounded so cool. I used to tell my friends that my mother helped to build space shuttle parts. Honeywell did build space shuttle parts, but not in my mother's department. She worked there until massive layoffs in the '90s sent hundreds of jobs overseas and out west, ironically to Phoenix, where we live now. Honeywell let hundreds of working-class parents go. Fortunately, Honeywell offered a severance package and school discounts to their employees, so Mom began a second career in nursing while working part time at a department store during her schooling.

Both jobs kept her out of our home for long periods, which meant that until I was old enough to be trusted with a key I had to stay with our next-door neighbor, Miss Gertrude, and later Miss Evelyn. Looking back... I'm not exactly sure that was better for me than staying home alone.

In kindergarten, Miss Gertrude's niece, Kiki, looked after me while Miss Gert picked up more hours working at the senior living center. Kiki was fun, so I usually enjoyed my time with her. As a rambunctious teen herself, she let me stay up late to watch *Knight Rider* or have an extra cookie before bedtime, while she chatted on the phone or occasionally snuck boys into the house. When word got around about Kiki's babysitting service, she added more clients, usually boys, with the exception being Annie.

Annie was a cute, shy, brown-skinned, girl with pigtails. She was six-years-old, about a year younger than I was. One slow Tuesday night, Kiki decided to get adventurous. She asked Annie and I to come to the living room, where she and a guy had been cuddling while they watched *Love Connection*. She asked Annie if she'd ever kissed a boy. Annie shyly shook her head. I responded just as awkwardly when Kiki asked me the same question. Using a phrase Kevin Hart would make famous almost thirty years later, Kiki told the two of us, "You gon' learn today."

She made Annie and I stand in front of the TV, grabbed our two heads, and pushed them together to make us lock lips. I don't remember much about the kiss, but it must not have met Kiki's expectations because she instantly demanded more action.

"Stick your tongue out, Ra."

"Give him some back Annie!"

Kiki and her male playmate then got adventurous and made us get on the floor.

I laid down first with Annie on top of me, as Kiki used her bare foot to push Annie's rear end left to right, creating an uncomfortable amount of friction as we waddled on the shag carpet. I wasn't enjoying this at all.

I lay on the floor getting dry humped by a girl I hardly knew, awkwardly bumping hips for fifteen minutes or so, until Kiki and her friend grew bored and started talking about something else. Kiki then commanded us, "Okay, y'all can go back upstairs now."

I left to resume my self-directed, all-toy version of *GI Joe: The Movie* and tried not to think about what just happened. On my way upstairs, I heard Kiki say to her male friend, "I'm horny now."

At the time I had no idea what that meant. I didn't even know what we were doing, let alone how to explain it. I remember my favorite TV shows in the 90s all having episodes where they talk about inappropriate touching, demonstrating with dolls… It took me a long time to realize that this incident with Kiki was sexual abuse, and I came to dread mentioning those two words for my entire life.

Throughout the years I was never in a position where I felt I was in a safe enough space to discuss something so private without it getting back to Annie or Kiki who was much older and would certainly deny it. Even later in life, I imagined her coming back, finding me, and getting her boy toy to pound me for besmirching their good names. Because of this I never told anyone about Kiki and what she did, and although I came close to telling my mother, and counselors in the past several times over the years, I now realize that out of fear I'd pushed the incident so far down into my gut that I'd almost completely forgotten it.

Feels good getting it out now.

That experience and not being able to talk about it honestly altered me in ways that I was not prepared for. My behavior changed following that incident. Mom was convinced I had become mentally unstable. I went from being gifted and introverted to being wild and uncontrollable. I vandalized property, I threw rocks, I lied and I stole. I did anything I could to get attention. At the time, on any given day, I didn't spend more than two hours with my mom due to her schedule. The only way I knew to get more of her time was to act out, which meant having to spend less time at the babysitter. Mom didn't understand what was going on with me, so she took away the only thing that might have kept me from going nuts: my video games. I snapped, yelled, and even cursed at her which got me in worse trouble.

To find a solution to the sudden changes in my personality and behavior, my mother enrolled me in a special group at school called

Gateways. I was pulled from class two to three times a week to sit in a circle with "the special kids" and explain why we do what we do. After a month or so of that, my instructor determined I wasn't mentally disabled. In fact, he determined that the lack of challenges in school had driven me to act out. This realization, along with Kiki getting caught with drugs and not babysitting anymore, led to a positive change and put me in a more stable state of mind. Soon, I was back in class, attaining the same high marks as before the "incident." I only became a problem child again in middle school, but everyone is crazy in middle school, right?

Eventually, I became a latchkey kid raised by the entire block.

Through middle school, Mom would come in from a shift at 6:30 a.m., just in time to wake me up, check my homework, fix my breakfast, and watch an episode of *Inspector Gadget* or *The Flintstones* with me before school. If I hadn't done my chores or finished my homework the previous evening, I would have to wash dishes, do homework, or clean my room instead of watching TV with her. By the time I got home from school at 3:15 p.m., Mom had already left for work. That meant that I had one hour per day tops to spend with her.

I had to let myself into the house and follow three simple rules after school:

1) Don't touch the stove,
2) Don't let anyone into the house, and
3) Keep our business out of the street.

Outside of that, I was a free man – well, pre-teen. If any of the neighbors saw me outside doing something I had no business doing, they had permission to blow the whistle, and even break out a switch or belt to whip me, even though I was generally a well-behaved kid.[1] Meanwhile, Mom would leave me with the words "be good" usually

---

[1] Switch (n): A small wooden twig with all branches and leaves removed, used for whipping a child's buttocks. Not to be confused with a Nintendo Switch.

followed by "don't make me come home and embarrass you." Even at twelve years of age and having long since surpassed her in size, I believed her.

My mom worked extremely hard to provide for herself and me, and still works extremely hard to this day, though now it is more for the things she loves, like casino trips and new earrings. She showed me the value of hard work at an early age. Back then she worked the graveyard shift, so I often didn't see her beyond a few weekday moments, and occasionally on the weekend. Once, when she purchased a new car, I complained because she worked so much that I never got a chance to ride in it.

As an only child, I never had to ask for much; she made sure I had anything I desired. I'm not saying I was spoiled, but I was spoiled. Recently, I asked her why she had been so generous in my youth. She said it was because she didn't want me to be so desperate for something that I would consider stealing it. When I was a child, I knew other kids who stole, but at the time I didn't think it was because they couldn't afford to buy what they took. Rather, I assumed it was the rush of adrenaline of the theft and the feeling of living up to the "bad boy" images of themselves that fueled their fires.

I didn't have that fire. I never wanted to be bad. I was a clever and creative child as far back as I can remember. I remember testing for gifted classes in elementary school. While my third-grade compatriots were reading books around that rank, I enjoyed a twelfth-grade reading level, which I maintained alone, in the corner of the classroom on a tattered beanbag.

At first, it was fun being the smartest kid in the class, sort of a mental *One Punch Man*, but after a while being smart just made me an outcast. I had to prove to my peers that I was just as cool as them. My efforts to do so started by talking back to and mocking adults. (I'm still way too good at impersonations thanks to that phase.) Then, my efforts elevated to pulling small, juvenile pranks in the classroom. At some point though, those pranks got out of control, and some even became dangerous. Turns out spraying spray paint on paper, then poking holes in it with a soldering iron starts a fire.

I grew up on the sixty-five hundred block of Woodstock Street in

West Oak Lane, a small almost-suburb like area within the Northwest section of Philadelphia. West Oak Lane was developed primarily between the early 1920s and late 1930s. Although the neighborhood was predominantly White from its inception until the mid-1960s, West Oak Lane is now one of Philadelphia's few middle-class, primarily African-American communities.

On a good travel day, West Oak Lane is about twenty-five minutes from the center of Philadelphia, but about five minutes from the suburbs, so, although we had a Philadelphia mailing address, it's barely Philly, geographically speaking.

Many people from the heart of the city thought our area was full of stuffy rich folks and uncool rich kids, so the younger generations in the area gave our area a nickname. Also, West Oak Lane sounded like West Philly, so to avoid any mix-up, we needed a distinction between the two areas. West Oak Lane became known as "Uptown." The name may not have had the pizazz of North Philly or the reputation of Southwest, but it sounded dope, so we stuck with it.

Most of my friends grew up in the stereotypical households you read about: single-parent homes, with household incomes at or below the poverty line. While most of my crew were the nerds of the block, we maintained relationships with some people who kept some pretty dangerous lifestyles. Although the kids on the block didn't need the newest and best of everything, everyone dreamed of gaining more, one way or the other.

Ant, our neighborhood bully, even got the nickname "Gooch" from us, based on the character from the TV series *Diff'rent Strokes*. On the show, "The Gooch" would take lunch money, clothes, and anything else he wanted from people, usually Arnold Drummond and his friend Dudley, and so did Ant. The only difference was that we didn't have a "Mr. Drummond" to come to the school and handle things at the end of the episode. We had to handle it ourselves, usually by laughing at Ant's bad jokes and kindly giving him whatever he wanted to avoid getting beat down. I recall moving out of the way when he played basketball to give him a clear path to the basket and avoid a conflict for obstructing him. "Whoa, you got me again, Ant! I'm just too slow."

I want to believe Ant had a good heart, deep inside. In elementary school, I shared a class with him. He acted out to get out of completing assignments, which is how I knew he suffered from a learning disability and had learned to avoid revealing his deficiencies by behaving badly. I felt bad for him. I tried to befriend him, which led to me having to explain his actions to folks on more than one occasion.

One day while outside playing Freeze Tag, Ant came down the block and said, "I wanna play." This wasn't a request; he was letting us know that he was in the game. This meant no one would ever tag him. On top of being an intimidating figure because of his stature, Ant was incredibly quick on his feet. He was known to hop over fences in a single bound in the pursuit of children to beat up. Ant's stories on the block are a series of John Henry-like phenomenal stories of lore; he was a living urban legend. There was the story about the time he threw a football the entire length of the street. There was another about the time he fought thirty guys from the neighboring block and won. There was also a story about him beating up a guy who punched his sister and making him strip naked and run down the block. No one saw these events happen, but we all knew someone who swore they were true.

Before joining the game, Ant asked—no, told—me to take his duffle bag to my stoop while he played with us. When I grabbed the bag, I almost keeled over from its weight. Ant laughed and said, "My books are inside, man!" I don't know if I looked skeptical, or if he just wanted to show off, but he added, "go ahead and open it up; see for yourself."

I unzipped the sack to find it full of guns. Pistols, rifles, shotguns, Uzis. It looked like a bag of props from the A-Team's TV set. I gasped and quickly closed the bag, anxious to set it down. Ant laughed and moved on.

Despite the high level of tension in the neighborhood, the basketball court was our Mecca. The court was our home away from home, our mostly peaceful refuge, where every argument was settled even though we couldn't keep it together for too long. First, there was the schoolyard at John L. Kinsey, my elementary school, which contained a full court on a bit of a hill, replete with cracked pavement, glass bottles and crack vials strewn across it at any given time. One summer day, a few rival kids from another neighborhood came through and ripped the baskets down. The baskets were replaced, and then the kids ripped them down again.

That happened three or four times at least. Sensing a pattern eventually, Kinsey decided not to replace the rims, and our local sanctuary was gone. Today, Kinsey School is closed indefinitely, basketball courts and all, and it breaks my heart a little when I pass by during visits to the neighborhood.

Next, we traveled up the hill to Simons Recreation Center, the site of my first-ever job as a summer camp counselor. It was a little farther, about ten blocks from the house, so we had to get permission to travel there. Often, we ran into bigger kids we didn't know, but no problems ever arose, at least none that a game of Twenty-One couldn't settle. We called Simons our home until one day, during summer league, an angry player decided to let off no less than four rounds from his .32 caliber pistol in broad daylight on the court. Simons was off limits to us after that.

Our third basketball haven was the courts at Morris Estate, about seven blocks from home. The Morris Estate courts were in a wooded park, secluded by trees and a gated area. This basketball court looked like the ones in New York that we saw in classic movies like *Above the Rim*. The court's surface was smooth, the rims were sturdy, and they even had nets attached. It was on this court that I learned some of my best moves. I had a mean, left-handed skyhook, patented after Kareem Abdul-Jabbar's; the kids dubbed it "The Meat Hook." It was also on this court that I heard some of my favorite hip-hop tracks for the first time. These came from the boomboxes that spectators brought to play the newest DJ Clue and Ron G mixtapes. Wu-Tang, Redman and so many more became my favorites because of these trips to the basketball court.

Unfortunately, Morris Estate was full of kids who didn't appreciate a bunch of new folks impeding on their turf, bringing new rules and customs. We ended up in our fair share of fights, which we often either lost or ran from—again, we were the nerds of the block. We were lovers, not fighters. Morris Estate also had its fair share of beatdowns, police raids and even shootings that occurred every summer. After a few incidents, we were forced back into our neighborhood to devise a plan.

That was when the idea of "Crateball" hit the block. We would grab milk crates from the local corner store, use a hammer to bang out the bottom, nail the hollow crate onto a tree or light pole, and voila! Basketball returned to the hood. Later, we got extra creative and nailed two different crates to adjacent trees starting what we called "Full Crate" basketball. Dr. James Naismith would be proud. The neighbors hated it because of the noise and traffic it brought to the block, but our parents appreciated that we were at least in plain sight. Thanks to crack cocaine and the ensuing violence, the streets of Uptown were getting worse. We were all looking for a creative and safe outlet. We just played hip-hop tracks on the block when we were relegated to Stoop Kid status. We didn't need family; we had each other. Stock for Life.

At home, what we had wasn't the best, but I never went without anything. I honestly never thought we were poor; I just knew we didn't need much. Even on frigid winter nights when our heat would go out due to non-payment, we made a way with a kerosene heater with a pot of water on top, and when that heated up, we had warm water for a bird bath before school and mom's coffee. I thought everyone grew up as we did until I went to friends' homes for sleepovers.

Congress created the Low-Income Home Energy Assistance Program (LIHEAP) in 1980 as part of the Crude Oil Windfall Profits Tax Act to answer the concerns of the rising energy prices of the 1970s. Its goal was to help keep families safe and healthy through initiatives that assisted them with increasing energy costs. Every winter we heard about deadly house fires caused by space heaters, so my mother was encouraged to apply for LIHEAP. Unfortunately, even in a single parent household, despite struggling to keep the lights and heat on, her yearly income was too high to be eligible for state assistance. Life in the middle class.

In the late 1980s a new lifestyle and a new way to participate in the economy swept through Philadelphia, courtesy of crack cocaine. It sold cheaper than rock cocaine but was similarly addictive. Crack houses began popping up on Philadelphia blocks, distinguishable by the high volume of traffic well into the night, with both drug users and dealers walking in and out or pulling cars up to the house. Our quiet block of Woodstock Street was no exception. An abandoned row home right across from our house quickly transformed into a crack house right before our eyes. Zombie-like drug addicts we called "fiends" or "baseheads" walked the night streets, jeopardizing the safety of our neighborhood.

To us, drugs represented dilapidation and fear, but on the other side of the game were luxury and opulence. Raymond, who ran the

Woodstock crack house, was never spotted without the newest pair of Cazal shades, a furry Kangol hat, and a new Adidas sweatsuit. His haircut was crisp, his style was immaculate, and Raymond looked like he belonged in an Eric B and Rakim video. If he spotted us playing football on the block, he'd sometimes slide the kids fifty dollars, saying, "Get yourself something nice, and get your mom something too."

When he wasn't leaned back inside his pearl white 1987 BMW E28 M5, Raymond could be seen bopping down the street with a gigantic boombox, which probably took somewhere in the neighborhood of twenty D batteries to power it. He'd play the same song every day, in or out of his car, almost like clockwork: "It Takes Two" by Rob Base and DJ EZ Rock. Raymond's songs are probably my earliest hip-hop memory.

The beat was infectious. The use of the now-famous "Yeah Woo!" break, using a brilliant combination of Bobby Byrd and James Brown samples, played throughout the song, anchored by a neck-snapping drum track that made any listener want to do The Running Man. The lyrics, so boastful and proud, were sung with a swagger that made anyone repeating the words feel like a million cash.

> 'Cause I'm a winner, no, not a loser,
> To be an MC, it's what I choose-a
> Ladies love me, girls adore me,
> I mean, even the ones that never saw me,
> Like, the way that I rhyme at a show,
> The reason why, man I don't know,
> So let's go

Raymond played the song repeatedly and mouthed the words like they were his mantra. The Woodstock Street crack house lasted until later in the year, when a police sting took down the house and made several arrests four months later. The officers knocked the door down at 2 a.m. with a battering ram. While they were downstairs, Raymond somehow managed to jump from the second-floor window, land on his back, miraculously get up, and bolt down the block, dropping money and crack vials as he ran. The stuff of legend. Raymond was never seen again after that morning.

Witnessing this firsthand was more effective as a deterrent than any scared straight program. Many experts blame the rise of hip-hop music alongside drug culture as the beginning of a dangerous type of hyper-masculinity in urban America. I wasn't a fighter, but I can't lie, a hard rap song could do wonders for the psyche of a mild-mannered listener. Don't believe me? Just throw on M.O.P's "Ante Up" in a crowded club. Honestly, though, I attribute my reckless behavior as much to the impact of pro-wrestling as to hip-hop music.

The WWF (World Wrestling Federation) programming dominated more of my Saturdays than cartoons. Although they started each broadcast with a "Don't Try This at Home" warning that I can still recite verbatim to this day. After the broadcast Chuck, Ant, the rest of the block kids and I went outside and started our own WWF (Woodstock Wrestling Federation) on the cold, hard concrete. We tried all of what we saw. High flying maneuvers, dramatic storylines, you name it. We even drew and cut out championship title belts from large refrigerator cardboard, previously used for our attempts at breakdancing. I'd say that "Macho Man" Randy Savage flying off the top rope had influenced me just as much as KRS-ONE holding a MAC-10 on the cover of Boogie Down Productions's album *By Any Means Necessary* in 1988.

Hopped on hip-hop, I fought my best friend Patrick over a girl who I didn't even like. I stole from stores with friends. Riled up on Pro Wrestling, I got my front tooth knocked out when a kid who was bigger than I was dropped a Hulk Hogan leg drop on the back of my head while I lay on the concrete floor. I was even suspended for trying to impress a girl by punching a brick wall, emulating Ronnie "Hands of Stone" Garvin. KRS said, "'Cause where I'm at if you're soft you lost," and we believed it. Before video games, wrestling and hip-hop were the only things that mattered to my young mind.

Capping off the epic WrestleMania IV event, my guy, "Macho Man" Randy Savage would best "Million Dollar Man" Ted DiBiase at the end of a grueling tournament. We couldn't get to Jersey to watch the landmark event, but the Philadelphia Spectrum opened its doors to broadcast the pay-per-view on closed-circuit television. My mother allowed my cousin Howie to take me. I bought a Macho Man foam finger and cheered

Savage all the way to victory from my seat, repeating his trademark "Ooh Yeah" the entire subway ride home from South Philly.

1988 also marked the release of the Nintendo Entertainment System's Action Set, which included a Zapper light gun, and a dual game cartridge containing *Super Mario Bros* and *Duck Hunt*. The system was originally released in 1986 and after a strong debut sold over seven million systems in 1988 alone. Howie had the NES since its release. He had both a mother and father, who were separated. He got two separate birthdays and Christmases, and I loved it because he shared the wealth. I wanted my own, so my mother bought me the Action Set after months of cajoling. I couldn't purchase any of the top titles, as they all came with a forty-dollar price tag. If I had a good month—good grades, no trouble, all chores done with no backtalk—I could get a bargain bin game, nineteen dollars and ninety-nine cents max. That price point usually meant a poorly built, third party game that had little fanfare. These games usually made good trade fodder, although trades were prohibited in my household.

Although my absentee dad, the barbershops, the babysitters, the kids on my block, plus wrestling and video games all had a hand in raising me, by far the biggest contributor to shaping who I am today was, and still is, my mother. When I stop and think about it, it's truly miraculous how she was able to point me in the right direction while working so hard to provide food clothing and shelter for us. And despite me relying on these other sources while she was at work, she did an amazing job raising me. This is a bit of a flash-forward at this point, but one of the best examples that proves this is the story about my high school prom.

I remember seeing the sign on our bulletin board:

GET YOUR MONEY IN FOR SENIOR PROM!
DON'T MISS THE MOST SPECIAL MOMENT OF
    YOUR LIFE!

Despite the near fights and drama of high school, prom time was probably the most stressful moment of all. My group of friends went from completely disinterested in attending, calling it "lame" and "for the posers" to extremely interested in two seconds, once Tariq, my best friend/sometimes rival, had mustered up the courage to ask an older girl to prom, and she shockingly said yes. Tariq had the guts I wished I had.

The competition was on. Once that happened, my entire friend group kicked into gear and made prom a priority, with less than two weeks to go. I wrote a letter for Mom and left it on the coffee table that said:

MOM. I HAVE TO GO TO PROM.
Please help me figure it out. Thank you – Ra

Like she always did, she figured it out. She got a tux, a limo and flowers arranged, in almost no time. We were prom ready, but I just needed one thing, the most important thing of all... a date.

Because I'd waited so long, I had slim pickings of women in our class, as most had decided they were either going with boyfriends, with groups of girls, alone or not at all, as it was much harder for a girl to find a dress on such short notice. As opposed to guys who could just hit Men's Wearhouse, women's dresses had to be unique.

I searched and searched until I eventually asked a mentor, a teacher on campus who has usually helped us out whenever we had issues. He recommended Michelle, a girl who was two years older, and seemed to really like proms, because he had photos of her at not only last year's, but the year before, so both years since she had graduated, she'd returned. *Interesting hobby,* I thought. But she was interested, and she was hot, so I was in. I said yes before I'd even met her.

When I told the boys, they were impressed by me not only managing to find a date, but one that was older, and attractive. I'd won the imaginary game. Turned out the thrill of victory was short-lived, because as time went on, the rest of the boys in the crew dropped out of prom, citing low funds or inability to find dates. Just Tariq and I went from our friend group.

Before we left for prom, our parents both talked it out, and we were set for a limo pickup. Mom pinned my corsage on while telling me the rules of engagement:

1) No touching;
2) No drinking;
3) Keep her safe at all times; and
4) Bring yourself back by midnight

The last one wasn't even debatable; the limo driver had strict rules to return me home by 11:45 or he wouldn't get paid. So he was motivated to stick to the rules.

The most memorable part of prom for me was the ride to the banquet hall. The limo driver played Power 99 FM, my favorite radio station, and at the moment we tuned in, the radio jock announced the debut of The Notorious B.I.G.'s "One More Chance" Remix, which became the hit of the summer. We sang along all the way to the prom, though Michelle told me she didn't like rap, which should have been the first sign of trouble.

She said something like, "Are you ready to have fun?" and I said, "absolutely!" while looking down into my hands. She could tell I was shy and withdrawn. The limo ride might have been one of a handful of times I'd been alone with a girl in high school, and the first with an older girl. She said things like, "Loosen up, it's gonna be wild!" as I sat hunched on the corner of the limo seat, cautious to give her room. Rule #1 and all.

The moment we exited the limo, I walked Michelle inside and instantly things got wild, as she said. She opened her purse and pulled out a small fifty milliliter bottle of *99 Bananas* and guzzled it in seconds, offering me her second bottle. I refused the drink politely, considering rule #2.

Keeping rule #3 closely in mind, I asked, "Are you sure you should be doing that?"

But Michelle was grown. She wasn't trying to take advice from me. "I'm good, I came here to have a good time; I don't know what you came for."

After we walked through the threshold and took photos, I saw a few friends from school and engaged in some idle chatter, but Michelle completely dominated the prom dance floor. R&B, hip-hop, reggae… the song hit and she knew the dance, and killed it. Michelle knew everyone, from the school staff, the banquet hall workers and even some of the parent chaperones; and if they didn't know her they wanted to get to know her afterward. I had no idea she was this popular.

Michelle was a professional prom-hopper. I didn't know this type of person even existed. She had been to at least three other proms post-graduation, and since most Philadelphia public schools used the same venues, Michelle had made herself very familiar with the layout of the high school prom.

Because she'd had such a good relationship with most the adults on site, they placed an inordinate amount of trust in Michelle. They let her supervise when they took bathroom breaks, in which she'd pop more bottles (who knows how many she had) and pass them to other students. As the kids say, it was lit.

I kept thinking of rule #3 from my mother, but through all the chaos Michelle seemed completely in control. She directed traffic like a pro; she glided along the dance floor like J.Lo and maintained the elegance of Michelle Obama. It was a sight to see.

Tariq and his date arrived a little later, and I spent some time talking with them while Michelle danced. I didn't want to become a burden on anyone else, and I wasn't much of a dancer, so I sat down, sunk my fork into some cheesecake and watched Michelle dance with any and everyone that was interested. Needless to say, it wasn't my finest hour.

The prom ended at 10 p.m., capping off a fun night. By 9:45 p.m., as everyone collected their coats, Michelle ran over to me with an amazing idea. "Hey, I'm gonna go down the shore for the night with some friends; I hope that's okay. You want to come?"

"Down the shore" refers to Atlantic City, New Jersey, approximately ninety miles from Philadelphia, full of casinos and beaches. It's a fun place to hang out while not too far from the hustle and bustle of the city. I thought about it, but I knew the truth. There was no way I could even make it to AC and return on time.

Michelle knew that, as she was there when Mom gave me the rules, including my curfew. I declined and told them to go and have fun. She asked, "Are you sure?"

I reiterated that it was fine. Michelle grabbed her coat, gave me a kiss on the cheek, thanked me for inviting her and joined the three boys and two girls to head to the beach. I noticed the smell of marijuana on Michelle as she closed in. If it wasn't a party yet, it was about to be.

I shook hands with Tariq and a few other friends, then hopped into the limo alone. The driver reminded me that I had another ninety minutes, and asked if I wanted to see the city… I didn't. "Just take me home, please," I responded. "You're alone!" the driver noted as we took off. "Yep." The rest of the ride was silent.

I got in at 11 p.m., beating curfew. Mom asked how it went, and as I was about to reply, I remembered that she had spent hundreds of dollars on this night, at my last-minute request, to make sure that it was perfect for her only son… so I wasn't about to tell her I had a bad time. I told her it was awesome, and that I had a fun time that wasn't too crazy.

Despite my mother's rules affecting how much fun I could have had, that was hardly regrettable compared to what would have happened if I had come home late with Michelle in my arms, both of us drunk, and her safety in question. That's not to say that Mom's punishment wouldn't have sucked, because it would have. But her negative reaction wasn't the chief incentive to why I behaved the way that I did. If prom was the last big high school test showing how good a son I was turning out to be, then being respectful to others, punctual and grateful for her effort was worth every effort on my part. Looking back, I see that Mom raised me so when I sacrificed a little for her peace of mind, I wouldn't regret a thing. And I still don't.

CHAPTER TWO

HOME COOKING

You'd probably be impressed
How I managed to cheat death
And make it out the hood with no regrets

—"Forever," *Forever Famicom* (2010)

THE POLITICS OF 1980S PHILADELPHIA were strange. We elected our first Black mayor, Wilson Goode, after a racially polarizing election in 1984. He defeated Frank Rizzo, an accused racist with alleged mob ties and a volatile relationship with the local African-American community. When Goode won, Black people partied in the streets, excited because they had taken the city back. The unofficial theme song of Goode's campaign was the Willie Hutch classic, "Brother's Gonna Work It Out."

However, Goode's tenure was marred by the now infamous MOVE disaster of 1985. MOVE was a Black Liberation group founded by John Africa (born Vincent Leaphart) in 1972. The group lived in a communal setting, abiding by philosophies of anarcho-primitivism. MOVE's headquarters was an entire block, Osage Avenue, which turned into a bit of a fortress for the outfit. Once the group refused to follow police orders, a standoff led to a bombing that rocked the city. Goode approved the dropping of a bomb from a helicopter, live on the news, that leveled four entire blocks on Osage Avenue in West Philadelphia, killing eleven African-Americans and destroying sixty homes. By the end of Goode's final term, Philadelphia was a month away from being completely bankrupt. Willie Hutch would say that Brother didn't work it out.

Every summer, the city got hotter, literally, and figuratively. Crime increased, and sweltering temperatures exacerbated the situation. Mom was desperate to keep me out of trouble and connect me to the family. We took trips every June or July, usually to South Carolina, then later to Washington, DC to visit my Aunt Willie Mae, who had moved to DC to take a government job at the U.S. Mint. I loved our trips to DC where we saw the monuments and museums. Those visits made me the history buff that I am today. I particularly enjoyed the Smithsonian museums. I never imagined that I would one day perform at that very museum many years later.

I remember riding the bus with my aunt one day and seeing a man hop on with a shirt that said, "Run Jesse Run." The faded blue tee depicted a Black man with an afro and a thick mustache. Something significant in my young brain made me ask for more information about the shirt. That was when my aunt told me about Jesse Jackson, the first African-American man to make a serious run at the presidency. She told me how he challenged Americans to turn off the television for two hours a night to read, how his Operation PUSH (People United to Serve Humanity) had worked to improve the economic status for Blacks since the 1970s, and how he was Dr. Martin Luther King's right-hand man and worked with him until the day of his fateful assassination. It was safe to say that most of Washington DC's Black population was rooting for Jesse.

In 1984, Jesse Jackson became the second African-American (after Shirley Chisholm) to mount a nationwide campaign for President of the United States. He ran as a Democrat. In the primaries, Jackson, who had been written off by pundits as a fringe candidate with little chance of winning the nomination, surprised many when he took third place behind Senator Gary Hart and former Vice President Walter Mondale; Mondale eventually won the nomination. In 1984, Jackson garnered over three million primary votes, or 18.2 percent of the total, and won five primaries and caucuses, including Louisiana, the District of Columbia, South Carolina, Virginia, and one of two separate contests in Mississippi.

My seven-year-old mind couldn't process elections, primaries, or caucuses, but I remember watching a few speeches on television while in DC and seeing a man who talked the way my uncles talked, and who possessed a perfect combination of wit and charm. Jesse Jackson was a man of fire and fury. However, what Jesse possessed in style, he lacked in substance. His inexperience showed when he was constantly outclassed in debates. I remember my uncles and aunts having conversations over cans of Miller High Life and Newports, stating that no Black person would ever be president.

I returned to school that fall with a new attitude, empowered and motivated by Jesse's work, limiting my disruptions, and achieving at new levels. I won the school's spelling bee in 1986, beating several older students. I won a shiny green dictionary that I showed off to everyone. It was my prized possession. Despite its huge size, I carried it to school every day. I was the top student in Kinsey Elementary for the next few years; I was laser-beam focused on schoolwork and achievement.

I later went from carrying that dictionary to rocking a Walkman and headphones, which earned me the nickname "Radio Raheem," based on the hulking, boombox-curling character in the Spike Lee classic *Do the Right Thing*. I wanted to be by myself, and as long as I had music, I was fine. I wanted to stay as far away from the opposite sex as possible. This was because of Christina.

Christina was cute. She was short and spunky with a bob haircut that was a little unkempt, but not too wild. Most importantly, she was hilarious. She always made everyone at our table bust out laughing. She sat next to me in sixth grade, and although I never made a move, she must have known something was up.

Truthfully, I didn't like her or any girl enough to want to be in a relationship. I was content with my video games and sketchbooks. With my relationship batting average sitting at a strong .000, I wasn't in any hurry. I was all right with my single status. I could spend my candy money on myself.

One day, though, things escalated quickly. For the first time that year, Christina was absent. I asked one or two people who walked to school with her if she was coming in. Absences are rare in elementary school, so I was just a concerned classmate. But my inquiries got blown way out of proportion, and people told that I had asked about her constantly while she was gone. The gossip led to the lunchtime revelation that Raheem liked Christina. As juicy gossip is wont to do, this revelation was all over the classroom in a matter of seconds.

Giggles, snickers, none-too-subtle pointing fingers and more became my existence. Everyone had an opinion on the news of the day, which was that the dork of the class had a crush. I tried my best to deny it, but there was no use. I just moved on, hoping the story would die down by the end of the day, and it did.

Christina returned the next day, and everything picked up all over again; I couldn't get a break. Worse, Christina sat right next to me. Thankfully she was a really good sport about it, or so I thought.

As that tumultuous day ended, Christina shoved a note into my desk. It contained those famous four words, "Do you like me?" There was a checkbox for "yes" or "no."

I didn't know how to answer, because I did in fact like her, but I didn't want to move on it. If I checked "no," she might never want to talk to me again. If I checked "yes" and she didn't feel the same, it was curtains. I'd be ridiculed. Lose-Lose.

In typical Raheem Jarbo fashion, I added a third option and wrote, "I don't know." Then I asked her if she liked me. Real smooth.

She wrote, "Yes!"

I was in.

I responded with an all-caps "YES," and, just like that, I had a girlfriend. *Now what?* I wondered.

At age twelve there isn't much a "couple" can do besides hold hands when teachers aren't looking and draw their names joined together by a plus sign with hearts around them. I couldn't bring Christina to my house; I couldn't even call girls yet. And I definitely couldn't let her big brother find out about us. But in a way, keeping the secret was the most fun part of the relationship. At least that was the case for a few days.

My friend, Kwame, who I would draw prototypes of new Transformer designs with, told me one day, "Yo, Christina is trying to play you!"

I didn't understand what he meant, but I heard the same thing from my boy Tyrone. I couldn't see how she could be playing me when we weren't doing anything. I figured they were jealous because they didn't have girlfriends.

Soon after though, I noticed people smiling when we walked by holding hands. Later, those smiles turned to giggles. It all came to a head at the end of the week, right after lunch, on Friday afternoon when I found a crumpled note stuffed into my desk. It said, "Do you really really like me".

"Yes of course. Why?" I said back.

"'Cause I don't really like you, I was doing it because Nicole dared me to. I thought it would be funny. Better luck next time, fats."

Christina had played me. The only female attention I had garnered in six years of elementary school was a ruse. Christina and her friends laughed it up after school that Friday and my boys could only offer "I told you so" as comfort.

I requested that my seat be changed the next Monday. I sat alone from then on, with my sketchbooks and advanced level reading material to keep me company in class, and my Walkman while outside of it. There would be more Christinas as time went on, but I barely noticed as I spent my school-age years chasing baseball cards, comic books, video games, and cartoons. Life progressed just fine, and I didn't even think of this event again until it was time to write a song called "Dream Master." Christina might have a cameo in that song. I probably should have changed her first name.

I became the quickest, wittiest jokester in John L. Kinsey School after the Christina incident, because it was no fun being a target. I learned how to be sneaky with my taunts, but constantly being on guard for insults makes it hard to know who your true friends are. I'd let loose on anyone if the opportunity presented itself.

My best friend in elementary school was Harold, a tall, lanky kid with a huge overbite and protruding lips; girls said that Harold looked like an extra from Fat Albert's Junkyard Gang. But Harold and I loved all the same things: G.I. Joes, Mega Man, drawing, and we were both grade-A outcasts. Harold and I had great times – we traded toys and video games, talked on the phone over the weekend about movies and cartoons, and even helped each other with homework assignments.

Harold had experienced his fair share of teasing in school just as I had, and I think that was why we bonded. When the cool kids took jabs at us, sometimes literally, we had each other's back. I tried to teach Harold to shoot back. Then, one day, a small incident turned huge.

Harold traded one of his G.I. Joe figures for one of mine, as we had often done temporarily, for a week or two tops. But this time we traded "for keeps." I was all for it, and so was Harold. All was well until the next day when Harold came to school and requested a "trade-back" when we had specifically stated there were to be no "trade-backs."[2] Kid rule is legally binding. Harold gave me a long sob story about his mother finding out he had traded his toys and whipping him good over it, but I didn't want to hear it. I refused the trade-back.

Harold was persistent. When he realized that I wouldn't budge and that he couldn't tell the teacher, he decided he didn't want any more whippings, so he followed me home from school to get his toy back.

"I'm not trading back, Harold! Just go home!" I yelled with increasing desperation in my voice at the gangly giant who was three steps behind me.

Harold responded, "I need it back!"

We arrived at my house, and my mother was outside.

Harold told her the whole story. My mother hadn't known that I was trading toys either, but I didn't think she'd mind. She not only minded, but she also proceeded to whip me both for the whipping that I caused Harold and again over trading toys that she spent her hard-earned money. Our friendship was over because of a toy.

For the next few days, I unleashed every insult I could at Harold, but only when the cool kids were around, so my insults would sting harder. I was determined to make Harold the most hated kid in the fifth grade. I was relentless. Unfortunately, I was so relentless that my strategy backfired. A girl, Melanie, came to Harold's rescue.

A girl! None of us had any luck with girls, but my insults had gotten him female attention. All of the effects I'd hoped for, *that* was certainly

---

[2] Trade back (v): A request to cancel a previously agreed upon trade.

not one of them. I was infuriated. There had to be drastic measures taken. I plotted for the remainder of the day.

During an art project in class, Harold left his seat to get additional help. I picked up his bottle of Elmer's Glue for the perfect prank.

I squirted the white bottle of glue all over the seat of his chair, emptying it, hoping that when he sat down, the chair would be stuck to his butt forever, like something out of a Three Stooges sketch. I laughed out loud at the thought of awkward, dorky Harold yelling, "It's stuck, it's stuck!" and the whole class cracking up and then carrying me out on their shoulders as some stupid prank king.

Harold approached the chair and was still engaged in a conversation. Perfect. He wasn't even looking at the chair! Then, as he stood right above the milky, white mess, I had the worst feeling of regret come over me. It was a strange feeling because the worst hadn't even happened yet. *What did I do?*

I sprang into action. Just as Harold was sitting down and was not even three inches from contact, I slipped a piece of yellow construction paper over the glue spill. Crisis averted. He had no idea that I saved both his pants and his life. That is, he had no idea until a girl next to him saw the paper. She pulled it up, and they saw all the glue on the seat. I got my worst punishment and beating from my mother and babysitter. Worse though, I lost a good friend.

My mother only showed up at school to embarrass me twice that I can recall. The first time was in third grade after I got in trouble for playing with a special pen Mom had bought me from the casino. During class, my teacher Mrs. Branch told me to put it in her closet. When I got there, I saw the mother lode—a basket of trinkets and toys she collected from different students all year long. My eyes lit up when I saw the pile of G.I. Joe figures, tennis balls, key chains, and Garbage Pail Kids cards. On top though, was a GoBot. GoBots were bootleg Transformers. They haven't gotten any cool remakes or movies yet. But it wasn't just any GoBot; it was Cy-Kill, leader of the bad guys. I knew that toy belonged to Tyrece, the cool kid who sat at my table but didn't speak to me much.

I knew if I could rescue Cy-Kill, I could open a friendship with Tyrece. Without another thought, I grabbed the GoBot and broke out.

I didn't get three steps from the closet before Mrs. Branch said, "Re-heem?" (She never pronounced my name correctly), "what's that in your hand?"

The whole class sounded a long "ooooooooh" in unison, and it was over. Worse than getting busted in front of the whole class was the fact Tyrece thought I was attempting to steal his toy instead of returning it to him. Mrs. Branch decided to turn my crime into a teachable moment by allowing the entire class to vote on my punishment. Way to ostracize me, Mrs. Branch! My chosen punishment was to write "I will not take things that do not belong to me from the teacher's closet" five hundred times, Bart Simpson style, over the coming weekend. I voted for "I will behave," but that was overruled unanimously. Mom came to school, with Miss Gertrude, my super strict babysitter. I instantly burst into tears the moment I saw her. Mom dropped me off at Miss Gertrude's where the punishment began. Miss Gertrude made me stand while completing the writing assignment, as I cried.

The second time Mom got called to school was because I'd gotten suspended for the silliest thing imaginable. When leaving class one day in middle school, I thought it would be hilarious to turn the lights out on the teacher, old Mr. Addison, a wily Black man north of seventy and arguably senile. He was the science instructor, but all we did in his class was issue out spelling tests. He refused to learn anyone's names correctly and chastised any attempt to correct his pronunciation. He called me "Jab-O" over and over, and eventually, my fellow students adopted it, so I was Jab-O for the rest of the school year. I hated it. That's why, as a form of passive-aggressive retaliation, I turned the lights out on him. Of course, I got caught. My principal said that I endangered the life and safety of every student in the class, so I was rewarded with a three-day suspension. Mom had to leave work and travel twenty-five miles up the expressway to pick me up, and she was not happy at all. I could hear my mother from down the school halls yelling, "Where is that boy?" I knew this wouldn't be good. She berated me in front of the class, telling me how hard she works, how I'm never going to see the light of day and how I was going to get my butt "worn out" when I got home that day.

The classroom can be a lot like the jungle. You learn quickly in school that there are two types of kids: predators and prey. If you aren't at the top of the food chain, you are bound to get eaten by the lion of the classroom. I found a third personality type that I fit into quite neatly: comic. I would be the hyena of the situation. As a jokester who was pretty good at impressions, I could make kids laugh and talk my way out of the tensest of situations. Being a funny guy saved my skin more than a few times, but it often backfired.

During gym class in fourth grade, the class clown in me had to show its face the most, as I was about as far from an athlete as one could be. Bad enough my chubby legs were exposed in the way-too-short gym shorts we wore, but climbing ropes and running were not my forte, so diversions were most necessary here.

During some type of circuit training exercises, I remember hanging upside down on the parallel bars like an uncoordinated ape, under instruction from Mrs. Jones, a mean Black woman in her early forties who had no time for any foolishness. She called everyone by their last name and hated my jokes and silliness. I tried every excuse I could to get out of running and jumping in class but to no avail. Her favorite line was, "Don't play games with me, Jarbo."

As I hung, I could see the coolest kid in class approaching me, Tyrone Dorman. He was the kid in fourth grade who had the smoothest skin, the brightest smile, and the newest fashions every day of the week. To loosely quote the song "It Takes Two," ladies loved him; girls adored him. He approached me in his new Adidas sweat suit, fresh shell toes, and his herringbone chain glistening in the low light of the gymnasium.

In a playful, harmless manner, he lightly tapped me on the arm, simulating a shove. His tap wasn't enough to make me fall, or to hurt me; it was meant to be a quick motion to gain a quick chuckle and be forgotten about a second later. But not for class clown Jarbo.

When Tyrone tapped me, I had a delayed reaction; when I realized the potential to make a moment with a cool kid, I snapped into action. I immediately let go of the parallel bars and yelled. I imagined myself hitting the ground, Tyrone seeing me in a crumpled heap on the crash pad, and us sharing a hearty belly laugh that we'd be able to reminisce on later over a square pizza at lunch. That's not the way it happened. I didn't judge my landing when I let go, and I fell directly on my left arm, separating my shoulder in the process. I instantly let out a howl, and the tears ran down my face.

To add insult to injury, a few bystanders saw the act go down, and all pointed out Tyrone as the culprit, so even if I hadn't wanted to out him, the damage was done. I didn't know how bad the injury was; I just knew I was hurting. I walked over to Ms. Jones to tell her I'd broken my arm. In true "The Boy Who Cried Wolf" fashion, she didn't believe I was injured. "Don't play games with me, Jarbo!"

I cried, "It's broken, it's broken!"

Ms. Jones told me to sit on the Bench and shut up. I struggled to hold back the tears as the children watched. When I sat down, another student asked, "Are you really hurt?"

"YES!"

Luckily, this student was more trustworthy than I, because when she told Ms. Jones, the teacher said, "Take him to the nurse's office. But if you're faking Jarbo, I'm writing you up."

I had my arm in a sling for three weeks following the accident. Tyrone was blamed for the injury and was suspended from school. He lived a few blocks away from me. One weekend when I was sitting outside, Tyrone walked up. When I told Mom who he was, she started yelling at him, and it got intense. I tried to calm the situation down.

Just when I was about to tell Tyrone the truth about why I'd fallen, he interrupted me with his announcement. "Uh, I uh, just wanted to let you know... I'm sorry, man. I really shouldn't have done that. I feel so bad." Tyrone's voice began to crack. "Look, man, I didn't mean it." Tyrone began to cry, wracked with guilt over something that he didn't even technically do. As he talked and the tears rolled, I realized that I didn't need to say anything. Instead, I decided to wait and see how it would play out.

The next two weeks at school were awesome. When anyone teased me about my arm being jacked up, Tyrone hopped in and defended me. We became best friends that year in school, and I never had to talk my way out of a fight again because Tyrone had my back. I wanted to tell him that he hadn't pushed me off the parallel bars and I injured myself in a silly attempt to make him laugh, but I didn't see the need to complicate matters. Maybe he'll read this book and chuckle about it.

My being such a troublemaker in school led to a lot of alone time, even more than you'd imagine an only child with a workaholic mother would have. I was constantly grounded or put on restriction. I spent so much time in my room that I began talking to myself. I had a doll that I called my brother. I named him Scott. Scott was a White male doll with freckles and light brown yarn for hair, and his blue eyes would close when he laid down. He wore blue corduroy overalls and brown boots. I'd talk to Scott and he always encouraged me. I'd sit Scott down with me on the floor as I filled sketch books with new GI Joes, Transformers, and video game ideas. With time, sketches got so impressive that my friends in school would ask me to draw for them. One day I came home and I thought I heard Scott suggest that I send these sketches to Hasbro.

That was the only time Scott and I argued, because I disagreed and didn't think Hasbro would want to see some nine-year old's drawings. But he was persistent so I decided I'd try. I drew six new Transformers designs with names, ability rankings and back stories, and put them in an envelope with a neatly typed letter that I'd printed on my neighbor's word processor. I copied the address to Hasbro from the back of my toys and sent it out to Pawtucket, Rhode Island, asking Hasbro, Inc. to "please make these toys."

Months later, I got the first piece of mail addressed to me that I'd ever received, and inside it was a letter to "Mr. Raheem Jarbo." It was the first time I'd ever been addressed as "Mr." and "sir." Although the letter was a very nice rejection, it did inspire me. Hasbro told me to seek a Patent for these designs, then resubmit in the future. They included information on how patents worked, and were way nicer to me than they had to be. They don't know it, but Hasbro's letter is the very first time I'd thought my work was good enough to be shared with others. I thanked Scott for the encouragement.

I started middle school in 1988. It was the first year that a voluntary school desegregation busing bill passed in Philadelphia. The bill allowed the city to offer bus services to inner city (read: Black) students who wanted to attend schools other than their neighborhood schools (read: White schools). The deseg bill as it was known caused quite a bit of upheaval in the city, as suburban parents argued heavily against busing. It's strange this didn't happen until the '80s in a big, liberal progressive city like Philadelphia. I mean, Brown v. Board of Education, the landmark case that segregated American public schools, was passed in 1954.

The proverbial floodgates opened. The finest schools in the Northeast came to our schools and presented state-of-the-art (in 1990) slideshows to recruit us. Everyone in my sixth grade class was excited about the opportunity to attend fancy, formerly all-White schools in Northeast Philadelphia, which housed amenities our neighborhood schools could only dream of, such as chess clubs, home economics, wood and metal shop, current textbooks, edible lunchroom food... you know, the works.

I attended Benjamin Rush Middle School, which was named after a man who opposed the idea of slavery, argued for free public schools, improved education for women, and supported a more enlightened penal system. Rush Middle had all the amenities we dreamed of, but with more racial tension than I'd ever seen previously in my life. Coincidentally "Rush" was also a Philadelphia slang term for a beatdown, which I saw plenty of when I got there. Things got serious for me when I noticed none of my middle school friends had toys. *It's time to be a man,* I thought, so I gave away most of my toys to younger kids in the neighborhood, including Scott.

School in a predominantly White neighborhood was a lot different than I was used to. First, it wasn't the suburbs we saw on television.

The houses in the Northeast were nicer, but our White classmates lived in low-income housing like us and shared our parents' disdain for government. We didn't know where they lived, however. All we knew was that we didn't look alike, which made us sworn enemies for some reason. People wonder where children learn to hate. I'd heard my relatives at home talking about the evils of White people, and I'm sure they heard the same things at home about Black people. I saw the environment that fosters bigotry firsthand. Racially charged epithets flew every day, in both directions, and there was almost always a fight in the bathroom over the smallest things—a glare or sometimes even a smile.

The racial separation was apparent, even to me. I'd never been taught to dislike anyone based on their physiological makeup, so I made friends wherever I could. But a strange thing happened every day. Each morning at 7 a.m., I'd meet my Black classmates at our old elementary school where we waited for the school bus that would ferry us away to the Burbs. Along the way we chatted about hip-hop music or the previous night's episode of *In Living Color*. When I got to school, I'd talk video games, *The Simpsons*, WWF wrestling, and comic books with my White friends, because I was nowhere near cool enough to hang with the Black kids I'd just talked to and laughed with on the bus. Fascinating.

I'd usually come bearing a mixtape I'd made the previous night with my trusty General Electric brand Kid-Corder, a bright red and yellow cassette recorder. I'd sit next to the TV and record the latest mix of the *Hot 9 at 9*, the radio's countdown show, Cosmic Kev's RadioActive mix show on Power 99FM, or the top ten videos on *Yo! MTV Raps*. But the game changed once Mom let me rent *Mega Man 2* from Blockbuster one weekend.

Mega Man 2's music was unlike anything I had ever heard. One day, when playing on Air Man's stage, I realized the music continued to play when you hit pause, and it gave me a crazy idea. I used the Kid-Corder to capture music from the game, but I accidentally recorded it over the same ninety-minute Maxell cassette I used to record all my classic hip-hop jams.

This fortuitous mistake proved one of the most instrumental moves I'd ever made and helped shape the artist I am today. The Sony

Walkman had a feature called auto reverse, which I had never really seen the point of using; auto reverse allowed you to play the opposite side of the cassette without removing and flipping it over. While I switched between Takashi Tateishi's sparse, yet lush, eight-bit melodies of *Mega Man 2* and Hank Shocklee and the Bomb Squad's hard-hitting, funk-laced soundscapes of Public Enemy tracks, something clicked. Hip-hop and video games become the soundtrack to my forty-five minute bus rides, and later, my life.

The friends I made that year also turned me into the sports fan that I am today. It all started in eighth grade math class when Mr. Docktor told us to pick the score of the Eagles playoff game; whoever guessed the closest would get an extra five points toward their most recent test score. I needed those points, so I sat through that game and watched the Eagles fall to the Redskins, six to twenty, on my thirteen-inch black and white TV. I had picked a point total of twenty-five, so I was closest. I kept watching as the Redskins eventually make it to the Super Bowl and win, led by the first African-American quarterback ever to win an NFL championship, Doug Williams. My aunt lived in DC, and they were still feeling the sting of Jesse Jackson's failed presidential run, so I didn't mind the 'Skins winning. Run, Doug, Run.

Despite the daily conflicts and drama, I made plenty of friends at Benjamin Rush. I left eighth grade early to move to South Carolina with my mother so she could take care of my ill grandfather who was very close to the end. My mother was the baby of the family. Since she had the fewest number of family members who would be inconvenienced by a move, we had to move to handle Pop-Pop's final business.

Throughout most of the '80s and '90s, traveling to South Carolina was an annual tradition for mother and me. We'd pack her 1987 Buick Skylark with coolers, gifts for the family, and a week's worth of clothing for our annual excursion down I-95. We did this until Uncle Bobby was murdered. After that, we didn't take as many trips, as the dark roads reminded us of what could be the worst-case scenario on a road trip.

Before I left for SC, the students at Rush threw me a going away party, overseen by my teacher, Mrs. Green. As the cake and Hawaiian Punch were being passed around, Mrs. Green called me to the front of the classroom to make a speech. When I finished, each student gave me a homemade card they had been secretly working on since homeroom. Some were elaborate, and some were crude, but each had been made with love. I accepted the gifts and trinkets.

The last person to approach the podium was Malaika, a girl who I had liked all school year. Malaika whispered in my ear, "We're going to miss you, Jarbo."

I stood speechless. After I collected my cards and devoured my cake and punch, I asked to use the restroom. Typically, one student was required to walk with another student to the bathroom, per school policy. Malaika jumped up and volunteered to accompany me, for the first time.

When we got outside the classroom, it happened. Malaika moved in for what would be my first kiss ever. It was sweet and warm, and the scent of her cherry Lip Smackers lip gloss remained on my face for the rest of the school day. I spent most of the day blushing, but no one could tell. My lips were on fire. Malaika gave me her phone number and address. Although we communicated occasionally, I never saw her again. I resented Mom and Pop-Pop for robbing me of the chance for a first real girlfriend.

The road trip to South Carolina was a party. Mom would blast her Motown Greatest Hits cassette on repeat until I knew every Temptations, Jacksons, and Stevie Wonder jam like the back of my hand. Then we'd switch to her old standby, Harold Melvin and the Blue Notes' Greatest Classics. I believe it was on these trips that music became such an integral part of my lifeblood. Those ten-plus hour drives were a bonding exercise for Mom and me, as they represented the most consecutive number of hours that I would spend with her, beating out the hour on school days by a long shot. We'd make each other laugh attempting to emulate young Michael Jackson's falsetto, or Teddy Pendergrass's signature growling holler on "Wake Up Everybody."

Located twenty-five miles south of Charlotte, Mom's hometown of Rock Hill, South Carolina began as a transfer point for Confederate soldiers during the Civil War. The city was racked with debt after the war. She grew up in a section called Boyd Hill, a low-income, majority Black neighborhood on the southern side of the city where she attended segregated schools.

Rock Hill was the setting for two significant events in the civil rights movement. In February 1961, nine African-American men went to jail at the York County prison farm after staging a sit-in at a segregated restaurant lunch counter in downtown Rock Hill. Their offense was reported to be "refusing to stop singing hymns during their morning devotions." The event gained nationwide attention as the men adopted a new and untested strategy called "jail, no bail."

Rejecting bail was a way to lessen the huge financial burden that civil rights groups were facing as the sit-in movement spread across the South; after an arrest, it was the organization's funds that were used to bail people out. As their actions gained widespread national news coverage, other civil rights groups adopted the tactic. The men became known as the Friendship Nine because eight of the nine men were students at Rock Hill's Friendship Junior College.

Later, in 1961, Rock Hill was the first stop in the Deep South for a group of thirteen Freedom Riders who boarded buses in Washington, DC and headed south to test the 1960 ruling by the U.S. Supreme Court outlawing racial segregation in all interstate public facilities. When civil rights leader John Lewis and another Black man stepped off the bus at Rock Hill, they were beaten by a White mob that was uncontrolled by police. The event drew national attention. Mom watched this on television as an eleven-year-old southern girl.

When we arrived in Rock Hill, the word seemed to spread instantly. It was as if Paul Revere hopped in a Cadillac with a bullhorn and hit the neighborhood ahead of us. Once we visited one aunt or uncle, the whole city was on notice. Folks in the South make family visits into a big deal, so that meant more hugs, cheek squeezing, gifts, and most importantly, more food than one person could ever handle. I think I gained most of my weight in the South.

Every night of the week was special. There were fresh-caught shrimp and stone-ground corn grits with biscuits and gravy for breakfast, fish fries at the local Veterans of Foreign Wars organization on Tuesdays, and chicken and dumplings on a random Wednesday just because. But, Sunday dinners in the South were the stuff of legend.

On any given day after church, my aunts would somehow make it home in time to prepare the most immaculate of meals in what seemed like seconds. The table would be full of amazing colors: golden fried chicken, beautifully browned macaroni and cheese, bright green collards, all of which was to be chased by sun-drenched homemade iced tea. The tables were set perfectly, covered with the finest of linens and adorned with hand-stitched lace doilies. We would join hands over the smorgasbord and thank the Lord for the goodness we were about to consume, and dig in.

Being a kid from up north, moving down South elevated my coolness level immensely, as the students at Rawlinson Road Middle School were instantly intrigued by the kid from the big, scary city of Philly who wore name brand sneakers and a Starter jacket. Ironically, my mother only bought me those things so I wouldn't be teased in school, and they wound up making me the coolest kid in my Southern surroundings.

While everyone up north sported the short satin jackets with a team name emblazoned across, mine was different. It was a newer release, a three-quarter length black and white Los Angeles Raiders coat stuffed with goose feathers. It had kept me warm on many blustery Philadelphia mornings. It instantly made me a hit with the Rawlinson Road boys, who admired my sports know-how. Even the girls were impressed. I made friends more quickly than I ever had in the past. I felt like Cinderella at the ball with my silver and black glass slippers. Bo Jackson could've been my fairy godmother, I guess.

Midnight would soon strike on this puffy advantage in the form of the a blistering hot, humid summer. While this coat was essential in the cold north, as the school year went on, temperatures rose in Rock Hill. On top of the heat, the sweltering humidity made it much too hot to wear the coat. I prolonged the moment as long as I could, wearing it well into the spring with short sleeve t-shirts underneath, and even shorts on a few days, until eventually, I sweat my way through them. Didn't matter, I begged my mother to wear the coat, no matter how high the forecast would go. I feared no one would like me without it. Luckily, I'd made enough friends in the first few months that when I finally hung the Starter up for the season, they hung around.

In the spring of 1990, Fairy Godmother Bo Jackson hung up his Raiders jersey temporarily to play baseball, and UNLV's Runnin' Rebels became the talk of college basketball, and beyond. Coached by Jerry Tarkanian, aka "Tark the Shark," the Rebels consistently led the NCAA in points; they turned most games into blowouts quickly. They managed to rack up two of the most impressive college basketball seasons of all time in 1990 and 1991 before things crumbled. UNLV was full of off the court recruiting violations and misconduct allegations that constantly put the team's chances of playing in jeopardy. Power forward Larry Johnson led the team to a near flawless record.

Larry was a six foot five, two-hundred-and-fifty-pound monster on the court, and was never seen without a fresh fade haircut with a part directly in the center of his head, and his sparkling gold tooth. He was outspoken in interviews and threw down thunderous dunks at game time. Larry made waves when he referred to himself and his teammates as "rebellious slaves." The UNLV Rebels forged a connection between sports and hip-hop culture, which was something that had never been done before. The Rebels became the blueprint for teams such as Michigan's Fab Five, who adopted the look and swagger of hip-hop and brought it to the court.

Rock Hill was only thirty minutes from Charlotte, and the city was abuzz when the NBA awarded the town a franchise, the Charlotte Hornets, in 1989. The franchise was placed in the hands of a man with perhaps the worst name ever in sports, Coach Dick Harter. After two rough seasons, led by blue-collar no-names like Kelly Tripucka and Earl Cureton, the Hornets managed to land the number one pick in the NBA draft in 1991. As expected, they drafted Larry Johnson who went on to become an All-Star in his rookie year and a full-blown superstar the next. I traded in my Raiders Starter coat for a satin Hornets jacket that summer.

As nerdy as I had become about sports, I maintained my love for video games, which put me in a unique position. At almost the same time, *Mega Man 3* was released for the Nintendo Entertainment System, and early reviews declared it another huge step in innovation for the franchise. New weapons and gameplay enhancements were added (Mega could slide out of sticky situations!), story gaps were filled in using cartoon-like cut scenes, and the music was as outstanding as ever. I needed every trick in my arsenal to get this game, which retailed for forty-nine dollars and ninety-nine cents.

After several failed attempts to rent the game at Blockbuster, I wound up trading every NES game I owned with a kid at school to get *Mega Man 3*. I remember arguing with the student about video game music; he said it was stupid, and that the game sucked. I was determined to get it, so I agreed with him and suggest he trade *Mega Man 3* away, which I thought was incredible. He made the trade with me. Since it was so early in its release, there were no cheat codes or walkthroughs available. I spent my time blindly attacking the game, which I found extremely difficult.

Meanwhile, back on the east coast, the hip-hop group Public Enemy was gearing up to release their fourth studio album, *Apocalypse 91...The Enemy Strikes Black*. Powered by the fiery singles "Bring the Noise" and "Can't Truss It," P.E. was on fire. The album managed to garner significant radio play and present a strong and positive message about cleaning up and taking back the African-American community; that was a combination that most bands, even today, cannot manage. The album contained the controversial cut "By the Time I Get to Arizona," which is a song about the state's unwillingness to observe Martin Luther King Jr.'s birthday as a national holiday. "I'll never go to Arizona," my foolish fourteen-year-old self said, as I bobbed my head to the sensational beats.

P.E. member Chuck D. was brash, yet articulate. He got his point across by placing his booming voice over dope beats. In 1991, my heroes had shifted from Stan Lee to Spike Lee and from Spider-Man and Wolverine to Larry Johnson and Chuck D. South Carolina had surprisingly shaped so many hobbies and habits that have stuck with me to this day. As much as I dreaded moving to Rock Hill initially, those eight months proved essential to my upbringing. After handling Pop Pop's final affairs and selling his South Carolina home, Mom and I moved back to Philadelphia, where the block and the house I grew up in awaited.

CHAPTER THREE

KING

Never thought that I would be in demand
High school they wouldn't let me in the band
Something 'bout believing you can...

—"Journey," Extra Credit (2017)

I N 2001 THE U.S. CONGRESS passed the No Child Left Behind Act, reauthorizing the Elementary and Secondary Education Act; it included Title I provisions applying to disadvantaged students. It supported standards-based education reform based on the premise that setting high standards and establishing measurable goals could improve individual outcomes in education.

The Act did plenty to improve education. The problem was, I went to school before it passed. I lived through the reasons why it was needed. This was especially true while I was in eighth grade.

After arriving back in Philadelphia in 1992, I attended Martin Luther King High School, which became not so affectionately known as "AIDS High" after a Philadelphia urban legend ran rampant. In 1990, two years before I attended the school, seniors were encouraged to give blood, and one of the seventy-eight samples came back positive for HIV, the virus that causes AIDS. This got out through local news, and the story traveled like stories do. One student turned into ten, then half the school supposedly had it. Just like that, the school's reputation became tainted.

Not so ironically, it wasn't until almost four years into my time at "AIDS High," when ready to graduate and senioritis was at a fever pitch, did my class spend a period researching AIDS and its causes. And not because it was part of the curriculum, but because our homeroom teacher shared with us that Eazy-E of the group NWA had died from complications related to HIV/AIDS, just one month after his diagnosis.

We were stunned. I'd heard some NWA records at my cousin's house. I remember sneaking into his cassette stash and playing "Straight Outta Compton" in 1989 before bed and being terrified of the ultra-violent and vulgar content. When I finally got to sleep that night, I dreamed that I was in a drive-by shooting with NWA. I heard Dr. Dre yelling, "DAMN THAT SH*T WAS DOPE!" like he does at the end of the title track. It's a very vivid memory. In 1995, Eazy and Dr. Dre were embroiled in a very public feud in which the two exchanged diss tracks. Eazy's "Real Compton City G's" (that's the edited version's title) got plenty of burn on The BOX, a music video program powered by phone-in requests, which ran twenty-four seven.

Knowing Eazy-E meant something to his students, my instructor wisely turned his death into a teachable moment. But this was the only time AIDS was ever discussed in class. And teachable moments like these were few when, every day of my high school tenure, there were many instances of gang-related fights. Students and staff even wound up hospitalized. The fights always went down at lunchtime. Once I watched two students pound on the discipline coach, a fifty-year-old man, until he was bloodied.

Worst of all, during my senior year, a teacher was raped at the school. On a Friday morning one April, around 6:30 a.m., someone broke into the school with a knife, cornered a teacher, and had his way with her. It was believed that the perpetrator was not a student at the school, but no one really knows. Classes were canceled the following Monday and counseling was offered to students.

My many escape routes sheltered me from most of the violence at school. The place was massive, with four floors and over two hundred rooms spread across a building that was the size of half a city block. There were bullies around every corner at King, just waiting for an excuse to pound on a nerd. Students who were easy prey had to avoid the most common areas at all costs. The nerdy kids like myself were in a charter called Academics Plus, and we spent our lunch period trading basketball cards or playing chess, far away from any cafeteria drama. Our teacher, Mr. Green, would buy boxes of baseball, basketball, and Marvel Comics cards wholesale, and sell us packs for a dollar each during lunch. Every day we worked on our collections and traded in a safe environment. But if anyone had to go to the bathroom, we never walked alone.

I watched my friend Stanley get punched square in the chest during a lunch break when we wandered past the wrong restroom. The kid asked all of us if we had fifty cents; we all said no, but Stan hesitated a bit.

The bully sensed weakness and moved in like a shark. "Yo, you don't want to help me out?"

Stan stammered, "I don't-I don't have anything."

The goon then suggested we find out exactly what Stan had, by demanding that he empty his pockets. "Rabbit Ears" was the exact request. Stan pulled the pockets of his stonewashed Lee jeans, and we all sunk when we heard the jingling of change in his pants. Stan had made an egregious mistake.

"Why you lie, yo?" the bully asked, clenching his fists, and stepping closer to Stan.

"I-I-I didn't—"

—POW!

A jarring blow to Stan's solar plexus. He tried hard not to cry in front of us, and I appreciated that at the time, but the tears escaped and crept down his cheeks. The two other kids and I just looked forward, unflinchingly, prepared for the same fate as Stan. The bully took about seventy-five cents in change from Stan and moved on as we all exhaled a sigh of relief. I feel bad about not stepping up for Stan, but I think he and the others with me all understood what would have happened had any of us made a move.

Sometimes I don't know how we made it out. In the midst of this literal war zone where gangs collided and weapons were drawn, we had some incredible lights, in the form of instructors who constantly pushed us to the limit. While many teachers gave the bare minimum, Mr. Jones, though he cursed up a storm at us, gave us the economic know how we needed, going above and beyond the state mandates. Mrs.

Dixon, my English teacher, used to give us college-level assignments and challenged us. She taught Kevin Eubanks, a famous jazz musician who, for many years, worked as Jay Leno's bandleader on *The Tonight Show*. I met Kevin later in life and discovered that he also credits Mrs. Dixon for inspiring him to succeed.

In 1992, my freshman year at King, I was still a huge video game lover. I subscribed to *Electronic Gaming Monthly*, *Game Pro*, and several other video game magazines. I would bring those to school and study new techniques on *Street Fighter II* to try out at the arcade after school let out.

It was through those books that I met Tariq, who would become my best friend in high school and college. Tariq was often teased, much like me. He had a birthmark on his forehead that caused a discoloration almost perfectly symmetrical on each side, which made kids call him "Two-Face," after the Batman villain. I was teased about my weight and called "Jumbo" as a clever play on my last name, so I understood what being teased felt like; we shared a common bond.

Tariq was incredibly smart and challenged traditional thought at every turn. He would even stump the teachers with his questions. I was so impressed with his intelligence that after tests, I'd ask him what he scored, hoping I had beat him. We made a game of trying to prove who was the smartest. We constantly quizzed each other on facts we learned both in and out of the classroom.

We both knew how to talk our way into and out of pretty much anything, but we began ostracizing ourselves when our intelligence competitions went too far. We went from trying to best each other's test scores to mocking students who failed to reach our level. Our friend Darrell wasn't pictured in the early version of the yearbook because he failed Algebra II, and we never let him live it down. He told us he would make it up in summer school, but we continued teasing him. When I couldn't compete on basketball courts or collecting girls' phone numbers, I would make the report card become my battleground.

As the years went on though, I began to struggle academically, even falling behind a bit while Tariq continued to excel. Rather than trust the teachers to help me, I learned a trick from Tariq to manage the heavy workload.

He said, "Just be nice." It's a mantra I use to this day.

Tariq told me to be the first person to get to class and the last one to leave. He advised me to offer help to the instructor whenever I could. This behavior resulted in our being called "Teacher's Pets," but by then that was just another name to add to the sticks and stones we caught daily. After a few weeks of being early to classes and staying late to help, the teachers appreciated my efforts so much that, miraculously, my grades began to rise.

At the time I was excited, but later I was angry at the teachers who let me slide by with Cs, and at my physics teacher Mr. Gettys who put a ridiculous curve on our tests, using a formula of the square root of the score times ten. By that scale a forty-nine, an F, becomes a seventy or a C, a thirty-six becomes a sixty or a D. Like I said, it was ridiculous. It was also extremely effective at increasing my grades. I passed high school geometry just because I was the only person who came every day on time to our first period class. I got a C on the first exam and failed every single one after that. Somehow, however, I ended the year with that same C. I didn't know anything, but being nice got me farther than studying did.

Being on the King Cougars football team would have made me less of a target for bullies, and as a big guy, I was encouraged to try out. I tried to tell them I could catch, and I was faster than I looked, but they were determined that all big men worked the front lines. They worked the big men. It was the most fun I never wanted to have again. On the first day of practice, I split my pants, dislocated my thumb by incorrectly holding a tackling sled, and threw up after running the track. Mom wouldn't let me return to practice after that, despite the coach's attempts to get me back.

Sports weren't the only ways students came to define themselves outside of academics. I was in my junior year in 1993 when the hip-hop bug caught me. It was the beginning of what was about to become a second golden age of hip-hop music; the first being in 1988. It all began for us when we noticed during homeroom class that if we turned the television to channel sixty-eight, we could get The BOX, my favorite station. OutKast dropped smooth rhymes over funky beats, and Common (then known as Common Sense), had a quirky single running the airwaves called "Soul by The Pound," which caught my attention when he dropped a line that said, "I never saw CB4 'cause I heard that sh*t was whack." I hadn't seen it either because it was Rated R. I chuckled, and I wanted more.

Our homeroom teacher allowed The BOX to run as students socialized and completed (read: copied) homework assignments while tunes from Onyx, Dr. Dre, and Wu-Tang Clan ran in the background. Hip-hop was slowly and surely seeping into my pores, and sometimes it ran into the foreground.

On one occasion during lunchtime at King, I heard rumblings about a devastating female rapper. She was the talk of the school. We snuck into a different lunch period and hopped in the cafeteria to watch our school's resident rapper Eve Jeffers tear through opposing MCs daily. Donning a short blond 'do,' and a mid-length denim skirt, almost matching the school's colors perfectly, Eve was fly and ferocious. The self-proclaimed "Pitbull in a skirt" took no prisoners, as she dropped impressive line after line. We all knew she'd be famous one day and we were right. Eve would go on to work with Dr. Dre and be known as the first lady of the Ruff Ryders crew. Eve dropped several platinum and gold albums before moving on to TV and film. She is an integral part of Philadelphia's hip-hop history. Today, Wikipedia says I'm the second most notable rapper from my high school behind Eve. I'm totally fine with that.

On top of this, during my high school tenure legendary hip-hop band The Roots was making a name for themselves in South Philly, dropping impressive singles like "Proceed," and gearing up for their major label debut. I had to get some of this action; it was so close, I felt it.

I secretly wrote raps at home, hopped up off the rush of Eve, then Wu-Tang Clan, Nas, Notorious B.I.G., and other legendary east coast rhyme slingers. The cadence, the patterns, the punchlines – I did whatever I could to keep up with the intense rap displays I heard while managing to keep it clean. I don't know why, but I just knew I had to keep the lyrics PG-13. If Mom heard me cussing, I don't think I would've been ready for the repercussions. I wanted raps my family could listen to. But first, I needed a code name.

I started out as "The R," a tribute to Rakim, who was my favorite rapper. I never thought about how disrespectful (let alone unoriginal) it was to use an existing, legendary artist's nickname as my own name. Imagine a new rapper today naming himself Young Biggie, or Lil Jay-Z – foolish. At the time though I didn't take it seriously, so it didn't matter. But when I began recording, I realized that I couldn't fully invest in a name that was borrowed from another rapper, especially one of legendary proportions.

It's hardly a coincidence that my next moniker came from comic books since everyone around me at the time read comics faithfully. The '90s were home to a huge boom as *Marvel Comics*, led by visionaries such as Todd McFarlane, Jim Lee, Rob Liefield and more, churned out comics that sold millions of copies. My favorites were *Spider-Man*, *X-Men*, and *X-Factor*. Of these, *X-Factor* had a very intriguing story arc that introduced a character by the name of Random, a shape-shifter. Not only was he cool looking, but he also had an awesome power. Not long after that issue was done, I had a new name. I became Random.

In my very first rap verse – which was terrible by the way – I made references to all of the things I love. I recall a particular set of couplets:

> I throw down like Shaq does a dunk
> Then I got another surprise for dumb punks.
> When you hit the ground, it goes THOOM
> Then hit you with a SHORYUKEN or a SONIC BOOM!

I'd managed to fit in sports as well a *Street Fighter II* reference, which confused my rap partners. This was rap, after all. A gladiator's sport. No time for that nerdy stuff. My rap was whack, but I got flack for all the wrong reasons. They all said I was too geeky to be an MC.

Street Fighter II hit arcades in 1991 and was such a runaway hit that an updated version was released each successive year. The 1992 iterations, *Street Fighter II: Champion Edition* and *Street Fighter II Turbo: Hyper Fighting* (a faster version of *Champion Edition*) became my favorite, and a game I will plunk a quarter into without thinking to this day.

SFII dominated arcades and spawned a fighting game resurgence in the industry. This led to games such as *Mortal Kombat* and many more. The home version of the game was the most expensive game ever released, dropping on a sixteen-megabit cartridge, unthinkable at the time, and with a seventy-five-dollar price point. My next-door neighbor, Zane, got the game for Christmas and we'd play rounds for hours over a soundtrack of Redman, Das Efx, and Beastie Boys albums. Afterward, we'd write rhymes and share.

The crew was born and consisted of Zane, Big Al, his brother Chuck, and my friend Ant who lived around the corner. We became The Firm, a rap group named after the 1993 John Grisham novel about a law firm with mob ties. We somehow transmogrified it to fit our persona of intellectual MCs. We later changed it to The N.E.T., which stood for "Never Ending Talent." It was an intricate web of verbal scientists, assassins, and generally smart dudes. Think *Mission Impossible* for rappers. Pretty geeky, when I look back on it.

We recorded together on four-track recorders and a Radio Shack mic. At first, we rapped over existing rappers' instrumental tracks, obtained by the purchase of maxi-single cassettes that included an instrumental version. We also got creative and looped the end of a beat with the beginning of its next measure through the creative use of the "Record" and "Rec Pause" buttons on our boomboxes. Later, once I got the hang of MTV Music Generator, I was making beats for the crew, as well as dropping verses. I was like the RZA of The N.E.T. The RZA served as the Abbot of Wu-Tang, claiming his place at the head of the table. The King. I just didn't know it yet.

Not sure of what to do after high school, I visited my advisor to talk about college options. She broke it down for me, much like I had heard the year before, almost word for word.

"Raheem…You're gonna have to work ten times harder, ten times faster, and ten times BETTER just to get the same opportunities as a White student. Your best has to be better."

I knew this well because I'd heard it so many times. But when the smoke cleared in 1995, I ranked nineteenth in my class of over three hundred graduates at an achieving high school, and I was taking college prep courses. I maintained a B+ average throughout my high school career, with only one C, ever. Basically, I looked like the perfect college candidate.

But the truth of it was these college prep courses should have been called "Try Not to Get Beat Up 101," because that's what I spent most of high school doing. The teachers appreciated how much potential we had, but because they were too busy keeping the warzones out of their classrooms to than give us the consideration, we needed to succeed they let us slide by with great grades, even when we had little grasp of the material.

When you think of who needed the No Child Left Behind Act, the first image you might think of could be the kids who created those warzones. That is true, but they weren't the only ones. Who is getting left behind? The kids who don't pass, or the kids who succeed just to get thrown to the wolves a year later? Thanks to the existing system, I soared through high school academically, but in college I slowed to a limp.

CHAPTER FOUR

LIONS

Thanks to the NCLB, they can't fail me,
So I ain't gotta listen to a thing they tell me.

—"Still Ain't Good Enough," *The Call* (2006)

REGARDLESS OF HOW PREPARED I was, going to college was not a choice in my household; the only question was where I would go.

Even though my father worked at Temple University for twenty-plus years, he took some time to let me know that, as a relative of an employee, I would likely be eligible for reduced or even free tuition to attend Temple, the alma mater of such luminaries as Bob Saget, Ted Bundy, and Bill Cosby. I was honored and appreciated the hook-up, but I didn't want anything from my father. Again, I didn't dislike him, but there was a part of me that didn't want to be in a situation where I owed him any more than I already did. My mother's years of poisoning had worked, and I wasn't interested in mending our relationship.

Additionally, Temple's campus is about five miles from the home I grew up in, and I didn't want to be in what would essentially be the thirteenth grade; I didn't want to use the bus to get to college like I did for middle and high school. I didn't want to continue going to the same malls and movie theaters I'd been going to my whole life. I wanted a new, on-campus experience, and Temple wouldn't provide that. Thanks, but no thanks. I wanted to explore.

As seniors in high school, my friend Tariq and I took a bus trip to Penn State to get a lay of the land. As wide-eyed freshmen-to-be, we were wined (literally – I definitely got drunk underage) and dined by the university and escorted around campus by the coolest students. We hit the hottest parties, and experienced college life from their ideal, scripted viewpoint. We even met two girls who were also prospective freshmen from Philly like us. We walked the campus like big shots, ready to take this place over in a year. We'd have been fools not to accept Penn State's generous offer to attend after such a showing, so we did.

I applied to three colleges and was accepted to each: Morgan State, Kent State, and Penn State. Tariq and I had an agreement that if accepted, we would attend the same school. Morgan State University was off the table because our high school advisors told us that Historically Black Colleges and Universities (HBCUs) were traditionally less competitive than others and that finding a job after college would be significantly more difficult coming from an HBCU than any other school type, due to employers' propensity to look down on Black schools. I don't know how true that was, but it definitely changed my young mind.

Kent State in Ohio had the programs I'd wanted but was a little farther than I wanted to be from home. So, while I appreciated their acceptance, it wasn't really an option. Penn State is three and a half hours from Philadelphia on a series of one-lane highways through farm towns, and that was just far enough that my mother could come get me if I needed a ride, but also too far to show up, last minute, unannounced. It wasn't a perfect fit academically, but I made it work.

It also didn't hurt that Penn State's football team was coming off a historic season. The 1994 Nittany Lions, led by future NFL starters Kerry Collins, Ki-Jana Carter, and Kyle Brady, finished the season with twelve wins and zero losses, including a blowout Rose Bowl win. Because the NCAA hadn't yet come around on a playoff system, PSU lost in a coaches-and-press-only vote to end the season as the number two team in the nation, losing to also-undefeated Nebraska. Coached by the late Joe Paterno, Penn State's season ended in controversy but left room for bragging rights by them finishing a season without blemish for the first time in history. Record flawless, zero losses.

Since I was a huge football fan, the glamour and glitz of big-time football attracted me. This was especially the case when I saw Beaver Stadium up close, knowing that every Saturday, ninety-three thousand screaming fans would fill the stands, creating an electric atmosphere, the likes of nothing I had seen before. However, I didn't realize that most of the 1994 team's standout players were seniors. That meant they were all leaving the campus as soon as I arrived. Though the football team maintained respectable records, the heyday of Penn State football was slowly coming to an end in more ways than one... more on that later. Anyway, Penn State, here I come.

Mom gave me an affirmation during the drive to college, which was the first time I'd ever been inside her new 1995 Ford Contour. She told me the same thing that my guidance counselor told me throughout high school. I almost knew the talk verbatim. I would hear it several more times in my lifetime. It's probably one that every prospective Black college student gets.

"Ra Ra...You're gonna have to work ten times harder, ten times faster, and ten times BETTER just to get the same opportunities as a White student. You can never EVER let them catch you slipping. Always do your best."

I unpacked my things, kissed Mom on the cheek and began the first day of the rest of my life as an independent student, a college man.

We sat through hours of lectures about orientation, and after that, the fun began. Penn State had scheduled a freshman pep rally in the basketball gym for us to meet other students and get hyped up for the years to come. While at the party, they played Prince's "1999" way too many times, to signify that the class of 1999 was coming through, while the Nittany Lion mascot cartwheeled across the dance floor when we chanted "WE WANT THE LION" enough times. We were on the way.

During the pep rally, I began itching, like I never had before and haven't since. I got an itch that no matter how much I scratched, could not be soothed. I scratched and scratched until my legs, my arms, and my elbows were chalky white messes. I looked like I'd been in a fight with Wolverine. The itch was so bad that I had to leave the pep rally early to head back to my dorm.

My dorm room was still empty, as my roommate to be, Sean Segal, a Golf Management major from small Danville, PA, hadn't arrived yet; yet his preselected schedule was already on the bed awaiting him, full of entrepreneurial classes. I hadn't even heard of Danville, but the tiny Northeastern Pennsylvania town was comprised of just five thousand people, 97 percent of whom were White. Sean was about to get a rude awakening when he arrived.

I crashed on the bed to the right, unable to shake the unexplainable itch fit I had been having. I stripped down and showered immediately, but that had no effect. Phase two of whatever I was experiencing was ready to begin. What seemed like hundreds of tiny hives appeared on my skin; small to medium sized swollen, pale bumps popped up on my legs, my arms, my hands, and my face within fifteen minutes. Additionally, the itching never stopped. I checked my unpacked bags for some sort of remedy and found nothing. Ultimately, I opened the micro-fridge and found a half-full ice tray. I rubbed ice cubes on my skin to attempt to soothe the discomfort.

To this day, I have no idea what I experienced; my mother says it likely was a nervous outbreak based on my anxiety about college. I've never been diagnosed with an allergy, so that made the most sense. I also had never been alone before in an unfamiliar location: I was inside a dormitory half-filled with freshmen I didn't know, in a city I had never been to before. I've performed on stages in front of thousands and never felt like I felt that day at the basketball court. I still get a twitch when "1999" plays too loudly near me.

My roommate Sean arrived the next morning, golf clubs in hand, ready for college life. He had it all—a new television, a tricked-out PC, and all kinds of gadgets to go with his expensive, name brand clothing. He seemed to be taken aback by my presence in the room. His father gave me a few dirty looks as they entered. He refused any help from me to move his fancy things in. From the beginning, he and I had a tumultuous relationship that would maintain throughout year one.

On the first day of college, I had a consultation with my advisor. He encouraged me to pick a biology class with an accompanying lab. Unfortunately, because Penn State is so massive, with a yearly enrollment of over forty thousand, every lab was full except for one at 8 a.m. I didn't want to take this course, but as a pre-dentistry major, science was a must. I filled out my roster with a freshman English class, mythology, African-American Studies, and a volleyball class.

My very first taste of college life was in an auditorium of three thousand people, listening to a biology professor read off notes under the crackle of a clipped-on mic, watching a poorly crafted, and four shades-too-dim slideshow. The professor was going a mile a minute, and you couldn't stop him or ask a question. Questions were to be saved for your lab breakout session in which a nineteen-year old teacher's assistant would attempt to find the answers to questions by contacting the professor. I failed that class with flying colors. It went by so fast that it made my head spin. This was when I realized that nothing would be easy at the college level.

Sean did inadvertently help me keep up with my love for writing and recording rap songs. At some point during the school year, Sean let me borrow his handheld tape recorder to record my biology lectures, which were delivered faster than I could write. I kept the recorder for a week and then began using it to record myself rapping new songs I'd written, acapella, while walking to class. Occasionally, when the dorm was empty, I would set the recorder next to my stereo and record my newly written rhymes over an instrumental by Method Man or Jay-Z.

One day after a rough night of classes, I entered the room and noticed the instruction booklet from the recorder sitting on my desk. Sean sat it on my desk, perfectly folded, and in a place where I would notice it. I took it as a sign that he wanted the recorder back but didn't want to ask me for it. I returned the recorder with a note inside of it that said, "All you had to do was tell me you wanted it back. Thank you." I had had it about two weeks by that time, so I didn't mind returning it.

To return the favor of petty, the next day when I came in from class, the recorder was back on my desk, with a note inside of it, saying "No, I was giving you the booklet. You can keep the recorder. You obviously need it more than I do."

I was heated… because he was right. I thought he was making a crack at my financial situation or my race. Who knows? I was ready to throw down. I called Tariq and asked him to come by.

"This dude is trippin'!" I yelled to Tariq in the common area. "I'm ready to hit him. He doesn't even know me!"

But Tariq wasn't even paying attention. He had his own problems.

Things got worse. One day, Tariq and I were in my room with Sean. There was dead silence. To break the tension, I asked, "Hey. Do you know any other Black people?"

He did not.

Tariq took it a step further and asked, "Man I'm sure you know a ton of Black jokes, then."

I didn't know where this was going.

Sean said, "Well, yeah I guess I'd heard one or two in my life."

"Let's hear one, man," Tariq pleaded.

"Uh.... Nah." After several requests, Sean obliged. He stood up, adjusted his Dockers, and cleared his throat, as if ready for his moment to shine. "How are Black People and Tornadoes the same?" he asked, anxiously.

We shrugged.

"It only takes one to ruin the whole neighborhood."

I chuckled a bit, if for no reason other than to ease the tension in the room.

Tariq exploded with laughter. "Yo! That's great! Got any more?"

Sean got a little more comfortable and let out another. "Okay… uh, what did the little Black boy get for Christmas? My bike! HA!"

Sean was feeling himself. We didn't ask for a third, fourth, or even fifth Black joke, but he kept going.

"Naked White women get on Playboy, but where do naked Black women go? NATIONAL GEOGRAPHIC!"

"Why do Black men get shot so often? Because when someone says, 'get down,' they all start dancing!"

Sean turned red from laughing so hard between wisecracks. Meanwhile, Tariq, after laughing hysterically at the first two, tightened up. You could cut the tension in the room with a knife.

As he ripped off joke after joke, the comfort on Sean's face turned our laughs to silence. I wanted to leave. Not just the room, but the dorm completely.

Not surprisingly, by the end of the semester Sean and I were no longer speaking. To avoid the awkwardness in my dorm, I spent my late nights in the twenty-four-hour computer lab. Due to the advent and accessibility of the World Wide Web in 1995, most of that time was spent in chat rooms discussing hip-hop lyrics or participating in online written rap battles. This made it hard to wake up for my 8 a.m. lab. Those were the days when my Eudora mail was popping, and Netscape Navigator was my best friend. At that time, my major was called bio-behavioral health. Penn State did not have a dentistry program so that major was the only path to pursuing a Doctorate in dental surgery (DDS) degree. Eventually, after failing a few more science classes, I decided dentistry was not for me. I changed my major to journalism because I thought I could write.

I got a D on my first English paper, which was about Courtney Love, but I didn't even know who she was until I started writing. I struggled so hard that I contacted my old English teacher from high school for help. I managed to get a B on a paper I wrote to convince my professor that KRS One's self-titled album was one of the greatest hip-hop albums of all time. I hope she actually listened to it because I still stand by that statement today. Rap music was still my life.

Unfortunately, to get to where I needed to get, I had to sit through classes in which I was the only Black student and answer questions on behalf of my entire race. This was pretty normal in college, and I hated it. I stayed to myself for as long as I could because I was worried about making a scene and being embarrassed academically or intellectually.

African-American students who attended Penn State were given "Diversity Grants" to offset tuition costs, simply because of the color of our skin. They needed more Black students on campus, so they did it by any means. So many friends of mine dropped out and even more spent nights crying after realizing they were in way over their heads, cursing the very thing that people stereotypically think that minorities want more than anything – a handout. College was extremely difficult. I had such a tough time adjusting to the speed of life without mom over my shoulder making sure my homework was completed. I messed it up big time.

I pretty much flunked out of my freshman year at Penn State, racking up a ton of debt in the process. I was advised to withdraw from the semester, which would mean I'd have "W's" instead of the D's and F's I was going to receive otherwise. School had been so effortless to me up until that point. My mom was so disappointed. She moved me closer to home to a branch campus right outside of Philly. I was back where I didn't want to be: thirteenth grade, living at home and commuting to college. It sucked. I had to prove myself worthy of the freedom I was given a year ago. If I could get my GPA up, Mom would let me go back to the dorm life. After a year of feeling like an adult, I was back to being a child again – a much faster Benjamin Button. I would have to do two years of hard time at the Abington Campus near home before I could get back to the main campus.

To make the transition even more embarrassing, the Philly campus started sending a yellow school bus to the Olney bus depot to save commuting students money as they traveled from home to classes. I appreciated the free rides, but it took me back to seventh grade, being bussed to Rush Middle School as a scared, twelve-year old. At least the buses were peaceful.

1996 started off smooth school-wise, as I pulled in above-average grades but I didn't make many friends. I think the lack of distractions kept my GPA rising, as my focus was at an all-time high on the Abington Campus. Things eventually got tumultuous for me after my favorite rapper at the time, Tupac Shakur, was murdered in Las Vegas. I was working at the TJ Maxx department store as a clerk when a girl came into the store yelling and crying hysterically that 2Pac had been shot. We all assumed that 2Pac would pull through this, as he had done when he was shot in 1995. 'Pac was a mythical superhero of a rap star, and we believed his five foot nine, one hundred seventy-pound frame was somehow invincible.

I didn't believe it to be real until the Philadelphia Daily News' epic cover story on September 14, 1996 featured a picture of 2Pac and callously read "IT'S A RAP". I even wrote a letter to the editor of the Daily News about how insensitive that headline was. That was someone's son, someone's friend... and a lot of people's hero. I brought the paper to my English teacher and tried to get her to speak about Tupac's death in class, but she refused. As a self-proclaimed "thug," it turned out that 2Pac's own words would turn many people against him.

2Pac spent most of his final days blaming everything on rival rapper The Notorious B.I.G, so many people believed that Biggie's days were numbered. I jumped into every online hip-hop forum I could find to defend the honor of my favorite rappers between classes at Penn State. Unfortunately, the many prognostications came true, as the rapper also known as Biggie Smalls was gunned down in Los Angeles. I was at home asleep when my mother called me from work to share the news. "Biggie Big (she never did get his name right) got shot! Ra, wake up! Turn on the radio!" I turned on Power 99, as I had in the past to hear new songs from 2Pac, Biggie and many more, to hear my favorite radio jocks on air crying and reminiscing about encounters with the six foot two, three hundred seventy-five-pound artist born Christopher Wallace. I wept for Biggie, for 2Pac and for hip-hop. The final straw had been plucked.

For the three months that followed, I stopped writing raps. I stopped posting on hip-hop message boards and I'd honestly thought that hip-hop was dead as I'd known it in 1997. I stopped listening to new hip-hop as well. When I did start writing again, I made very strange abstract, almost unintelligible rap songs that I never recorded. I wrote one strange song about myself being murdered, behind my high school, over a misconstrued rap lyric. After that I realized I was done. I didn't like what I had become. Rap would have to undergo a serious change for me to get back into it. I just didn't like how the gangster tales of drugs, fast living and murder began to get reflected in real life. I wanted no parts of that.

While home in the summer of 1997 and 1998, I took what would turn out to be my favorite job I've ever worked, as a College Monitor at the Boys and Girls Clubs of Philadelphia. Our task was to help high school students in the inner-city gain employment with neighborhood businesses, and then we would travel to their jobs to check up on their progress while on the clock. We were given free bus passes every week and being paid twelve dollars an hour, much more than the Pennsylvania minimum wage of five dollars and fifteen cents at the time.

My supervisor, Bill Singletary, was a burly Black man who commanded respect. When he saw the children slacking off at the Club, he'd simply say "LEADERSHIP!" and they'd all fall into line like privates when a drill sergeant enters the barracks. We traveled the entire city on the Boys and Girls Club's dime, and after a while, the employers didn't want us stopping in too often, but agreed to sign our time slips, so we were free to catch a movie or hit an arcade while still racking up hours. Good times. At that time, the winds of change began to catch up to the music that I loved so dearly.

1998 is when I came back to rap. It was one of the most exceptional post-golden era years I recall in hip-hop, where I felt a true shift in focus. A year ago, although there were a few groundbreaking rap albums that hit the market like *Wu-Tang Forever*, Company Flow's *Funcrusher Plus*, and Busta Rhymes's *When Disaster Strikes*, the hip-hop I'd known and loved was dead and gone. The murders of 2Pac and The Notorious B.I.G. rocked the entire music industry. We were desperate to find our way out of the darkness. I began writing rap songs again in my spare time, but the fire was waning. Hip-hop was in a state of transition. Gangsta Rap was out, and the people wanted to hear something fresh and new. I wrote weird rap songs about the end of the rap world as we know it, in a land where hip-hop is banned and forced underground because that was where I saw it going.

Then, in 1998, the release of Lauryn Hill's phenomenal solo debut, *The Miseducation of Lauryn Hill,* was when music's shift was fully felt. Lauryn rhymed, but mostly sang, beautifully, and told the stories of relationships, fame, and religion through a woman's eyes like no one had ever done at that time. The numbers backed the claims of its greatness. The album debuted at number one on the Billboard 200 chart, selling over four hundred thousand copies in its first week, which broke a record for first-week sales by a female artist.

In the next month, we would see phenomenal releases from Outkast, Mos Def, Talib Kweli and others. Those albums confirmed the changing of the guard in Hip-hop. Of course, Jay-Z still sold records, and Big Pun arrived and became a megastar, but there was an overall movement toward fun and consciousness in rap that had not been seen since 1988. That's why I'm not worried about hip-hop today when I hear the music that artists release. Everything runs in cycles.

Video games followed with some legendary releases as well: *Metal Gear Solid* dropped and was widely regarded as one of the greatest PlayStation games ever. While I bumped Black Star and Outkast, getting my knowledge of self on, I spent my evenings sneaking through enemy hideouts on *Metal Gear*. Both forms of media, while unrelated, shaped my identity in ways I didn't realize at the time.

When I was back on the main campus in 1998, I didn't return to Pennypacker. Due to the fact that year's freshman class was larger than the previous, every dorm was full. This time, I resided at nearby Snyder Hall, on the top floor, in a study room that had been repurposed and transformed into a dorm. It meant my room was bigger than most, but we had two doors to remember to lock. This time around, I shared my room with Jude, an easygoing Jewish kid from nearby Easton, PA, who loved football and video games just as much as I did. Every Saturday morning, I awoke to the cheers of ninety-three thousand Penn State football fans, marching their way to Beaver Stadium, donning their war paint and screaming "WE ARE!" at the passersby to get a "PENN STATE!" in response. Once the game started, I could hear the announcer's PA system registering who carried the ball, who tackled who, and the normal game-day chatter. From my seventh-floor dorm room at Snyder, I could peek into the open mouth of Beaver Stadium and spot a sea of navy blue and white, a sea of people larger than I had ever seen, going ballistic over football. I wanted to explain what I saw and felt about sports to people who had no idea. I wanted to be a sportscaster. It was time to change my major. I entered the College of Journalism.

My advisor, Dr. Frasier, told me that sports journalism was a difficult career path because ex-athletes are the primary candidates for such jobs. Sarcastically, I thought sure, a guy who has been hit in the head over and over can definitely offer better insight into sports than a guy who sat in front of the TV and watched for twenty years.

Deep down though, I knew the truth. He was right. So, I changed my major one more time to African and African-American studies (AAAS). My advisor asked what I planned to do with that. I had prepared for this question my entire semester. I repeated what my instructor, Dr. Ahmed, said when he prepared me to answer this very question: I could become a park ranger, a museum curator, or I could teach African-American History.

As I recited the options, none of them sounded particularly appealing. I loved to read and write though, and the AAAS major challenged me in those areas more than any other had previously. The best part about the major was that after three years of coursework, Penn State notified me that because of an overlap in the curriculum I was close to attaining an English major as well.

I ended my college career as a double major in English and AAAS. More letters, same confusion. I still didn't know what I wanted to do. But someone I knew had a good idea.

CHAPTER FIVE

WORK HARD, PLAY HARD

Homie I pen great,
Not the state pen, I went to Penn State.

—"Been a Long Time (The Returners' Anthem)," *The Returners EP* (2014)

I REMEMBER IT CLEARLY. SENIOR YEAR, sociology class. "I think you'd make a great teacher, Jarbo."

I really thought Dr. Sam Richards, a wiry, energetic hippie of a Sociology professor at Penn State, was yanking my chain when he mentioned this, glancing over my midterm. He continued, "I know of a program, and I think you'd be a perfect fit. I'd be happy to recommend you." It was as if he knew I was a senior with no clue what to do next.

I really enjoyed Dr. Richards's class, with our heated debates on race, gender, and political matters. It was during his class that I first encountered Elie Wiesel's *Night* and actually shed a tear while reading it. I found it interesting that Wiesel, while a spectacular writer, at first refused to write about his Holocaust experiences because he felt he couldn't explain what he'd seen. A close friend encouraged him to tell his story so that all who read it would become intrigued, and so moved as to ensure it never happened again. Wiesel's story was one of my main sources of motivation to finish my own novel, though for less noble reasons.

The opportunity Dr. Richards spoke of was Teach Philadelphia, a local division of Teach for America, which was a program that allowed students who didn't major in education the opportunity to teach in the inner city. I didn't have anything else going on, so I considered the offer.

But what did I, as a teacher, have to offer? What lessons did I have to share? The next few years would define my identity as a man, as an educator and later as a performer, as I soaked up more knowledge than any other point in my life.

Throughout the late '90s, there were two warring wrestling programs, the WWF and WCW (World Championship Wrestling). These two multi-million-dollar juggernauts slugged it out on TV week in and week out, on different networks running at the same time slot. For a moment, WCW had bested WWF in the ratings department for an impressive eighty-three weeks, led by stars such as Hulk Hogan, Ric Flair, and Goldberg. The WWF was forced to create new stars to compete.

My roommate John, who I'd gone to the Philadelphia campus with, and I would flip the television channels back and forth for two hours every Monday night to keep up with the happenings on both shows until January 4, 1999.

On that day, WCW tried an underhanded tactic on live TV to keep viewers like us from hitting the FLASHBACK button on the remote control. They spoiled the results of WWE's program, which was pre-taped. Announcer Tony Schiavone updated us smugly,

"If you're even thinking about changing the channel to our competition, do not. Mick Foley, a guy who wrestled here one time, is going to win their title tonight. That's gonna put butts in seats, yuck."

I think it was the "yuck" that made me and one hundred thousand others in the world change the channel at that exact moment. People cite this as the pivotal moment in the wrestling wars. I knew what that word meant. Hell, I'd heard it before.

Mick Foley did not "look" like a wrestler. He didn't have the physique, sex appeal, or amazing body that the champions of the time did. He was overweight. He wore sweatpants and a dirty white dress shirt. He wore a mask to cover his face, was missing teeth and kept his hair long and ratty. He didn't boast phenomenal strength or speed, and prior to this match, his biggest claim to fame was how brutally he would get beaten in losses. He famously wrestled in death matches and lost an ear. He was thrown off the top of a cage through a table. He was bounced onto thumbtacks and lit on fire in crazy matches. People called Mick a "glorified stuntman."

Somehow, despite his shortcomings, Mick made people believe in him. He worked hard and got to the top. He made kids like me feel that anyone could wear that title belt. I saw a bit of myself in Foley as he hoisted the WWE's world championship that night. I tuned into WWE's show to see a man who'd likely been called fat and got "yuck" when mentioned; who was told he'd never win the big one, prove everyone wrong. After that, I never went back to WCW. Fast forward, to today and WWE owns WCW. Poetic.

That's what wrestling did for me more than anything else. It challenged my imagination in ways I didn't think possible. It wasn't the larger than life characters and ridiculous over the top sexual innuendos. Through storylines and drama, I realized you can achieve anything you can imagine. And there's no better feeling than completely surprising your audience. So, when we heard Mick Foley was slated to win, we absolutely wanted to see this manifested and witness a part of history. Whether the outcome is predetermined or not, as a comic book fan, what's better than live action comic books?

Wrestling dominated most of my college life from the start.

While I lived with Sean at Snyder Hall dormitory, Tariq lived in a different dorm in East Halls called Pennypacker Hall. This was the dorm to which most of the African-American freshmen class were assigned. In an immersion technique, 90 percent of the students that represented 5 percent of the college's population resided in one dorm. I was also in East Halls but in a building next door to Pennypacker. Snyder Hall was much quieter and more diverse. People in Snyder referred to Pennypacker as "the Projects," because of the number of Black and Brown students there. I'd get offended because all of my friends stayed at Pennypacker. I spent every evening after class there, watching TV and catching up on the latest gossip with my people. We played spades, traded hip-hop albums, and talked and laughed louder and longer than anyone I'd met on campus.

Tariq's roommate, Kwesi, was a tall, articulate, sharp-dressed brother from North Jersey. Make no mistake, though; he was a hip-hop head through and through. He put me on to so much new music, most of which I loved as our tastes were almost the same. Since he was from a place so close to New York, he had access to new, exclusive mixtapes that were relegated to the area. After every break, he would come back with new Wu-Tang, Redman, or Biggie freestyles that were like currency in the dorms. I often joked that Tariq and I should've swapped roommates.

Tariq had made an enemy in Pennypacker of Simon, a Korean-American student with a rep as a tough guy, who was dating Ady, the resident advisor of his floor and a very good friend to most students in the dorm. Turns out, Simon was jealous of the attention that Ady got from other males, particularly Tariq. Ady just happened to be R.A. on a co-ed floor. She needed to speak to men and women; it was part of her job and no one's fault.

One thing most people didn't know was that Tariq could fight if he needed to. He was known as a geek like me in high school, but he was in great shape. Growing up in North Philly will definitely teach a person to hold his hands if he has to. He had taken boxing classes and was a big fan of the sweet science. Simon had told Tariq something like, "stay away from my girl, or else." Tariq didn't take kindly to threats. Tariq was dating someone else in the building, Ady's roommate LaRay, who wanted to try to bring peace.

LaRay begged the two to squash it, but it got worse by the day. Tariq decided to bring his own petty to the party, and on the dry erase board outside of Ady and LaRay's door, he wrote "Simon is a bum," in his classic *Sign O' The Times*, New Roman font inspired by Prince's album track lists and liner notes. He was confident that Simon would see it and know who had written it.

Tariq wanted to test Simon's mettle. It was on.

One day later, while Tariq and I were in Ady and LaRay's room, Simon walked in, slowly. The scene played out like a classic movie.

"You think you funny, huh?" Simon asked in a low tone, cool and focused.

"What you mean, man?" Tariq responded, laughing nervously.

"You gonna die, bro. Tonight. I'm gonna hurt you bad, man." Simon's threat was cold and direct.

"Word?" Tariq asked. "Okay, why don't you come in here and do it?"

LaRay screamed, "No!"

I held her back, explaining that this had to go down or it would never be resolved. I insisted, "They have to live together all semester. Let's get this out of their systems. As long as no one gets seriously hurt, a scrap can be a good thing." I hoped I wouldn't regret these words.

Simon rushed at Tariq, head locking him, until Tariq pushed him away, into LaRay's bookshelf. Tariq then landed three straight left jabs directly to Simon's eye, followed by a counter punch with a right to the cheek. Simon went down, but the two wrestled some more until I stepped in and broke them up. A clear winner was not yet declared, but everyone knew it was over. We didn't know for sure who'd won until a party in Pennypacker that weekend. Simon showed up with shades on, covering up a shiner and a few bruises. Tariq was clean and scratch free. It was the classic wrestling story of good versus evil, with good prevailing in a grudge match on campus.

Wrestling dominated my life even more when I returned to the main campus, and it even got me out of trouble once. But, a bit of back story first. After one semester with Jude in Snyder, I won a housing lottery and moved my things down the hill to Nittany Apartments, the swanky on-campus housing usually reserved for student athletes. I wound up rooming with John who was joining me at main campus, but while it was his first time, I was making the most of a second chance.

John and I took jobs as clerks at the local supermarket to make some extra money to pay for apartment living costs. The hours weren't bad, and the pay sucked, but we needed money to live like bosses in our new fancy apartment. We had a fully functional kitchen and were determined to make the most of it. Unfortunately, up until that point, I had never cooked. My mother always gave me specific orders never to turn the stove on when she was out of the house, even when I was seventeen. So, I didn't. I'd bring home the bacon, but John and my other roommates would fry it. I started a kitchen fire the first time I tried to make eggs. Yes, eggs.

Once we got comfortable in the market, John and I got a little sneaky. Ramen Noodles weren't good enough. We began sliding extra items onto each other's conveyor belts and not scanning them. We picked up rib-eye steaks for the grill and many other delicacies for cheap or free. This practice became addictive, so we started hooking up our friends as well. We met a girl who worked at the campus bookstore who agreed to do the same for us there, so our small ring of thieves grew. Once, one of our friends was pulled into the back for questioning. After an hour-long session, he was sent home. It was getting too hot. Time to quit.

I got a phone call about a week later from the State College Police Department. They were inquiring about a series of fraudulent transactions at our market and wanted to ask me a few questions, on site. The problem was, if an item that was too expensive got scanned and we wanted to void it, we'd have to sign off on the void. They had my handwriting. They asked me to come in the next day after classes ended.

The entire day I was racked with anxiety and nervousness. I just knew I was going to jail. The most we would take were a few steaks and some frozen seafood, but the total was probably well into the hundreds with the amount of food we took over the months I'd worked at Weis. There was one day though where I clearly recalled John telling me he wrote down a shopper's credit card number and then used that to buy the groceries. He even used it to get cash back that night. *Oh crap,* I thought, *I'm going down.*

Telling on someone else when you are just as guilty as they are is a serious violation, bordering on a beatdown-worthy offense, so I knew that this was one that I was just going to have to eat myself. I thought about how disappointed my mother would be. How my second chance was ruined all because of a stupid supermarket job.

I remember sitting in my *South Africa Today* course thinking of excuses I could use to cancel going to the station house that afternoon. I could say a pop quiz came up or I started a new job. Anything to keep me from walking into a jail and never coming out. I'd heard so many horror stories about the police force on campus being racist and mistreating students of color. But I did the crime, so I was ready to do the time. Since this was a credit card investigation, I figured he would want to see my writing. In the margin of my notebook, I wrote my name, over and over again, in a different handwriting style than normal, in case he asked me to write there on the spot. Class ended, and I headed downtown, prepared for the worst as I walked up the police station stairs.

I met the officer who had called me. He asked me if I knew anything about people using credit cards that weren't theirs at my location, and I said I did not. He didn't buy it. He showed me a receipt, signed by someone, probably John. Sure enough, the officer asked me to open my backpack and give him my notebook to see if my handwriting matched the scribble on the receipt. He opened right up to my practice page. "Hmm."

As the officer sat and studied my notebook, I looked around the room nervously. I spotted his cup of pencils and pens, and at the very top was a brand-new WWE pencil, with The Undertaker, Stone Cold, and The Rock all over it. This was my moment.

"Hey… uh… you a fan of WWE?" I asked with a smile.

"Oh my God! Man, I'm a huge fan. Did you see the pay-per-view last week?"

"Yeah, dude, that was nuts. I can't believe they let Stone Cold win, wow."

A fifteen-minute enthusiastic wrestling conversation ensued in the police station. We talked about storylines, about which women were the hottest, who would win the next title match. When we were finally done, the officer ended his chat with "Well, thanks for coming in, if you hear anything please give us a call, okay?"

"Of course. See you at the next WWE show on campus?"

The officer nodded. "You know it, I'll be out there with my Stone Cold Steve Austin tee."

I'd made it out of the lion's den unscathed, and with my knowledge of wrestling to thank. When I got a few blocks away, I hit my knees and prayed out loud for probably the first time in my life. "God, THANK YOU for getting me out of this. I promise, I'll NEVER do anything like this again!"

It was time to get focused and try to graduate without any more close calls. It seemed like there was a force over me, giving me chance after chance, so it was finally time to make this count. AGAIN, I was ready to make the most of the opportunity I was given. Back to class I went, determined to succeed.

John and I invited friends over to watch WWF Pay Per Views one Sunday per month. Nittany Apartments were where the Penn State football team also lived so many of them stoped by to watch games and matches. Since John and I were big guys, people, including the ladies began to think we were members of the football team. Not a bad perk.

During hangout sessions, I would overhear the football players razzing each other, the way teammates are wont to do, but this particular conversation made my ears perk:

> Player One: "Why were you late getting out of practice, man?"
>
> Player Two: "Man, coach had me stay after to work on some drills."
>
> Player One: (Laughs) "Yeah, alright…. You got caught up with Sandusky in them showers again?
>
> (Hysterical laughter by both)
>
> Player Two: "Nah man, not me! Never that, bro!"

We brushed it off as normal guy talk, but when the news came out many years later, my jaw dropped.

In 2011, after an intense two-year investigation, Jerry Sandusky, then the assistant football coach at Penn State University, was arrested and charged with fifty-two counts of sexual abuse of young boys over fifteen years old from 1994 to 2009. He met most of his molestation victims through The Second Mile, a non-profit serving at-risk boys in Central Pennsylvania. Several of them testified against Sandusky in his sexual abuse trial. Four of the charges were dropped, and Sandusky was found guilty on forty-five of the forty-eight remaining charges. Sandusky was sentenced to thirty to sixty years in prison – at his age of seventy-four, it was effectively a life sentence.

Penn State assistant coach, Mike McQueary, who I shared a senior year science lab with, testified that in 2002 he walked in on Sandusky having anal sex with a young boy in the university's showers. Mr. Sandusky later admitted to showering with boys on campus. McQueary told head coach Joe Paterno, who later told athletic director Tim Curley.

Curley denied hearing this from McQueary and was found guilty of perjury during the trial.

Coach Paterno, known as "JoePa," a legendary figure on Penn State's campus for forty-five years, submitted his resignation, effective at the end of the season when the Sandusky scandal began unraveling. The resignation was refused, and Paterno was fired immediately in 2011 when an investigation determined that Paterno may have attempted to persuade university officials not to turn Sandusky in. Joe Paterno died seventy-four days after the firing; then after his death, one hundred eleven of his NCAA record wins were removed from his record, taking him from first to twelfth all-time.

Penn State President Graham Spanier, who welcomed us to the university in 1995 during our "Class of 1999" pep rally, was sentenced to four to twelve months in jail, a seventy-five hundred dollar fine, and two years of probation. Penn State football was given five years of probation, a four-year post-season ban, and lost forty scholarships. Like dominoes in a row, they all fell down, one after another.

This was another teachable moment for me that I later brought into my classrooms. I learned the safety of students is our number one priority, or at least should be. If I'd heard of anything like this happening on my watch, I would have spent my every breath ensuring that anyone who had hurt or abused children would be fired, suspended, and even prosecuted to the fullest extent of the law. The last thing I'd do is cover up for someone doing such horrible things, which is why JoePa's part in this scandal was the most hurtful to me. It made me question everything and everyone. Humans are imperfect and flawed though – and personal relationships and bias probably play a part in most decisions we make. But no matter what, the number one rule in education is that the students come first, at all times. Joe didn't hold true to that and paid the consequences.

Penn State football died in 2011 as we knew it. Anyone connected to this tragedy would never be the same. I had long since graduated but couldn't fight a feeling of guilt and helplessness. I wish I'd inquired a little more during those conversations on my couch. I wish I could have done more to help those boys in their time of need. I can imagine how awkward it might have been if I'd raised the point of helping those kids, but I just didn't know if it was my place to act so aggressively on what, as far as I knew, were just rumors at the time. I still keep up with this case, and hope and pray all the victims have somehow found peace and closure with the outcome.

After returning to campus in 1998 for my last year in college, I became a serial dater—I met women, hung out with them for a few weeks, then got bored and inexplicably sought another. Constantly wanting to meet new women was a strange new thing. I'd went from introvert to social butterfly overnight. There were times I'd "date" five or six women at once—maybe two on campus and three more I'd met online in a chat room. I ran up a ridiculously high phone bill falling asleep on the phone talking with girls, only to awaken, and then forget who I had been talking to. This lifestyle turned out to be too much for me; it became tiring and confusing and got me in a lot of trouble.

I continued to date, but I'd decided to become a one-woman man when I met Tisha in Philly over a break. Tisha was a brilliant and talented girl. She was a year older than me. She danced ballet, had really great art skills, had won all kinds of awards in school, and constantly challenged me to read and learn more. I spent time at her place consistently, having dinner there, and later, meeting her parents and sleeping over.

Tisha was different than most girls I'd known because she had a two-year-old son. My mother and friends immediately wrote her off as a fast-tailed girl whose sole purpose was to get college kids with potential caught up, or to find a new daddy for her son and they warned me to stay away from her. Of course, I didn't listen and tried to convince them otherwise. Tisha and I dated for four months, going to the movies, the library, and wherever else twenty-year-olds went. I wasn't allowed to meet her son until I had been around for a while, which was fair. Once I did, I found him charming and engaging. We had great times together.

Tisha's early pregnancy forced her to drop out of school, so she was taking night classes to complete her GED requirements while raising a son. This made her priorities much different than mine, and there were some weeks we didn't have much time to hang out. Our date time dwindled from twice a week to an hour or two on the weekend, to none.

I was young, so once the phone stopped ringing, I didn't give chase. I moved on.

We went about two weeks without talking, and she stopped answering calls. I assumed she was busy. It was a mutual ghosting. I went on about my life, attempting to make my second chance at college count, but I never stopped thinking about Tisha. I called her on Mother's Day, just to say hello, and to send some good wishes, after almost a month of radio silence.

She apologized for not calling me and said she had a lot of work to do and had had a medical procedure that kept her from being as active as she'd liked. Out of genuine concern I asked, "what kind of medical procedure?"

"An abortion."

Silence. *What did this mean?* I stammered as I tried to figure out what to say next. "Yeah... It was yours." I was too shocked to say anything. "Raheem... you have your whole life ahead of you, and I'm trying to get mine together. Let's not talk about this anymore."

So, we didn't.

Stunned, I hung up the phone and spent the entire day in my room, wondering what could have been. A child that looked like me. Becoming a twenty-one-year-old daddy. Dropping out of school, forsaking *Mega Man*, *Final Fantasy VII*, and *X-Men* to support a human that I helped to create. Canceling concerts and missing album deadlines to be there for my son or daughter. Would Mega Ran even exist?

I don't know if a part of me was relieved, though I would never ask Tisha to do what she did – or if I was angry at her for not giving me a chance to decide on something that would affect both of our futures. As I approach forty, still childless, I have to wonder how different things would be if I had a child all those years ago. For now though, the songs I've created are like my children. I've nurtured them, then released them into the world to hopefully go out and make a difference. Some have soared to unreal heights, taking me to places I never thought I'd see in my dreams, while some have remained close to my heart—not huge commercial successes, but songs that mark moments of personal growth. Songs like "A Poet," which I didn't have the heart to write until seventeen years after this event:

> I recall back when I was 19,
> Dating the girl that I thought I would wed.

Couldn't get her touches out of my head
Till the day that on my heart she would tread.
A couple of years my senior, shorty even had a little son.
I loved him like he was my own, made a house a home.
To put it short I was sprung.
My momma thought I was an idiot
Just for falling for a fast girl,
So, on the day she stopped calling the crib
It hurt me like a hundred hammer curls.
Sat up in my room sulking, wishing I wasn't so open,
Even used my final bus token to go to visit her crib
    in Logan.
Sat on her steps till she walked up, told me she came
    from the doctor.
She had just an abortion, and she didn't want me to
    stop her.
I had my whole life ahead of me, and she didn't wanna
    complicate that.
Didn't really know what to say to her, so I sat there, had
    to take that,
Cause what would I do, drop out of school, to raise a
    baby when I am one?
I wanted to say it but deep down, the words just couldn't
    be found.
So if you get the same chance, don't sway a sister or
    brother's dream.
Gotta show them the entire palate, but let the child pick
    the color scheme.

I sobbed writing "A Poet," because of the memories. I didn't have a journal back then, so I didn't realize how painful these events were despite carrying their immense mass for so long. I know you're not supposed to pick a favorite child, but the ones that give me an emotional reaction are definitely my favorites.

I stayed the course and graduated college as a double major, with an English and African American Studies degree and without a plan, outside of Dr. Richards's Teach Philadelphia suggestion. It took me five years and four summers to finish my degree. Goodbye class of 1999; hello summer session of 2000. College was such a battle for me, between struggling with newly-found independence, navigating social groups and making the time to study. I barely staggered out of there alive. I didn't know what I wanted to do for a living but knew that I had enough schooling for one lifetime, at least on the student side of it. But as I jumped into the teacher's world, I realized that throughout my formative years, the best teachers weren't people who could just recite facts. The ones who stuck with me the most, even now, were the ones who went beyond – the ones who told me they weren't perfect, and did all they could to solve problems. The teachers that showed that they were people – human – just like me. That was the type of teacher I wanted to be.

CHAPTER SIX

SUBSTITUTES

The Natives are restless, borderline aggressive
And that's the educators,
They say a teacher's reward is in heaven

—"Faculty Lounge (Remix)," *The Visitor* (2018)

JUST A WEEK AFTER GRADUATING from Penn State, I jumped straight into four weeks of teacher training with Teach Philadelphia. This program somehow determined that this plucky young man, fresh out of college, was now certified to take on the most challenging kids in the roughest parts of Philly.

Teaching middle school is like the real-world version of playing *Dark Souls*. You suffer, a lot, but if you can make it through, you feel unstoppable – until the thing around the corner humbles you and scatters your body across the stage. And wouldn't you know, middle school was the area of most need, and where I eventually assigned to. I came in ready to be Joe Clark in this gritty reboot of *Lean on Me*. I was ready to make a difference, to be the positive Black male role model that these kids had never seen.

I had only one African-American male instructor in high school: Mr. Harmon who taught math. Harm, as we called him for short (he hated that), was a straightforward brother with a bald head and goatee, resembling Avery Brooks's Hawk from *Spenser: For Hire* and the short-lived spin-off *A Man Called Hawk*. Hawk, like Mr. Harmon, was a no-nonsense enforcer, solving problems with ease, and never losing his cool in the process, even when things got dirty.

Mr. Harmon shared many similarities with Hawk, the most important being that he was a brilliant man who refused to let anyone under his watch fall through the cracks. I needed that. Mr. Harmon pushed us to the limit in trigonometry class, and never gave up on even his roughest students. I felt I owed it to my students to be a little like Mr. Harmon both in and outside of the classroom. Unfortunately, a challenging setting can get the best of you, and problem children wound up changing me for the worse before I could change them for the better.

As a substitute teacher, I learned to carry a bag of tricks to get through the day. The "bag of tricks" phrase comes from the famed cartoon, *Felix the Cat*: "Felix, the cat. The wonderful, wonderful cat. Whenever he gets in a fix, he reaches into his bag of tricks."

My bag of tricks contained the following items: a stack of three by five cards, for makeshift flash cards of any kind. Spare pencils, because kids were never prepared, and there usually were none in the classroom. A ream of lined paper. Pencil sharpeners, so students wouldn't have to get up. Scissors, crayons, markers, and construction paper for creative purposes. Also important was a deck of playing cards for memory games, or good ole' blackjack (or twenty-one as we called it for legal reasons). Most full-time teachers are offered a stipend for supplies. Substitutes are not provided this luxury and are forced to create something from nothing, to work magic as it were. I think this is where I picked up a lot of performance experience – every day in class was, in a way, a performance. I've always said, "If you can entertain and capture the attention of a twelve-year old, you can do anything."

The powers that be sent me to substitute at Roberto Clemente Middle School in North Philly, notorious for being one of the roughest schools in Philadelphia. It was in a section of town that was always in the news, usually for stabbings or muggings, but most recently for an ecstasy ring that three eighth grade students ran, even selling drugs to teachers and staff members. They always sent me to middle schools to substitute. I think it's because, in middle school, teachers weren't concerned with getting perfect attendance bonuses; they just needed peace of mind. I recall one assignment, for which I received one hundred dollars in payment, a step up from the thirty-three dollars per day I'd previously gotten.

What's the worst that could happen in one day? I should have known of course. I had the unruliest seventh grade class ever. Before I arrived, they had chewed through two substitute teachers in as many days. Their full-time teacher kept calling in sick each morning. My predecessors thought they were only working a one-day assignment only to be asked to return at the end of the day. The children lacked structure, discipline, and fear.

I planned several memory games for first period, to try to get to know them, but those cunning brats thwarted each attempt. I looked for the teacher lesson plans, practically tearing the classroom apart to find them, to no avail. During training, I was told that teachers were required to leave emergency lesson plans. In all my years of substitute teaching, I never once found lesson plans in a classroom. So, there I was, a greenhorn teacher, thrown into the fire with gasoline underwear, no plan, and no escape.

During a five-minute lull before lunchtime, a simple game of hangman got way out of control. I turned to write the clue on the board and heard a scream. When I turned, a student was clutching his eye, injured from a thrown object. I observed the culprit "shushing" the injured kid, and several students implicated this student as the pitcher.

The perpetrator was a six-foot-tall, one hundred and eighty pound thirteen-year-old Puerto Rican student with a huge, bushy afro, who frequented the principal's office often. When I sent him to the discipline room for his actions, he left without issue.

I resumed class as scheduled, then later got a call from the discipline room's instructor who told me, "I just want you to know, the student you sent here told me, 'I'm going to f**k up Mr. Jarbo for snitching,' so be on the lookout." Then he shocked me when he added, "So uh… We're pretty full down here though, so we're going to have to send him back to you at the end of the period. Okay?"

"What?!"

As a substitute, I didn't know much about school policy or procedures, but I was fairly certain that any threat on a staff member should be taken seriously. Perhaps they were dealing with major behavioral challenges or criminal activity in there, like drugs, weapons, or otherwise – it was Clemente, after all – but I didn't expect a student who recently said, "I'm gonna f**k up Mr. Jarbo" to get sent back to my class not five minutes later.

Alas, Afroman returned as promised. I opened the door for him and greeted him. He asked, with a smile on his face, "Did the guy in room 105 say anything?"

Yeah," I answered, "but I don't remember what about." I smiled back.

What followed played out in a way that was similar to a scene from the movie *The Principal* starring James Belushi. I imagined that at some point that period I'd wind up with a knife at my neck while the entire class cheered him on. Needless to say, I made sure to stay frosty for the rest of the period.

But this boy only watched me. His eyes followed my every move. He didn't participate in any class activities that period, and I didn't force him to. It was a strange mental stand-off, where neither of us flinched. The rest of the day went by without much of a hitch. Finally, it was 3 p.m. and I was home free, saved by the bell, word to Zack Morris.

However, I learned that day never to leave school at the same time the students do, no matter how tempting it was to get out of there. As a substitute, you don't have staff meetings or anything else to hold you up, so you're free to split as soon as the day ends. However, that's not a wise decision. You don't want students to see what you drive, where you go, or anything that can be used against you in the court of the classroom. Your chances of awkward conversations about what you do after school increase big time if you leave when they do, as I did on that day.

All I wanted to do was leave as soon as possible; I didn't think that was asking too much. Unfortunately, I wasn't driving at the time, so I had to walk to a bus stop about three blocks away. Suddenly, I heard *Ping! Ping! Ping!* very near me. I looked up and realized I was hearing rocks hitting nearby cars. I looked across the street, and there was everyone's favorite problem child, Afroman, with a crew of kids, tossing rocks across the street in my direction. I sighed heavily and decided to confront the problem.

I walked across the street and asked, "Hey, are you trying to hit me?" They seemed scared and immediately denied the allegations. At that point, I was off campus and more than a little frustrated. I told them, "Because if you were, I'm right here, and I'm not running."

Afroman moped. "Nah, we won't hit you because you would tell the school on us."

I assured him that, since we were off school grounds, I wouldn't tell if they wouldn't. I removed my glasses, dropped my shoulder bag, full of tips and tricks on becoming a good substitute teacher (perhaps literally and figuratively) and prepared to throw down. If a rock had hit me, then I'd have a jail record, I'm sure of it.

Afroman got excited. "Oh, so it's on! Let's go!" He then huddled with the other two troublemakers a moment before remarking ominously, "We'll be right back!"

They sped off down the block, presumably to round up more kids to make the envisioned beating even bloodier.

I smiled and stayed put.

A lot of things go through your mind when you're preparing to do something stupid. When you get time to think about it, things usually calm down and hopefully, you realize the error in your ways and move on. After five minutes of standing there, I figured this was a ridiculous idea that, no matter what, would not end well. As a thought experiment, I imagined the possible outcomes:

1) I'd beat up a group of teenagers, they'd tell their parents, and I'd never teach again;
2) They'd come back with kids and/or adults, whip me, and I'd have to live with the embarrassment of getting beaten up by children; or
3) We'd start brawling, the police would come, and I'd get hit with an assault charge.

Not good. Any of them.

After five minutes, I realized my idea was a bad one – a true lose, lose, lose situation. But a teacher can never back down and show weakness, so I waited another five minutes. No one showed up. I waited for another five. Nothing. At that point, I decided it was best to go home, so I walked to the bus stop and sat, alone with my thoughts.

On the ride home, I thought about how I could extract myself from this situation. I had some dangerous thoughts. One idea was recruiting a younger kid from my block to accompany me to school and to assault the threatening student on my behalf. In the end, I knew I couldn't do that. I even thought about telling the principal I couldn't come back.

As a substitute, for better or worse, you always have the option of accepting or refusing work. I had a few deal breakers when it came to accepting jobs.

1) Never teach at a school in the neighborhood where I grew up.
2) Never teach kindergarten.

Rule number two was mercilessly tested the day I got four calls, all requests for kindergarten positions. I declined all four. Unfortunately, it was getting close to the "no call zone" in which I wouldn't get work and therefore wouldn't get paid. I got one more call at 7 a.m., which tested my resolve for both rules. The dry computerized voice on the phone informed me, "You have a kindergarten position at John L. Kinsey," which was a school I had once attended. It was a mere two blocks from my mother's house, which I visited every weekend. It was possible that, while walking to class, I would hear someone yell, "Ra Ra," which was my nickname on the block. Despite my trepidation, my rent was due soon, so I had to do what I had to do.

BRING IT ON.

I arrived at the school, already nervous about the position, but knowing I had to take it. I entered the office and gave my name. Not a second later, Camille, who was the niece of a childhood friend, saw me and said, "Hey, Ra Ra," just as predicted. Fortunately, Camille was in second grade, so there wasn't a chance that I'd be teaching her class. I'd gotten lucky, or so I thought.

I walked into class ten minutes late and saw the teacher's assistant leading the class in some activity. When I saw the work on the chalkboard, I was surprised that kids that age were able to handle that level of work. I nodded in approval and said, "Wow, this is very impressive."

Immediately, the assistant asked the class, "Boys and girls, based on what Mr. Jarbo said, do you think impressive is a good or bad thing?"

The kids conferred and deduced it was a good thing based on the context clues given. That was when I knew I was not prepared to teach kindergarten.

But it got worse.

When the assistant left, one of the students immediately raised his hand and asked to use the bathroom. I obliged. Not five seconds later, another asked to do the same thing. This began a chain reaction that resulted in eighteen out of thirty-six students needing to use the restroom. What I learned from this mild pandemonium was that even six-year-olds could smell blood in the water. The rest of day was mostly a blur, but I do remember the following: several kids cried, several fluids spilled on me, several kids complained that other kids refused to be their friends, crayons were stolen, and one student locked himself in the closet. For a good twenty minutes, I thought he was lost. That day showed me that kindergarten was simply too much for me. That was a five-day position, and I barely made it through the first.

At the end of the day, as a long-term substitute, you visit the office to sign out, and during this time the principal invited me into his office to debrief. When the young principal said, "see you tomorrow" I couldn't bring myself to say I wouldn't be back. Instead, I replied "Yup," left his office, flipped open my cell, and canceled the position.

When I walked out to the pavement, I stopped for a moment, exhaled deeply, and contemplated my future in education. At that moment, a woman walked up to me and read me better than anyone I had ever met in my life. She asked, "You're thinking about quitting, aren't you?" I couldn't even look her in the eye. She kept going. "Well, do what you need to do, but keep in mind that you are the only positive Black male role model that most of these kids are ever going to see. EVER. Whatever you do, don't give up on them. Don't give up on yourself."

I had tears in my eyes as I walked to the bus stop that day, and I replayed her words over and over again. That was quite a burden to have on my back: I not only had to be great for myself, and my family, but I also had to be great for the kids who were coming up after me just because they don't have positive role models. How unfair. I did just fine without a positive Black male role model. The men in my life up until this point were my dad, a chronic liar and drunk; my neighborhood hustlers who said and did anything they could to get a dollar or into a woman's pants; and my barbers, who spent the day cracking jokes about life and hiding their true income and occupation from the government. I realized I couldn't quit. I was determined to try again.

At the same time, my girlfriend, who was also a teacher, came home after Parent-Teacher Conferences and called me, hysterically crying.

"They changed my grades," she said.

I didn't understand so I asked what was going on.

"My grades, all of them. I wrote in one thing, and they gave them all a higher letter grade. I didn't see it until the conferences when I'm right in front of the student and their parent. What was I supposed to do?"

Confusion was all over my face. "Why would the school change your grades?"

Four words. No. Child. Left. Behind.

As a by-product of The No Child Left Behind Act, now in effect, schools must keep an overall average of a certain score or risk the entire school's achievement designation lowered to Low Performing or Failing. With that distinction, the school would receive significantly less funding the next year, which means tattered textbooks, outdated computers, and no money for extracurricular activities.

Her school had altered the grades of four failing students to C's. Those students' parents attended conferences thankfully, but when a student can't even read and is in danger of failing the grade, how does one explain that to a parent who sees C's on a report card? It made for a very difficult conversation. After a few conversations, she found out that several other teachers had their grades changed, for funding reasons. Students went from F to C. From C to B. From B to A.

Now I understood why she was livid. I was done. For real this time. I was certain that come the end of the school year, I wouldn't return to education. Now I just had to figure out what else to do.

CHAPTER SEVEN

SUMMER OF SCAMS

Imagine a warzone nobody wants to leave
Younger G's stay busting shots during summer league
—"Losses" *RNDM* (2015)

"THE TWO BEST THINGS ABOUT being a teacher? July and August." I remember an older woman saying that as we picked up our final paycheck for summer break 2001. Because I was a long-term substitute, this was my last payment for two months. I had to figure something out. With school out, I wasn't set to receive pay or Benefits over the summer break.

Mom gave me the best advice, which was simple. "You better find a job, boy."

So I got to work, filling out applications at every store in every mall in town. It put me in a tough spot, because outside of teaching I didn't feel like I had any other skills. My prior work experience was summer camp, the college monitor position and CVS. I could watch kids and watch a cash register. That skillset didn't leave me with many options.

Mom would go to work all day and night, and I'd be home alone most of the day, plotting and planning my next move, as an unemployed adult on the block. I found nothing most days, so I'd end up playing video games, walking the neighborhood or sitting on the stoop waving to the passersby. My girlfriend at the time was teaching summer school, leaving me plenty of time to figure things out.

Another old tale I'd heard growing up was that "idle time is the devil's playground." With so much free time from day to day, it was almost guaranteed I'd find myself in some trouble. One hot June day, my friend Rell who I hadn't seen him in quite some time walked by. Last I'd heard, his parents kicked him out of the house, and he'd moved across town. But here he was, back on the block, so he stopped on the stoop to chat. Rell casually offered me the opportunity of a lifetime.

"Yo… You wanna make some quick money?"

I perked up with interest. "Uh, yeah, what's up?"

Rell laid out the plan. "All you need is a bank account with no money in it, like five dollars or less, and I can bring you back a thousand."

Miss Gertrude told me another wise old saying during babysitting that came to mind here, "If it sounds too good to be true, then it probably is." I instantly declined. "Nah, I'm good, that sounds like a scam."

"Nah, man, it's legit! I just did it last week! Made a G, easy work!"

I don't know if it was the look of sincerity in his eyes, or my empty wallet that made me give this a try, but all I knew was that I'd had seven dollars and seventy-three cents in my account that was somehow to last through the whole summer, so I thought, *what do I have to lose?*

"Okay, man, I think I can do this. How does it work?"

"You get me your bank card, my guy deposits a five thousand dollar check into your account, then you go into the bank and withdraw the whole thing, and we split it. That's it."

Word.

Rell explained to me that he had a silent partner, who didn't want his identity known, who was connected inside the bank and could make it happen with no problem. Rell was just the middle man. I didn't want to do any business with anyone that I wouldn't see with my own two eyes. So I insisted meeting the man, or at least make the trip to make sure my card and money didn't get out of my sight too long.

I threw on some sweats, a tattered 76ers tee and ball cap and we hopped in Rell's car. After twenty minutes or so, we ended up at a seedy gas station in North Philly, and parked on the side. Rell hopped out and walked around the building. He came back in three minutes, letting me know that his partner absolutely could not be seen by me. "He can't take a chance yo; he doesn't know you like that. But he's right here and he's

ready to do this. Just hand me the card and I'll get it done real quick…
don't worry, we good, bro."

At this point, I was so close, and my seven dollars and seventy-three
cents wasn't doing much for me. I hand over the card to Rell.

"Oh, I need your pin, too."

Honestly, this should have been my last straw. *What would an insider
at the bank need my pin for?* Anyone should know to never give out a
PIN code, under any circumstances. This was the time to jump ship.
Instead I tore a piece off of a KFC receipt that I saw in the car and did
the one thing that banks tell you to never, ever do: I jotted down my pin.

Rell darted around the block to meet with the Mystery Man. He
returned in a second, with a check in hand. The plan had slightly
changed. Mr. X would take my card to the bank and use it to add six
thousand dollars to my account, then in an hour when we got the call
that the funds were in place, we would go into the bank and cash this
check, a five-thousand-dollar personal check that he had in hand. I'd
give Rell the five thousand, and then I'd be one thousand dollars richer.

Rell told me we were all set to go and that he would wait for the
wizard of Oz to call and it'd be fine. We drove back to the block, silently.
I had serious regrets about what I had done from this point on. And it
only took a few more minutes for the heat to come down.

Rell got a phone call from the Mystery Man, who told him to tell me to
take that check to the bank right now and cash it. I really wasn't expecting
to be in the bank with my tattered rags on, but very well. We arrived at the
bank and I signed the check and deposited it at the teller window.

"One second, please," the sweet bank teller said.

She returned a minute later and asked me, "Can you have a seat right
over there? We'll be with you in a minute."

After seven minutes of me sitting, Rell called my cell phone. "What's
taking so long man?"

I responded, "I don't know, I'm just waiting to be seen."

"To be seen? You're just cashing a check! I don't like it. Get out of
there, man!"

I laughed. "Wouldn't that look suspicious if I just walk out of a bank
without my check?"

Rell didn't laugh. "Yo man, GET OUT OF THERE!"

I told the teller I was in a hurry to get to work, and I needed to leave. She came back and explained that my recent bank activity was making it difficult to cash this check.

"Your balance is too low for me to clear this amount. Can you wait a couple days?"

"No problem, see you soon!" I left the bank so fast I forgot my hat.

I jumped back in the car, sweat beads beginning to form on my forehead.

As we pulled up to the neighborhood, my phone rang with an unknown one-eight hundred number calling me.

It was my bank. An automated call was alerting me that my checking account balance was low, and my account had been overdrawn. The call didn't give me any specifics, but told me to call the bank if I did not authorize this transaction. I called the bank's automated balance hotline and my jaw dropped.

"Your... balance... is... negative... two thousand... five hundred... seven dollars and... seventy-three cents."

Anger bubbled up within me. "What's going on man?" I asked Rell as he walked down the block.

"What's up?" he asked innocently.

"Yo, your guy just took money out of my account!"

Rell looks puzzled. "Are you sure, man?"

"Positive."

I put the phone on speaker and let Rell hear the latest transaction report. "Transaction... one... an... ATM withdrawal in North Philadelphia... for... two thousand five hundred dollars."

Mr. Blank Face had scammed me. He used my card and made a huge withdrawal knowing I couldn't cover it, and he walked away scot-free.

Rell began sharing my anger. "Yo, man! I'm so sorry, man. I'm gonna find him. He started calling Edward Nygma. "He's not answering." *Aw man, I can't believe this!*

It honestly took me two days of not hearing from Rell again until I realized that he was likely involved in the jig and received a portion of my money as a finder's fee for bringing the mystery man another victim to scam. I've not seen Rell since that day in 2001, and that's probably for the best. I hope he's not in jail. But as for me, I was back to square one. No money and no plan to make any.

A few days later I'd invited my friend Benny over to play video games during the day, and we played *NBA Live* for a few hours until he had to go to work. I'd needed work, so I asked what he was doing. He told me he was working for a new startup downtown called GoInternet.

"Basically, we sell websites to businesses... lot of phone work, and it's a hustle, but it's fun and I'm doing great, man! I'm on track to make three thousand dollars in bonuses this month!"

"What?" I couldn't believe it.

"Yeah, man, I'm leading my team in sales by a long shot. I think I could even move up to manager soon, they promote pretty fast."

I didn't know a thing about phone sales, but I wanted to give it a try, so I asked him to put a word in for me, and he did. I got a call back the next week and was brought into a training class.

After a three-day crash course on phone scripts and closing deals, and welcome videos, our training class of twenty-five were on the phones and working hard. We'd call small businesses, mostly mom and pop stores, and offer them a trial website sample. The problem was, the sample was a crude digital mock up that never actually made it online, and this sample packet would cost the customer twenty-nine dollars per month, easily and discreetly billed to their phone bill, and wouldn't be removed unless the customer called to cancel.

As the telemarketer, I was on the front line, explaining my services to anyone who would listen, from the elderly who didn't even know what a website was, to the sons and daughters of the business owner, cajoling them to authorize payments that they didn't even have the right to approve. When a telephone operator got a yes, we were instructed to stand up at our cubicle and clap our hands loudly, signaling for a supervisor to come over and close the call.

My supervisor was Shawn, a slim, well-dressed man about my age who drove a Mercedes. When he came to my cube to close a sale, he had a very smooth method of cupping his hand over the phone receiver when announcing that the customer would be billed monthly, or waving the phone away from his mouth, as if he was operating a church fan, to muffle his speech, then returning at the end of the script to ask, "Is that okay?" with clarity so that they could respond in affirmation. If he got an "okay" or "sure, all right," Shawn would respond with "Is that a yes?" and the deal was done. Once the call was closed, Shawn would activate a strobe light at the front of the office space and make a tally mark next to our name on the big board to make us feel special. It felt like the movie *Sorry To Bother You* to a tee.

As I looked at the big board, sure enough I saw Benny's name atop the leaderboards, far ahead of the number two salesperson. Although we worked the same nine to five shift, we were on opposite sides of the sales floor, so I'd see him on breaks or at the end of the day. All telemarketers made minimum wage while on the phone, which was five dollars and seventy-five cents per hour back then, but our sales bonuses were where the real money came from.

The checks weren't much, but my mother was happy I was working. However, I learned telemarketing wasn't the life for me after getting fired two weeks in. My violation was that I'd gone two days without a sale, which was grounds for termination. Nothing personal, but if you couldn't convert, you weren't needed. Benny held on though, and only needed to make it one more week to get the bonuses he had worked for in the month prior, and wouldn't you know it, he was terminated after going one day without a sale, and clocking in two minutes late the next. Because employees had to make it through a month with no corrective action, no bonus monies were accrued. He had gone from top earner to ex-employee in just two days. *It was all good just a week ago.*

I remember seeing a news story a few months later about GoInternet. The company's downtown Philly location didn't open its doors on a random Monday, leaving hundreds of workers wondering what was going on. The news reported that the company just shut down without telling everyone, and didn't even give the employees their last paycheck. GoInternet had other concerns.

I'll let the U.S. Attorney's Office take it from here. From 2003 court documents:

> The entire GoInternet business model was designed to
> defraud customers and potential customers into making

monthly $29 payments for Internet-related services without their knowledge or authorization. GoInternet's telemarketers duped customers into receiving a welcome packet without disclosing that the mailing would trigger monthly bills unless the customer called to cancel. The packets were then designed to look like bulk business mail to prompt it to be disregarded or thrown away. GoInternet engaged in "cramming." It would place monthly charges on its customers' local telephone bills, without authorization, which customers routinely paid without noticing. By approximately 2003, GoInternet employed over 1,000 telemarketers and was signing on approximately 7,500 new customers every week. By the end of 2003, GoInternet's customer base included more than 350,000 businesses.

In 2010, the president of GoInternet, Neal D. Saferstein, who we only saw in training videos, was sentenced to two hundred seventy-six months in prison for running a multi-million-dollar telemarketing scam that defrauded as many as four hundred thousand small businesses out of as much as seventy-five million dollars. On October 30, 2009 Saferstein pleaded guilty to wire fraud, mail fraud, and two counts of filing false tax returns. GoInternet was GoneInternet. I was back to unemployment, but in name only, because I hadn't worked long enough to actually receive unemployment compensation.

My summer ended without a lot of money made, but with plenty of experience earned.

CHAPTER EIGHT

GAMES, GAMES, GAMES

Though getting up for work is a struggle,
Playing all night till you come down with carpal tunnel
—"For the Gamers," *The Visitor* (2018)

FINALLY GOT A CALL BACK from EB Games (which would later become GameStop) at my local mall in early August, 2000. It was so close to the start of the school year, but I didn't know what my fall season would entail, so I took the job. As a video game lover, this was heaven. I got to be around for game releases, and we even got a whopping 10 percent discount on purchases. This almost made the white polo and black slacks worth it.

Judd, our assistant manager, was a soft-spoken family man who treasured gaming as much as I did. After he showed me how to use the heat gun and shrink-wrapping device in the stockroom one morning, he put me on to the best-kept secret.

"You know, you can just take a game home and play it, then bring it back and shrink wrap it back, no one's the wiser. It's important for us to know how these games play, so it's all good man." He was right. People asked us every day if a game was worth the money, and we had no way to accurately answer that if we hadn't played the game. We were just helping the customer. That's what I told myself. So, if you buy a "new" game at GameStop today, it very well could be a previously played game that you paid full price for.

EB Games got me back into playing video games hardcore, and

even got me into music production. If I hadn't been there on the day that one copy of the coveted MTV Music Generator came in, I wouldn't have been able to get it, and start making beats at home. Thanks to this, Random Beats was born. I learned how to manipulate the samples and loops in the game, and with help from a CD burner I bought from eBay, I could record beat-CDs that I would use to promote myself while out at concerts and even at work. If I'd overheard anyone in the store saying they made music, I'd run and grab a CD from my coat in the stock room and shoot my shot. I bought video game soundtrack CDs from EB with my paychecks and sampled sounds from games like Resident Evil, Final Fantasy, and Zelda, and somehow work them into my beats.

I held onto the job through the winter, working nights and weekends while I substituted during the day, if I found work. Other times I'd just go to EB Games instead of seeking a substitute position, I enjoyed the job so much. That's why I was at EB on September 11, 2001.

I asked Ronnie, our store manager, not to schedule me on weekdays, but because we were shorthanded, he had me open the store on Tuesday, September 11. I was given keys the previous night to open the gate, and would man the store alone until 2 p.m. when Ronnie came in.

We had a TV in the store, but it was required to run non-stop ads on a VCR loop for a device called the "Skip Doctor," an invention that would smoothly sand the bottom surface of your game discs to remove any scratches and prevent games from skipping. We sold them for thirty dollars, and employees who sold a Skip Doctor got an extra four dollars bonus on their paychecks, so we were encouraged to push the Skip Doctor and ordered to never change the television away from the commercials.

It was around 9:45 a.m. when our first customer entered the store to buy a PC game and asked me, "You heard about what's going on in New York?"

I had no idea. He mentioned a plane hitting a building, and I assumed it was an accident, much like everyone else probably did. I turned the television to the news station and a correspondent in front of the building talking to bystanders. After a while, someone shouted to move, reporters and people began running away, while the camera panned up to show the South Tower of the World Trade Center collapsing at 9:59 a.m.

After the horrific events of this day unfolded, people speculated there may have been more terror attacks planned, and if so, we assumed Philadelphia would be a target. Mall security told us every store would close early. People began closing shops, and I was on a bus, heading home by noon. If I was confused about my life's choices before, this didn't help much. I needed some stability, and education was the answer. I went back to school assignments for that month.

Life at EB got hectic that October when the game of the year released: *Grand Theft Auto 3* for the PlayStation 2. *GTA 3* was a sequel in name, but introduced a completely different gameplay and graphical style than the first two, and its open-world gameplay, street-smart story, and phenomenal voice acting and soundtrack made it a hit. The game went on to sell fourteen million copies, and we couldn't keep it in stock at EB. People would come by to purchase, and become livid if we didn't have a copy for them. We'd open the store with three hundred copies some days and were sold out by noon.

But as much as business was booming in October, things in the retail world can change quickly. In November our manager Ronnie shocked us with the news he had to cut our store hours due to a corporate command. I went from forty hours to twenty-five hours per week, then to just ten. It became too inconsistent for me to make decent money, but I really enjoyed the work, so I didn't quit, but I sought other employment. Enter Toys R Us.

I took a seasonal holiday-only job as a sales associate at Toys R Us in Franklin Mills Mall, the very same place that thirteen-year-old me used to play lookout while my middle school friends stole condoms from the drug store. The job started on Black Friday and ended the day after Christmas. I was now twenty-four, and looking to supplement my income to keep my apartment and car I had just acquired. Toys R Us had a few advantages over EB for me, the most important being they did not want me to work the cash register, which I was absolutely fine with. All I had to do was stand at the entrance to the video game section, greet customers and answer questions about the newest games, which thanks to my other job, I had a wealth of knowledge on.

The worst part of being at Toys R Us during the holidays and having no money was that it really made me want all the things I couldn't have. During the next year, a Playstation 2, which was the hottest item of the season, came into the store and I asked the associate to hold it for me so that I could buy it on payday. Payday came and went and my paycheck of one hundred and thirty dollars wouldn't even begin to put a dent in the four-hundred-dollar price tag on the PS2. So I asked them to hold it another week for me. They did, but when my next paycheck was even less than the previous week, they told me I needed to pick up the system or risk losing it. The next week I had rent due, so the PS2 eluded me, and never returned that entire holiday season.

I was such a great employee at Toys R Us that they told me I was welcome to return any holiday season after this, so I did in 2001 and 2002. But on days off, I still worked part time at EB, which paid less but was much closer to my home. Toys R Us was definitely my favorite of the two. I made sales, I extended sales, and I even made friends. One day though, I got a phone call while on the clock, which never happens, so I wondered why I'd ever get called to the phone via intercom system. The voice on the other side asked a few very minor questions that any Toys R Us associate could have answered. "Hey uh…Do you guys have Madden?" "How much is it?" "When do you guys close?" I answered, and noted that the voice sounded familiar but I ignored it.

The next day when I went to EB, my manager Ronnie asked me straight up, "Do you have another job?"

I said yes.

He followed up. "I called you while you were there. Did you recognize the voice? Judd told me you had another job so I had to see for myself." Ronnie told me that I'd violated a rule by working for a direct competitor.

"But how?" I asked. Toys R Us sells everything, from bikes to trains to video games, just like the store jingle used to say. EB Games just sold games… *how are they a competitor?*

Ronnie explained to me that my employment at Toys R Us was a conflict of interest and that I couldn't do both. No additional pay, no incentives. Just an ultimatum. I was told I couldn't serve two masters, which I would be told again ten years later by my school principal. I didn't understand. I'd only been working there because of the lack of hours at EB, so if they gave me more hours, I'd stay. I told him that it was a temporary seasonal job, and he agreed to let me stay there as long as it didn't affect my work at EB Games. In addition, I was also a day-to-day substitute teacher, but I enjoyed these jobs much more. Ronnie promised me more hours so I told him I'd leave Toys R Us after Christmas... which I'd planned on doing anyway.

In one of the more monumental moments of my adult gaming life, the Xbox dropped on November 15 with a game that changed the first-person shooter genre like nothing before or arguably after it: *Halo*. This game captured the hearts and minds of myself and everyone who played it. My group of friends would stay up all night, clocking twelve-hour gaming sessions on *Halo* during Christmas break. My friends would bring additional TVs to my house and set up in adjoining rooms and we would matchup for four on four Team Slayer all night at my bachelor pad. Any time not spent on *Halo* was spent working on beats and rhymes for what was to be my first "official" demo tape, recorded at home on a four-track recorder that I'd bought from the Radio Shack just four doors down from EB Games at the Cheltenham Mall.

My hours returned by January and I even thought I might be on track for a manager position at EB. One day though, EBX's corporate heads visited our store unannounced from West Chester, PA to address us personally. They told us that while our store had some of the best sales numbers in the region, it had an unreal amount of shrink. In the retail world, shrinkage, or shrink, is the term used to describe a reduction in inventory due to shoplifting, employee theft, or administrative errors such as record keeping, pricing, and cash counting, and supplier fraud. We were costing the company thousands of dollars due to either correctable errors or flat-out gross negligence. Changes had to be made.

The store stayed closed all day on a Sunday for us to count stock at the store, and the numbers came back worse than before. We were in the red by significant amounts. Corporate decided to take action. They invited each staff member into the back, one by one, and questioned each of us for as short as five minutes, and as long as an hour, until they got what they needed from us. When it was my turn to go to the back, I walked by Judd, who had a dejected look on his face, as if to say "we're done for." I was questioned for thirty minutes about what I'd seen my co-workers do, what they've seen me do, and if I wanted to make any confessions about retail theft going on at the store. I hadn't seen anything so I didn't say anything. The suited man then asked me if I'd ever heard of a pin-hole camera. I had not. He explained that the technology exists to record every transaction I've ever made in the store on a tiny camera the size of an ink pen. He asked me that now that I knew this existed, then would I have anything else to add to my confessional? I did not. They let me leave the room and called the next person in.

I don't know the results of this meeting, but I do know that the next time I tried to return to work a week later, my key didn't work in the gate, and there was a completely different staff working at the store. I asked for Ronnie, my manager, and the teenager at the register said, "I don't know who that is." Another manager emerged from the back at that time and invited me to the stockroom to let me know that my employment at EB Games had effectively ended as of this day, and I was asked to turn in my badge and key. My entire group of co-workers were replaced without another word. No goodbyes, nothing. I didn't have anyone's phone number from the store except my friend Dudley, who had quit one month before this had gone down.

I called Dudley and told him about what had happened with everyone at EB, and he laughed on the phone from South Carolina, where he had moved to. I didn't understand why he'd thought it was so funny. He told me that on his last day at the store, he walked out with a new XBOX and several games, unbeknownst to anyone at the store that day. He knew he wasn't coming back, so he had no concern of the consequences as he stuffed a huge XBOX console and games into his backpack. He'd caused at least $1000 in shrink that day, and who knows what else while working at the store, but he was long gone.

While working part-time, I spent weekends at my mother's house, mainly because that was where all my friends lived. We worked on beats and songs for my friends' albums as well as my demo project, which I had named "Archetype," meaning 'the original which has been imitated.' It's not a record that anyone has in their possession, and I really don't think it's that good, but it's the first time I was able to successfully transfer my thoughts from my composition notebook to a recorded medium. We recorded on cassettes and then, thanks to the CD burner, we could make one copy of our albums in real time. If anyone wanted more copies, they had to buy a five-pack of CD-R's from Walgreens and wait a week for me to do it, since it took a while. The sound quality was hideous however, and got far worse in the transfer from tape to CD. I made a CD cover in Microsoft Paint on my neighbor's computer, stealing a ClipArt image of a studio engineering console with headphones on top and reversing the image, to avoid being caught of course.

I sampled tons of video games within my beats, but I didn't dare let anyone know. I thought they'd laugh me out of the room. I somehow turned themes from Noboru Sugimora's terrifying *Resident Evil* 2 soundtrack into haunting, eerie hip-hop tracks, perfect for storytelling and it worked, somehow. My friends loved the beats so I wound up the producer for everyone on the block who wanted to rap. Random Beats was rolling. However, Raheem needed to make money.

To stay afloat, I did my best to maintain employment at the Philadelphia School District. But after hearing the news about grades being changed by higher ups at my girlfriend's school, I felt disgusted and conflicted. I had lost faith not just in public school, but in the educational system altogether. Still I felt stuck. My student loan companies wouldn't take kindly to me not paying them simply for moral reasons, so I had to work, and Toys R Us holiday shifts had ended. My last paycheck there went toward a GameBoy Advance and *Pokémon Gold*. Back to teaching I went, begrudgingly.

I couldn't take the uncertainty of substituting any longer, but I wanted to teach and help children. The drama of teaching in the city got to me though, and I was ready to move on. After weeks of filling out applications, and logging hundreds of hours on *Pokémon*, I interviewed at a few places. Eventually I wound up at a new school, Woods Services, far away from the city, ready to embark on a new beginning.

CHAPTER NINE

RANDOM

'05, RAHM Nation brought the thirst back,
Got the hunger I had when I wrote my first rap.
—"The Opening Movement," *The Call* (2006)

M ANY PEOPLE DON'T KNOW THIS about me, but I spent about three years of my life doing gospel rap. I did, and still do, identify as a Christian, though I'm more spiritual than religious. After college, while depressed about my life's direction, I went to church and re-dedicated my life to God. After this, I went through the "fired up" phase every new Christian goes through, when you are so excited about the changes you're making that you start to kill off the parts of you that feel are unworthy of a child of God. This usually starts healthily, with the new Christian swearing off of alcohol or refusing to hang out at the club as much. But after the initial honeymoon period, this lifestyle spring cleaning can build to extreme levels. My friends would throw out their comic books, and even get rid of hip-hop albums, video games, and anything representative of their 'old selves.' My friends' parents found the devil in everything, from nursery rhymes to Harry Potter

In my case though, hip-hop was something I couldn't shake off or toss aside, even when starting my new life. I decided instead that I would make Christian hip-hop, also known as gospel rap, or holy hip-hop. Our group was known as the Exit-Us Movement, led by Ohene, the lead emcee and producer of the squad. Ohene is probably the most talented musician I know, even to this day. We were hugely inspired by

Philadelphia-based Christian rap collective The Cross Movement, who ran the scene from the late '90s until about the mid-2000s, even signing on a tall dude from Houston named Lecrae, who helped turn Christian rap into the multi-million-dollar industry it is today.

The Cross Movement had a knack for creating gospel rap tracks that exhibited skill and weren't preachy. That was the recipe for making good Christian rap tracks, and they had it down. No "Cat-In-The-Hat, Jesus-Is-Where-It's-At" raps. Their 2004 album *Human Emergency* is still on my playlist. These guys made dope rap that just happened to exalt the Christian experience. We wanted to do that too with Exit-Us, and we had a great start.

We played at churches across the city, usually asking for a "free will offering" rather than a payment for our performance. The problem with this was we would kill it for a packed church of sometimes up to a thousand people, and at the end of the show, there wasn't even enough money for one of us, let alone a group of five, to eat a meal. After one show, we were waiting for a bus to take us home because we didn't have a car, and many of the very same folk who cheered for us and told us we did a great job, rode right by us standing at the bus stop. That infuriated Ohene in particular. Part of Ohene's concern about this was that his wife was pregnant. He felt it was time for a change.

I assumed the change would involve asking for a mandatory payment if we had to travel to perform, but no one felt that was an acceptable request of a church. So, instead of asking, we decided not to play shows in churches anymore, and then not to be a group anymore. Ohene was convinced that we weren't reaching the people who needed to hear our message; they didn't congregate at churches, but at the clubs, the bars, and in the streets. Jesus took his message to the people and we needed to do the same. By performing in those venues, we'd receive judgment from the Christian community, the same people who ghosted our free will offering and instead fed us exhaust at the bus stop. Within about a year the Exit-Us Movement was done.

I left that situation confused and lonely, uncertain about what to do next. I kept making music and began writing what would eventually manifest as my first album, *The Call*. It's very spiritual, in that it does make reference to God in an uplifting way and to my beliefs, but I wouldn't call it religious because it's not biblical per se; regardless I like to think it pleases Him. But the fight I experienced within myself at the time was making me wonder if gospel rap was the path for me. I had things to say some might not consider typical Christian rap album material. I asked my pastor if an album speaking on relationships between people who aren't married, crime, racism, sexism, and terrorism was considered gospel, but he didn't have an answer. So, I stopped calling my music gospel and started calling it rap music.

Rappers need original beats for their creations, but I didn't have the money for equipment. The MTV Music Generator was a godsend. Released in 1999 by Codemasters for the PlayStation console, this disc enabled music production for people who didn't have the budget for the expensive machines and keyboards, before music-making software was cheap and readily accessible. It was a hard game to find, so when it finally came into the stock at EB Games, I snatched it up quickly and purchased it at the end of my shift.

I tried to make beats for a week straight and got frustrated with the limitations of the software. First, I tried re-creating my favorite tracks, but something was always missing. I couldn't create the sounds I wanted, and the stock sounds were terrible. I needed something else to make this system work for me. Then, I found an edge. A life hack, if you will.

The best thing about MTV Music Generator, from my perspective, was that it allowed sampling, which is defined as the act of taking a portion, or sample, of a sound recording and reusing it as an instrument or a sound recording in a different song or piece. To sample on the Generator, you removed the game disc from the console, then inserted a music CD, and you could rip ten to twelve seconds of music or sound from the other disc, to use in your musical compositions. I recreated Mobb Deep's hit track "Quiet Storm" almost perfectly, so then I knew I could create my own tracks based on that process.

I was a huge fan of sample-based hip-hop production. Raised on Wu-Tang Clan, A Tribe Called Quest, Pete Rock and CL Smooth, and

Gang Starr, I was sure this was all I needed to create music like my idols. I grabbed my mother's Motown CDs, then took a trip to the library and picked up a few classical albums and soundtracks. The subsequent tracks I produced were so good, people offered to purchase them from me. I sold them beats that were made on a PlayStation. Of course, when people asked how I produced them I'd lie and say I made them on "a few programs."

The only problem was that sampling wound up creating a beat file way too large to save on the PlayStation's tiny memory cards. So, I was left with beats I couldn't save. I found the only way to keep these beats was to put them on CD, so I bought a Phillips CD Burner and burned my beats onto CD-Rs in real time, meaning if the beat was five minutes, it took me five minutes to put it on CD. I would make whole beat CDs with twenty-plus tracks on them, most of them saved on that CD only, as the original production file would have to be deleted because of my inability to save. That meant this beat was final once it went onto CD, so the worst thing I could hear from a potential customer was "I like it, but the (kick, snare, hi-hat, strings, you name it) is a little too loud. Can you fix that?"

"Nah, as-is, bro."

Like a kid with only one pair of pants, I couldn't change.

I was a college graduate teaching by day and chasing a silly dream of being a professional rapper and beat-maker by night. I couldn't pay my rent, so I lost my apartment, and my girlfriend at the time was not into the idea of shacking up. So, in 2004, back to the block I went, to live with Mom for the next two years. Her greeting: "I told you you'd be back." Even though she was right, to get away I worked days and wrote songs at night, making time for video games and extracurricular activities when I could.

I was writing and recording music as Random and making beats as Random Beats. Random Beats Productions was born years ago on a fall day in 1999. It beat the name of my original production company, Meehar Productions (my first name spelled backward), which I was certain would be my label and publishing name. In 2004, I made Random Beats Publishing official, as well as Random Beats Music LLC in 2011. I got new business cards made for Random Beats once I sold my first beat.

Somehow, and I wish I knew how, some of my beats got to a studio owner named Ali, who worked at Lab Addicts Studios in a suburb of Philly. Since my phone number was on the disc, Ali called and invited me to the studio, offering me an in-house engineer job, where I would record sessions for clients, and at the same time attempt to sell beats during sessions, with the studio getting a percentage. I did it with no hesitation.

That was my first time in a real studio, and I was hooked. I became obsessed with every nuance of the studio. Work nights, weekends, it didn't matter; I was there until 4 a.m. most mornings working on music, learning the ins and outs of recording techniques and then somehow waking up for work in a few hours. It was a thirty-minute drive each way, through the woods, and I didn't mind a bit. I'd invite my friends from the block up to the studio to record, mostly as practice, and in downtime I'd record my own demo album, giving it the amazing name "The Random Demo Project."

As the in-house producer, I'd give G-BAL Entertainment artists first pick of the beats, and then shop the rest to customers who came through. G-BAL was comprised of three members: Ali, the face; Lefty, the hustle; and Ki, the muscle. I didn't see Ki much unless we were all at the club networking, which to him was meeting women and bringing them back to the studio at unsightly hours. I spent most of my time learning from Ali, and later picking up Lefty to bring him to the studio to work on his album.

At that point, I was running with three teams: The group I started in high school, The N.E.T.; Exit-Us with Ohene in West Philly; and G-BAL at the studio and beyond.

Every weekend, with G-BAL, I'd hit the club with a stack of beat CDs I'd burned and get them to any notable artists in the city. I landed a few: Journalist, whose 2002 album, *Scribes of Life*, released on Motown Records; NH, a ferocious street battler who made his name tearing through rappers in the DVD era, and appeared on several of Meek Mill's early projects; and even Freeway, who had signed with Jay-Z's Roc-a-fella

Records. People in the lab thought I was a bit of a dual threat and began nicknaming me "Kanye East," based on Kanye's versatility with creating rap vocals and making the backing beats at the same time, and my penchant for sampling soul records, much like early Kanye.

Kanye's first album, *The College Dropout*, was my blueprint. Not content-wise, but it was super impressive to see a beat-maker jump seamlessly into making full-on rap songs that weren't just passable, but were undeniable hits. When it was released in 2004, the top songs on the rap charts were 50 Cent's "In Da Club" and "P.I.M.P," Bonecrusher's "Never Scared," along with several other aggressive, machismo rap jams. Kanye completely changed the game from his release, shifting the hip-hop landscape with his self-aware, everyman persona that shined through in his raps. Hip-hop was different now. I thought there was finally space for me. So, I got back on writing raps hardcore. I wrote about my struggles with religion, my job that I hated, and my life.

I recorded pretty much every day at Lab Addicts with friends, until the day I was locked out of my own studio. One afternoon, I pulled into the business park and noticed a yellow eviction letter on the studio door. I ignored it and inserted my key into the lock per usual, but it didn't work. The locks had been changed. A bigger problem arose when I realized we hadn't properly shut down last night's session, leaving data discs, my PlayStation, and several other important items in the studio on the previous evening.

While I fussed and cursed the crew and myself for not handling business correctly, I went to the adjacent building, a practice space, to see if our next-door neighbor could get me in touch with the property manager. In my frantic fury, I met a man named Samik, who worked on tunes with others in the same business park that held Lab Addicts. Samik was a talented producer who created lush, full jams that may have been considered a bit too layered and complex to be hit hip-hop tracks at the time, but which fit perfectly in the world of R&B, and with the expansive Kanye-inspired song ideas that I'd had for my first album. A brilliant musician with a great ear, he dropped into my life at just the right time. I maintained contact with Samik and vowed that we would work together soon.

I was able to get into the studio that evening for five minutes, enough time to burn one copy of "The Random Demo Project." I burned several more at my girlfriend's house, and she helped me with cover art in MS Paint and by placing labels with my name and phone number on a spindle of CD-Rs. One door locked and another door opened miraculously.

Ohene, whom I hadn't talked too much in the years since the Exit-Us Movement disbanded, somehow heard the demo CD I had created, and we reconnected. Particularly striking to him was the song that ended the demo CD, called "Goodbye." For the main part of the song, I sampled Jerry Butler's version of the song "Make It Easy On Yourself," which appeared on one of my mother's soul selection albums. With the use of my PlayStation, I sped up his lyrics and used them as my chorus:

> (If this is goodbye)
> If it's the last song that I get to rap on
> (Oh, I just know I'm gonna cry)
> I'll do my best not to cry, it's goodbye

In the song, I talked about how music wasn't fulfilling me, and that it had been a fun ride, but I was calling it quits, in 2004. Before my first release, before even embarking on a single tour, I'd talked about how much music was becoming a stressor for me, when it began as a carefree hobby. Ohene told me over the phone, "You can't quit man, you're just getting started." He told me there was so much more work to be done, and asked me to come by his house in West Philly to chat.

I took the hour-long bus and train ride to West Philly. At the meet-up, Ohene told me about his new record label RAHM Nation (Reform and Healing Movement), and said he thought my message and sound would work well there.

From the ashes of the Exit-Us Movement, RAHM Nation arose.

I still worked with many of the original members of that gospel group, but our focus shifted to community uplifting through hip-hop, influenced by KRS-One and The Temple of Hip Hop. RAHM Nation believed that, through strengthening the community and exuding positivity through hip-hop music and education, we could make a powerful impact on the inner-city community. RAHM Nation's first release, Ohene's album *The Rapademics* fused hip-hop culture with education so much that Ohene began teaching a class on hip-hop at a local university. All members of the label were invited to come in and assist.

During the release of this album, I reconnected with the crew and began working on my album, *The Call*, with RAHM Nation. This was a good time for us and for the movement, as Ohene's album gained rave reviews from the local scene's toughest critics. The top local rap site at the time, PhillyHipHop.com, praised *The Rapademics* as a classic. When it was time to work on my album, I knew I had to do something different. Whereas *The Rapademics* was top caliber "backpack" rapping, I wanted to make soulful, socially conscious music.

I went back to Samik for his help, and he produced the first single, "Raze the Bar," which bucked many trends of the time, and even included a verse targeted at the sound and subject matter of rap in the early 2000s:

> I'm sick of thugs, tired of pimps and players,
> Sick of Evisu Jeans, sick of Timbs and Gators
> Sick of singles with R&B chicks
> I'm tired of every hot rapper on your remix
> I'm sick of everybody talkin' bout they pack heat
> I'm tired of rappers coming off sweet over whack beats
> Sick of the same producers on everybody's record
> Tired of Black women getting disrespected
> I'm sick of the radio for playing the same song
> Ten minutes later "dang that just came on"
> Tired of kids who can't comprehend
> But know 50 Cent from beginning to end
> Sick of filling out these applications,
> Tired of going to more funerals than graduations
> And I'm sick of people who can't get inspired,
> And I'm sick and tired of being sick and tired.

The shot had been fired. The line in the sand drawn. The verse was a staple of my live shows in Philly, and I'd end with that verse acapella for full effect. People assumed I hated popular rap but I didn't; I just wanted to challenge traditional thought. To Raze (tear down) the Bar (the standard; the status quo).

In Philly, Jay-Z's style of rap ran the airwaves and the streets. Jay's Roc-a-fella records signed several rappers from Philly including Beanie Sigel, Freeway, Young Guns, and single-handedly changed the landscape of sound in the scene. Neo-soul (The Roots, et al) was out and "chipmunk soul" was in.[3]

Kanye West's 2005 album *Late Registration* was the first time I'd really noticed live instruments complimenting sample-based production. Kanye's beats were spiced up on that album by the co-production of Jon Brion, who brought so much out of tracks like "Hey Mama" and "Gone." He made those rap tracks sound like songs. I discovered the untapped potential to make unforgettable moments within hip-hop productions, much like what happens with some of the biggest rock and pop tunes. I wanted live instrumentation on many of the tracks for *The Call*, but that was a challenge on my limited budget.

Matt Weiss, also known as Storyville, has always been a genius in the field of sound. He can create magic from mere ideas or me beatboxing or making sounds with my mouth. He emailed me some tracks while he was away at Sarah Lawrence College. I thought they were just hip-hop beats, but they were not. He'd hired live viola players, bassists, and drummers from the college to create these tracks, which gave them a special touch. He also taught me to seek unconventional methods to create. The beat that would become "Push" was epic. I wanted to add a horn solo to the end of the song to wrap the perfect bow around it.

I didn't know anyone who played the saxophone, so I hit Craigslist. A young gentleman by the name of Frank Machos responded and was eager to lay some runs on "Push." He came to Mel's studio and nailed it, first take. I joked, "You may have a future in this music stuff." He really did. Frank went on to teach music and is now the head of the music department of the School District of Philadelphia.

---

[3] Chipmunk soul (n): A production technique in hip-hop, popularized by Kanye West, involves sampling music containing vocals, and pitching the singing's speed up until it sounds like the cast of *Alvin and the Chipmunks*. The best example is Kanye's song, "Through the Wire."

Though we were making great music, money was extremely tight. I'd been spending my entire paychecks on rent and had even applied for food stamps while living on my own before coming back to live with mom. The inconsistency of substituting led to me needing a second job. My friends who had stayed home from college had great jobs, cars, and were even starting families. Meanwhile, during a long winter break I had to pick up extra shifts at Toys R Us for a little holiday cash.

After teaching, I'd change clothes and put on a ridiculous red smock and take orders from twelve-year-old kids. The job wasn't all bad, but the fifth time you accidentally step on a skateboard or get caught with a stray Nerf football isn't so fun. I felt like such a loser, having to work what I considered to be a demeaning job while trying to make ends meet. I didn't know what depression was at the time, but I began to feel gloom creeping in. I struggled to keep up payments while chasing a fantasy of rap stardom.

I drove my rusty red 1989 Chevy Blazer to work and parked outside, disgusted, and disheartened by the day I'd had at school. Fifteen minutes before clock-in time, I sat at the wheel in the parking lot, stewing about life and how it wasn't how it was supposed to be. Here I was, a college graduate, no criminal record, who had done things the right way, struggling with two low-paying jobs.

I contemplated ending everything – the job, my day, even my existence. I envisioned the world going on without me, Raheem the employee, the teacher, or without Random the rapper. *Would anyone even notice I was gone?* I thought my life was so devoid of meaning that I couldn't imagine a world that I'd ever belong in. I didn't want to be anyone's burden any longer.

I turned on the car; maybe to drive away from the job, maybe to try to get a bit more heat out of the engine, maybe even to ram my decrepit Blazer into the Toys R Us front window and end it all, leaving a pile of twisted metal and glass. I really don't know why I turned that key. But when the crankshaft and pistons sent that charge of power to the Blazer to start it up, the CD in the vehicle played, and "Track 5" of Storyville's beat tape ran. A track that started off with an angelic vocal run, followed by a reverberated viola over hard live drums and bass played and sucked me in.

The concept for "Push" started to rack my brain. *With all that we've made it through, with all that your parents and ancestors have gone through, how could you give up now? We have so far to go, so we have to push to get there.* I knew I couldn't quit.

I wound up two hours late to work that evening, though I spent that time in the car right outside the building. I had something to give the world, whether it knew it or not.

I met Mel, aka DJ DN3, while working as Ohene's teacher's assistant at Temple. He was an associate of RAHM Nation and had produced most of *The Rapademics*. Mel made superb beats and engineered our recordings out of his studio, a two-bedroom apartment just outside the city. He invited me to hear some tracks and offered to help me work on my first album. In 2005, I'd teach until three, and then rush down the interstate to Mel's lab to work on music until about seven when he had to stop for dinner. Then, I'd return and work some more the next day. We had an extremely fluid work dynamic, recording for hours, occasionally taking breaks to talk hip-hop or play *Grand Theft Auto*, but otherwise working feverishly on new tracks.

It was during these sessions that Mel introduced me to the genius that was James "Jay Dee" Yancey, also known as J Dilla. If Mel was John Coltrane, Dilla was Thelonius Monk. Mel studied Dilla's intricate sample chopping techniques and, dare I say, mastered them. Mel learned how to make beats the best way however, by emulating one of the greatest to ever do it. When he played me his "re-flips" of some of Dilla's best beats, I was shocked. I couldn't tell the difference. Mel could re-create J Dilla's beats perfectly. He brought Jay Dee's signature swing and crunch to each of his productions on *The Call*, like "Salvation" and "Luminesence."

I became hooked on Dilla's beats, tracking down everything he had ever been a part of thanks to Fat Beats, UGHH.com, and HipHopSite. com, our online hip-hop stores. As an early member of The Roots' online message board forum, Okayplayer, I was privy to a few top-secret jewels and even got a hold of some of Dilla's beat tapes that circulated throughout the industry, which contained tracks used by De La Soul,

Pharcyde, Busta Rhymes, Common and others. That was the lighter fluid that kept our firestorm of recording sessions going.

Tragedy struck on the day that when Mel, after canceling a few sessions in a row by phone, told me that he had lost two months of work, due to a hard drive failure. We were about 75 percent done the album, and I was devastated.

Mel was beyond crushed, too. Over the three days that he had canceled our sessions, he had been contemplating the end of his life as a musician. He felt like he had let me down, and that it was a sign that making music wasn't meant to be his path in life. I felt just the opposite. I thought that the universe was saying those rhymes and beats weren't up to snuff; and was giving us a second chance to do it right... so we got back to work. Sammus, an artist I work and tour with frequently, has a song called "Reset" in which she talks about how losing everything is often necessary for growth.

We agreed to get back to work. When I got to Mel's the next day, he was playing a track he had made, with what sounded like a strumming harp sample, laid over a fat, buzzing bassline with awesome swinging drums. I shouted what I always shout when I hear something dope: "YOOOOOOOOOOOOOOO!" Then I asked, "What's good with this jawn?"

Mel responded, "It's yours you like it," and the track that would later become "The Opening Movement" was born. It became the intro-track that we didn't have before. It was far better than the earlier version of the album. We were back in business.

Though we re-recorded much of the album, the rejuvenation led to us recording ten new tracks in addition to what we had. His perseverance and beats on that album were what gave it such an identity. I'm glad he didn't quit.

While putting the album together, I traveled to upstate New York on a bus with a ton of my closest rap friends at the time. We were going to play a festival, with several notable MCs, including Dead Prez, Immortal Technique, and others. Technique even rode the bus with us. While the rest of us hopped on the mic and freestyle rapped the entire trip, Tech sat quietly and contemplative, as if the fate of the world was on his mind – it very well may have been. I had a few seconds to chat with him about Philly, and he instantly lit up when he told me he used to live there. Immortal Technique went to Penn State University, the same school I attended. While I was chasing girls, downloading hip-hop tracks off torrent sites, and struggling with classes, he had gotten kicked out for a racially motivated fight at the school, which checks out, based on the confrontations I'd had there.

The festival was vibrant, with kids, adults, balloons, food trucks, and everything that a festival should have. The vibe was interrupted when an emcee hit the stage and informed the turned-up crowd that, due to a run-in with the law on the way in, Dead Prez would not be attending the show. A collective groan traveled through the audience; the main reason they had attended was to hear the revolutionary raps of Dead Prez, and he wasn't there. No "Hip Hop," no "Mind Sex."

As my old babysitter, Miss Gertrude used to say, "when one door closes, another one might not open, but you better crack that thing." Dead Prez's absence from the show opened a gap in the performance schedule. I immediately stepped to the event organizer and asked if I could extend my performance time, and they obliged. I'd be playing in the spot previously reserved for the DPs.

The only problem was that I didn't have enough material for a full performance. I had signed up to perform as a part of a collective, not solo. I'd asked for and received something I wasn't even ready for. Since I had always had a way with words and freestyling was something, I did a bunch, even on the bus on the way to the show, I decided that I'd wing it and make it work.

Halfway into the set, I asked the DJ for a beat. Giving me a Dead Prez beat would've been a major faux pas, so he gave me something classic, "Tried by 12" by The East Flatbush Project, which everyone knows, but hardly anyone knows where it's from. I got busy. The DJ balanced the record perfectly on the two turntables and kept the groove going seamlessly as I dropped bars about what I was wearing, the name of the park, the event, and the fact that I wished Dead Prez were there. I even went into the crowd to speak directly to the audience in rhyme form.

After what seemed like a half hour (it was about six minutes), everything ended. I felt like The Incredible Hulk, slowly returning to my human form as Bruce Banner, clothes tattered, sweaty and confused as the adrenaline slowly winded down. The crowd let out a raucous cheer, and it was the first time in my life that I'd received an ovation like that. I knew I had something special. Thanks to the training I'd had as a teacher, I was always prepared at a show to bring the bag of tricks. The object freestyle was added then and has become a part of my set since. That 2004 trip upstate, the artists I met, and what I learned about myself on that stage made that one of the most incredible moments of my early story.

I had stopped performing in churches, and later stopped going altogether, but I didn't stop reading the Bible. The album title, *The Call*, came from Matthew 22:14, which says, "For many are called, but few are chosen." The chosen few are the ones who receive the call, act on it, and begin to live their purpose, walking a tougher path than the rest. I felt like I had a calling to serve, but I didn't necessarily know what to do with it, so I ran away from it. 2 Corinthians 5:17 says, "Therefore, if any man be in Christ, he is a new creature: old things are passed away; behold, all things are become new." I was a new creature with a new focus.

A friend told me that G.O.D. as an acronym could stand for Generator, Operator, and Destroyer; and that these are the traits of a god. Anyone who can generate, operate, and destroy is a person in control of their fate and decision-making. Much of the early hip-hop generation was raised in a religious sect called The Five Percent Nation, sometimes called the NGE, or Nation of Gods and Earths. The movement began in New York in the 1960s and is credited with giving young Black men confidence and courage in the face of a nation that constantly degraded and downplayed their existence and relevance.

The NGE teaches that Black people are the original inhabitants of the planet earth and must take their place as the Gods (men) and Earths (women) of civilization. As a Christian, I'd always been taught to seek God himself to gain a clearer understanding of the world, but the NGE teaches that there was no need to look any further than within to see God. The youth could transform and possess its true potential, thus enabling them to overthrow the overbearing oligarchy by becoming just rulers of themselves. This doctrine meshed especially well with conscious themes found in other golden-age hip-hop recordings. I didn't know an earth from the actual planet Earth, but it always sounded dope on records.

The Nation of Gods and Earth propagated its teachings throughout the US and abroad. In the early 1980s, this spread was in part due to early adherents teaching when away at college or in the military and, more famously, because of the rise of hip-hop music.

An astute listener could pick up the NGE tenets and terminology within so many classic rap songs by Brand Nubian, Eric B., and Rakim, Wu-Tang Clan, among many others. When we talk of 'ciphers' and 'dropping science,' or even use the word 'peace' to sign off, we are using terms straight from the glossary of the Five Percent Nation. Mike Tyson even credits a member of the NGE for setting him straight by encouraging him to stop stealing, to embrace his talents, and to love those who loved him. Whereas Christianity teaches that knowledge of Christ is the key to salvation, the NGE wholeheartedly believes that *you* are God, so therefore knowledge of self is the way. As a Christian man, though our viewpoints haven't aligned all the time, I've always had a great deal of respect for the NGE.

When making *The Call* between 2004-2005, I asked myself what kind of first impression I wanted to give. It's an introduction that can't be removed from the listeners' minds and memories, and it should leave no doubt what your intentions and abilities are. Time for everyone to hear what you, the artist, has to say. I had to answer the questions. Are you a one-hit wonder or are you here to stay? Style or substance? Who ARE you? What are you?

My first album taught me what I love to look for in music. I was highly influenced by a couple of great albums that I considered timeless classics: Public Enemy's *It Takes a Nation of Millions*, Ice Cube's *Death Certificate*, De La Soul's *De La Soul Is Dead*, A Tribe Called Quest's *The Low End Theory*, and Kanye's *Late Registration*. All these albums, while totally different, served the same purpose for me: they provided a balance of fun and substance, layered concepts that could take years to fully unpack, and most importantly, they satiated a need for dope beats and rhymes. *The Call* was my attempt at the sonics, rhymes, and beats of Kanye's *Late Registration*, but done with a significantly lower budget, and with DJ DN3 and Ohene serving as my Just Blaze and Jon Brion.

The album was complete. It sounded greater than I ever could have imagined it would. I was so pleased. I managed to capture my complete self in this hefty twenty-one track album (including bonus tracks that I'd been performing up until the release). We set our release date for February 21, 2006 and began promotion. One week later, Mel called me to tell me that his hero, J Dilla, had passed away due to complications of a rare blood disease and lupus. James Dewitt Yancey died at thirty-two years old. I'd had dreams of Mel one day getting the chance to play his beat-flips for Dilla, perhaps he and I sharing the same stage. But alas, that was not possible now.

In the months before his passing, Dilla toured Europe in a wheelchair, which raised speculation on his health. Shortly after he was hospitalized. On his hospital bed, he would create beats, then take breaks for his mother to massage his hands during moments of extreme pain so he could continue. His monumental release "Donuts" dropped on February 7, two weeks before my debut. I listened to "Donuts" every day before *The Call*'s release, and Mel and I said a prayer together for Dilla and his family. I began performing J Dilla dedication sets during my performances because I felt we were spiritually linked due to these releases being so close and his influence on Mel's production. It's the closest I've ever been to music as a religious experience. It felt like a return to our gospel rap days.

Today, I don't generally refer to my music as gospel. However, gospel means *good news* and I do attempt to bring good news to listeners in each of my songs. I guess, in that sense, my music is very much gospel.

The good news I have to share for you now is that no album put me through as much as this one. It all got easier after this. But *The Call*, released on February 21, 2006, was my *piece de la resistance*, my magnum opus. The strain and pressure I experienced in the creation of this album means that the best version of me created it, which makes it more important and closer to me than anything I created before and even after. They say pressure makes diamonds, and I felt the pressure – it helped us make a diamond. It helped us make The Gospel According to Ran.

Chapter Ten

GOODBYE

Northwest Philadelphia, born and raised,
But the transient spirit wouldn't allow me to stay.
—"Same as It Ever Was," *RNDM* (2015)

I WAS ALL GOOD JUST A few months ago. I moved to Phoenix in August 2006, six months after releasing *The Call*. I moved when musically, everything was where it was supposed to be for me. I was playing three to four shows a month, opening for all the mid-to-larger underground rap acts, and making waves on the Philadelphia hip-hop scene. DN3 and I didn't win the local awards that I'd hoped to with the album, but I was very proud at the sales and reach that the album had. We were on our way.

Philly was still Philly, for better or worse. Fears of violence in my neighborhood and the dead-end nature of my work and music lives were pushing me away from Philly, and they weren't the only things. I can't even lie – I moved because I was tired of snow.

Living on the east coast, you get the worst of both worlds, weather-wise. You get record-breaking heat waves in the summer and monumental blizzards in the winter. I had grown tired of it. I'd had enough, physically, and mentally. We'd all heard the stories of how people in the inner city act up when the temperatures rise, and how incidents that typically end in violence escalate during hotter months. The winter can be just as treacherous in the city.

I remember a blustery winter day when two teenage kids were killed for throwing snowballs at a passing vehicle. The driver double backed, popped the trunk to retrieve a weapon and shot them. Another aspect of city life in the winter is the unspoken rule of honoring the work it takes to dig one's car out of a snowy parking spot. In the city, when finished shoveling, you put one of your lawn chairs or trashcans in the spot where your car had been to hold it until you return from your destination. It's an honor system of sorts. If another car is in that spot when you return, trouble is on the way. Trust violations usually led to violence.

I had begun to hate both summer and winter equally.

On an unseasonably cold April night, my best friend Chuck, who had begun taking salsa dance lessons and quickly became a pro at it, invited me to go with him on his twenty-ninth birthday. I'd usually turn him down, thinking salsa just wasn't for me, a big guy with two left feet. But for his birthday we hit the Spanish nightclub in Chestnut Hill. I marveled at his dance moves as he glided across the floor looking like a peanut butter-skinned Marc Anthony and stared incredulously as the women lined up and begged for Chuck to be their dance partner. Chuck was a nerd like me, so to see him becoming the life of the party on salsa night was extremely shocking, and even inspiring.

After a fun time, we returned home, exhausted, but fulfilled. We parked the car near our friend Lorenzo's house at the top of the block. As we parked, I looked across the street and saw a man in a brown unzipped hoodie, sitting on an adjacent stoop, just staring into the fall night. I commented to Chuck, "This dude has got to be freezing," and we laughed. Chuck thanked me for rolling out with him and helping to make his birthday special.

We walked into our homes, Chuck first, as he lived toward the top of the block, and I went to my house at the center. I turned on the television to unwind and not even ten minutes later was interrupted by a loud sound.

BANG. BANG. BANG.

I'd learned not to be the nosy one to open a door when I heard gunshots, so I peered out the porch blinds to see if I saw anything; I did not. This one was a false alarm. I went back to watching television.

Twenty minutes later, a loud series of *THUD* sounds blasted from my front door. My friend Damien was knocking frantically to get my attention. I answered the door and could see Damien was visibly shaken.

"Yo Ra... uh, can you call the cops?"

"Why?" I asked. "What happened, man?"

Damien sighed. "Mr. Aquil. He got shot just now. I think he's dead, man."

I didn't know who he was referring to, but I learned later that Arien, My friend Lorenzo's brother, had changed his name to Aquil after a prison sentence and his conversion to Islam. He had served his time upstate and been released a week earlier. Arien had been at his mother's home on our block every day since the release, doing yard work, and taking care of the house. When I asked Damien what happened, he said he'd heard the shots, and when he peered out of his window across the street, he saw a man in a brown hoodie running down the block, while a man lay bloody in the street.

The man I had seen just twenty minutes earlier and made a passing wisecrack about, was a cold-blooded murderer, waiting patiently for his target and the right time to strike. His target was a newly released, newly reformed man, a father, a man who had paid his debt to society and was ready to claim a new place in a new world. Aquil, aka Arien Robinson, passed on April 26, 2006. He was one of four hundred and six homicides in Philadelphia that year. The murderer took a son away from a mother, right in front of her home.

The potential for violence didn't stop there. In my own mother's house, my friends and I had "Halo Parties" while she was at work. Six to ten of us would come together, bringing TVs and Xboxes to my house to link them up and play hours of *Halo*, filling my mother's living room with dozens of characters, both savory and unsavory. She'd kill me if she had known. But all were welcome at the Jarbo household.

Jamie, another friend of ours from a block over, would come to the house to play *Halo* or *Super Smash Bros.* with us in between his shifts as a drug dealer. I think we all knew what he did when he wasn't with us, but we agreed never to discuss it and to keep those elements as far away from us as possible.

Then one day, before an intense *Smash Bros.* match-up, Jamie made himself more comfortable so he could resume kicking our butts (he was pretty good at the game).

"This thing is heavy, man. I gotta take it off," he said as he removed his jacket to reveal a bulletproof vest. He unsnapped the vest and picked up the GameCube controller. I looked on, mortified, too shocked to speak until it got worse. Jamie reached in his Girbaud jeans and pulled out a .38 caliber handgun, which he placed on my mother's coffee table, right on top of the newest *Ebony* magazine.

I couldn't take it. I paused the game. "Yo, J, you can't, man. Not in my crib, remember?"

Jamie understood, but pleaded, "Yo, I know, but you don't know how it is out here. It's dangerous out here, man."

I knew how dangerous the neighborhood was getting. Arien's death was hard to process because I'd been so close to where it happened on the block. It could have been me, or Chuck, or both of us that night. The killer could have mistaken any of us for Arien. Deep inside of me, evil thoughts were brewing. I wanted revenge for Arien. I knew I wasn't the guy to do it, but I knew that the streets have a special breed of karma for people who violate the code, and every day I looked forward to someone coming onto the block to tell me that Arien's killer was brought to justice. It never happened…and that infuriated me. I was becoming a product of my environment rather than the change my environment needed to see.

I managed to tell Jamie as nicely as I could that maybe he should seek a new career path. Later, we chose to not be aligned with anyone who was into anything that could jeopardize our future. We decided it was best that Jamie not come to our homes after that. And I decided to shake up my own career path, culminating in my leaving the city three months later.

If this is goodbye, to quote Jerry Butler on the song I'd sampled a few years earlier; then I just know it won't be easy.

I had a great job in Philly working at Woods Services, an alternative school, teaching special education to pre-teens. I worked with attentive kids and staff, and they covered 75 percent of my tuition to go to grad school. I haven't been able to find a deal like that since I left. Interestingly, due to new law changes and stricter guidelines, Woods couldn't rehire me today even if they wanted to. I am not currently qualified for the position I held six years before, which sounds nuts.

One day, I spent an entire shift searching for teaching jobs in warm areas. That wasn't the best thing to do on the clock. I used one of those incognito browser windows and came up with a list of four places that fit my needs: warm weather, a relocation package, and open middle school positions. I developed a list of pros and cons for each.

Miami, Florida
PROS: Great weather, hot women, beaches, awesome nightlife
CONS: Language barrier, too much temptation, low student achievement numbers

Charlotte, North Carolina
PROS: My family is there, growing city
CONS: Not much of a music scene, the family is there – they get nosy

Las Vegas, Nevada
PROS: Cheap housing, casinos, know a few people there
CONS: A little too hot, casinos

Phoenix, Arizona
PROS: Fastest growing city in the US, lower violent crime than Philly
CONS: Too hot, no family or friends there, higher property crime numbers, low student achievement numbers

I interviewed over the phone with at least two schools in each city, but the choice was made for me. I went to Phoenix because it was the only school I interviewed with that was willing to hire me without a face-to-face interview. The rest of these schools wanted me to pack up and fly out to interview. If I were hired, I would have had to go back home, pack, and then go back for good. I didn't have the funds to make that kind of move, so I chose Phoenix where I had no friends or family. It was a reboot in the hardest of ways.

Right before I went to Phoenix, I made my first ever trip to the west coast. I attended Rock the Bells, a huge hip-hop concert in San Bernardino, south of LA. It was a trip that Missy, a friend from college and I had planned, well before I had decided to move west. I almost canceled when I told her I had to save for the move, but she wouldn't hear it and agreed to cover part of my costs to make the trip happen.

The lineup was incredible. Snoop Dogg, De La Soul, Wu-Tang Clan, Mos Def, Talib Kweli, and many others I'd listened to my entire life were all under one sweltering desert roof. A friend suggested I take some of my own CDs, just in case I ran into any rappers or producers. I stuffed a backpack with *The Call* and a few leftover business cards for Meehar Productions.

We got into the show, and after hours of incredible hip-hop, I decided to go for mine. I had Missy hold my backpack as I grabbed a handful of CDs and went for the side of the stage where a large security guard was opening and closing the gate to let staff through. I walked behind them like I belonged there.

"Where you are going?" A six foot eight, three-hundred-and-fifty-pound man asked me as he placed the back of his large hand on my chest.

"Um… just taking these CDs to some peeps."

"Oh, yeah? Who?"

"Uh… De La, Talib, Wu, you know, whoever." As if I were on first name basis with any of these bands, I thought my coolness would prevail.

This man must have seen the desire in my eyes, or he just had a soft spot for awkward dudes shooting their shot. "Okay, go ahead back there… But you gotta give me one of those CDs." He flashed a smile.

"Yeah, of course!" I replied as I handed him *The Call*. "Track three is the one, 'Raze the Bar!'"

He warned me, "Alright if you get caught back there, I don't know you."

I skipped to the backstage area where I immediately saw Immortal Technique, then Redman, then Ghostface Killah, and Raekwon. My nerves went into overdrive.

Then it happened. I saw them. De La Soul: the three men my cousin Howie had thrown on for me to explain how you didn't have to be a gangster from the hood to be a rapper. Three of the most creative rap artists ever. The soundtrack of my teen years. In the same room as me. They were standing right in front of me, taking photos and chatting with Kadeem Hardison, known to us as Dwayne Wayne from the show *A Different World*. I sat in the corner and just watched, incredulous at what was transpiring.

Mos Def walked by. Then Method Man and RZA. This was insanity. One after another, my childhood superheroes walked in, talking to each other, laughing, even eating, like normal people do. I couldn't believe what I was seeing.

I sent a text to Missy, "THIS IS NUTS!"

She said back, "Get a picture!" and I'm glad she did because I wouldn't have this story to tell otherwise.

I walked over to Mos Def, who was conversing with a very attractive woman, and asked him if he would take a picture with me because he's my friend's favorite rapper. Annoyed, Mos let out a deep sigh and said, "Yeah, sure, man."

No one was around to take the picture, so I asked the woman, who flatly refused.

"Oh, no, sweetie. I'm a model, not a photographer." She walked away. At that point, Mos was even more perturbed.

I grabbed a passerby and asked them to take a photo. Right before they did, Mos Def said, "Hold on, let me put my shades on." He proceeded to grab the largest, darkest shades I'd ever seen and pulled his hat down as far as it would go. "Okay, now you can take the picture."

The result was disappointing. I have a dark, blurry photo of myself and Mos that I took home, only to have my friends say, "That ain't Mos Def!" every time I show it. He made sure that the photo was as bad as possible, probably because I'd interrupted him and his lady friend, or he had been having a bad day. No idea. Thanks, Mos.

Regardless, the rest of the day was incredible. Even though no one emailed me or followed up from the business cards and CDs I had handed out, the fact that I got to talk to those guys gave me new inspiration to work on something new. Surprisingly the only person out of the room that I still talk to is Kadeem Hardison, who turned out to be just as big of a gamer as I was. We talked Xbox, and even how much of a fan we both were of a band called Panacea, who I would get introduced to in a much more intimate means later.

Right before Wu-Tang Clan headlined and closed out the night, the hosts of the event announced a secret surprise guest would soon hitting the stage. The weary crowd didn't want any surprises at 1 a.m., they wanted who they paid to see. The Wu.

"Introducing your special surprise… LAURYN HILL! … Playing an ACOUSTIC SET!"

Lauryn released a genre-bending album in 1998, *The Miseducation of Lauryn Hill*. It was the only official studio release for Lauryn, but the album sold millions of copies and still holds up as a classic.

She was a legend, undoubtedly, but this was unfortunately not the time or place for acoustic, soulful vocals. This was a rap concert, and this crowd was expecting the grimiest, muddiest rap there is. The Wu. The crowd booed so loudly that I never heard one note of Lauryn's performance.

She cut her set short, and after fifteen minutes of boos she left the stage to make way for the Clan. They ripped an hour-long set of hits, and we ended the night happy.

I flew home, consciously aware this was only one night of happiness. Back home I realized that music wasn't enough, being positive wasn't enough. I didn't think anything would change Philadelphia. I'd been displeased with my life up until that point. It was time to leave the city I'd been born and raised in and try something else. I repacked, and prepared to drive back out west to my new home.

CHAPTER ELEVEN

NERDCORE

Capcom sue the RAHM? Probably couldn't cover it.
Free 99, hope the whole world discover it.

—"Bubble Man," *Mega Ran* (2007)

I HADN'T PLANNED MY MUSIC CAREER past *The Call*. Musically, I had said everything in it that I'd ever wanted to say as a rapper. I had effectively translated everything from my Demo Project to a full-length album, and although I was very proud of what we had created, I just wanted to get out what was on my mind at the time. The world was crazy in late 2004-2005 when I started writing it, and it just got crazier: George W. Bush had just gotten a second term after a wild election, hundreds of US troops were killed in the Middle East, and global terrorist attacks reached a critical mass. At home, Hurricane Katrina capped off the deadliest hurricane season ever, education reform was being forgotten, and personally, I had just broken up with the girl who, at one time, I was certain I would marry. Once the record was done and out of my system, I wanted to move on. I stopped writing new songs and went into a silent, semi-retirement mode. Teaching and adjusting to a new environment were the only things on my mind.

I knew that a move of this magnitude had to be total, fresh start. Taking the things that I owned in Philly would have attached to a way of life I didn't want to return to. I sold everything that wasn't tied down when I made the move: my television, my Xbox, and my MPC (Music Production Center). After the harsh thirty-six-hour drive, I arrived in

Phoenix with only three storage bins full of clothes and a computer. The heat instantly strangled me.

In 2006, when I moved into the neighborhood on the south side, that was one of the roughest areas in town; I didn't even notice. There were four hundred fifty thousand-dollar homes developed just twelve hundred feet away from low-income housing. I'd never seen anything like it. Upon a closer look, I noticed that even the nicest homes had bars on the windows. Property crime was (and is) a very real thing in Phoenix.

The major housing boom of the early 2000s was just beginning to wind down. Everyone wanted a nice home, so land developers built thousands of similar looking structures on vacant or underdeveloped land and sold homes for cheap to people who couldn't afford them, through adjustable rate mortgages, or ARMs. The interest rates skyrocketed on those mortgages as the years went on. Sadly, in 2012, many of those homes were foreclosed on or abandoned. I roomed with my friend's brother, who lived on a block next to half-million-dollar abandoned homes, which were boarded up with missing AC units due to nighttime thieves. It was a sight to behold.

So were the plain t-shirts, flip-flops, and very few name brands worn. Few people rocked the newest Jordans. Guys hardly had super stylish haircuts, huge beards, and oversized t-shirts. I would surely get laughed out of the neighborhood if my toes were exposed in Philly, but apparently in Phoenix, that was not the case.

I had no problem adjusting to teaching in Phoenix though, because, all around the world, it's the same song. I saw the same students, parents, and teachers I had seen all my life; they just had different names and faces. I was a special education teacher at Santa Maria Middle School, which was about 99 percent Hispanic. There was one Black student in my class, Daequon, who accused me of giving him a harder time than any other student. That most likely was true, just because I wanted him to shine, and was probably so worried about anyone thinking I gave him preferential treatment. Adjusting to the students' cultural differences was a new experience.

It was hard to keep a positive attitude when you had no idea what would happen from one week to the next. I watched several co-workers resign early due to various school practices or terrible treatment by students. My top student dropped out of seventh grade because she was her family's only babysitter. My worst students fell victim to the temptations and peer pressure of gangs and enrolled. Weekly meetings for Special Education teachers were the worst. At any given time, the school could inform us that the practices exhibited every day in classrooms were now illegal, like suggesting a parent get a child tested to enter or leave special education services, or asking a child about their home life to make sure they were safe.

When I first moved to AZ, it was six months after the release of *The Call*. The buzz for it that had started so strong had faded. And traveling three thousand miles away from anyone or anything familiar isn't smart when you have an album to promote. No one in Arizona cared I had ripped open mics for months, or had shared stages and gotten props from established east coast MCs. As impressive as they were, they remained regional names, so I couldn't just hop on the big shows like I used to. Music videos in 2006 were too expensive to shoot, and I didn't have enough contacts to tour or go on a west coast press run. The album stopped dead in its tracks. If I were to make a footing out west, I would have to restart from zero.

I had a buzz, but I just didn't know how to make it last. Sustainability is the hardest part of the process as a musician. As tough as it may be to create a great album, it's probably a hundred times harder to get people to care about it. Once they do care about it, keeping their interest is almost impossible without a budget… or going viral doing something silly. I moved on from promoting *The Call* and started thinking about the next step, and if even hip-hop would be a part of it.

I began frequenting a downtown Phoenix hip-hop spot called The Hidden House, which held weekly rap events called Friday Night Live, where local DJs and MCs would hit the stage. After a few weeks, The Hidden House became our home. It was a dive bar in the most typical of ways, but the bar staff were friendly, the drinks were poured just right, and you always heard some good music there every week. I frequented The Hidden House and passed my CD off to Al Page, who ran the music events there. "Oh okay, I'll call you man," he said after reading the back cover of *The Call*. I knew by the music that played out of the speakers at The Hidden House that if given a chance to get onto that stage, I'd make the most of it. I wound up meeting everyone I still rap with today, like Mr. Miranda, Roqy Tyraid, and Penny, aka the Writers Guild.

I probably played one hundred shows at The Hidden House in the eight years it existed, to the point that whenever I'd show up, everyone in the place would expect me to grab the mic and freestyle, even if I was just attending to support a friend from the sidelines. I became Norm in *Cheers*, and The Hidden House was where everybody in the Phoenix scene knew your name. At its most packed, The Hidden House could probably hold sixty people, which was perfect because every show felt like a packed house, but at the same time, with the venue not having an elevated stage, the performer was at eye level with the crowd, which made it easy to create an intimate vibe in the building. It was the perfect place for a number of up and comers to hone their craft.

At the same time across town, the longest running event in Arizona, known as The Blunt Club, run by Universatile Music, was happening every Thursday at Hollywood Alley in Mesa. I wasn't able to attend as much due to it being farther from my home, but they boasted some incredible guests, such as the legendary December night in 2006 where arguably the most influential group in hip-hop, Public Enemy, performed at the two hundred-person venue.

It was truly the stuff of legend. Fate had shined on the one city that probably gets the least attention from the hip-hop gods. Public Enemy was in town and their show at the Marquee Theater, a fifteen hundred-person venue in town, was canceled. The Blunt Club staff persuaded PE to perform at Hollywood Alley on the same day, with one simple ask: "How is Public Enemy going to pass up an opportunity to play 'By the Time I Get to Arizona' IN Arizona?" With four hours' notice, a Public Enemy concert was happening in Arizona. Word spread quickly on MySpace, and I did all I could to get to that show. I arrived just after 9 p.m. and there was a line almost two miles long. Dejected, I drove home after people in line were informed no one else was getting in. I watched videos the next day in shock. People were on each other's shoulders, wall to wall, singing every word with fire in their bellies. I was determined to make moments like that happen in my new environment, somehow.

I came back to Phoenix after Rock The Bells and had one more show on my schedule that month, a monthly event called "RapStock" at a venue on the east side of town. At this show, fifty rappers – yes, fifty – would perform a seven-minute song set. Hardly enough time to convert a show goer into a supporter, the event was mostly to serve as a networking event for musicians, because Lord knows no fans were ever there. Rappers and entourages would meet up at the monthly show, mainly to fold arms and watch skeptically as upstart rappers worked their hardest to gain the crowd's approval. I had managed a few head nods and handshakes during my set, which was about the most success one could leave a RapStock with. After this show, I knew that something about my approach had to change. I watched forty-nine other rappers dress alike, perform on the same beats (literally – many had re-used the popular beat of the moment or even had downloaded the same popular beats from the website SoundClick to perform over) and it really hit me that not many of these artists had given any thought to seriously standing out. I went back home and took some notes.

These show experiences, along with the high that remained from that trip to Rock the Bells, enlightened and inspired me in amazing ways. Suddenly, I was ready to try to change the game like Wu-Tang Clan did. Instead of kung fu flicks, my avenue would be through video games. I had a unique perspective that I could bring to the marketplace, I just had to trust myself to execute it.

The *Mega Man* rapper was born on a winter evening in 2006 in Phoenix. I was at the computer surfing the internet, when I discovered emulators. A video game console emulator is a type of emulator that allows a computing device to act as a video game console's hardware and play its games on the emulating platform. With this, I could play classic NES games on my PC, without a new console. Now, this wasn't totally legal; the law says you must own any game that you emulate. I told myself it was legit because, at one time or another, I'd owned the games.

I fired up *Mega Man 2* and discovered that I remembered all the old tricks and traps from 1990; sixteen years later, it was as if I hadn't left my NES behind all those years ago. The music was still phenomenal. I hummed it while blasting boss robots to oblivion. Who needs friends when you have retro classics?

Playing through this game gave me the idea of all ideas. As I hummed along with the music, I began muttering words, then phrases, and then chorus notes. I began crafting songs in my head to high-speed, eight-bit chiptunes while I struggled through the game's levels.

Later, in search of *Mega Man* music mp3s online, I came across a website called Atomic Fire, a comprehensive *Mega Man* fan site, full of information, tips, and a section for soundtracks. The owner, known simply as "DaHeatMan," had compiled every piece of information and media on the *Mega Man* series, much like I had, but he put it all in one place on the internet.

I had found nirvana. I downloaded one track, then another, and then another. Before I knew it, I had spent three hours on the page, playing and downloading songs from the classic *Mega Man* series. When the smoke cleared, I had neatly organized folders of over two hundred tracks. I had spent more time listening to *Mega Man 2*'s soundtrack than any other. Its tunes took me back to those challenging levels, and the cold mornings on the bus with my Sony Walkman.

Next step, I quickly booted up my music production program, Reason 3.0, and loaded a song from *Mega Man 2*, Wood Man's stage theme into the interface. I stretched it, added some new drums, strings, and synths, and began humming a tune that would eventually be called "Grow Up." I felt like a California miner in 1849. I was onto something so different that would eventually change my life, though I didn't know it at the time. I wrote lyrics about remaining child-like and immature and recorded the song at my engineer's home. With that, the Mega Ran idea was born.

I didn't plan to be the first person to rap on video game, specifically *Mega Man* themes, making full-on hip-hop bangers from these tunes. I searched Google to see if anyone had made anything like this before. Surely, they had, right? They hadn't. The closest I found was a band called The Megas, who replayed *Mega Man* music and added rock lyrics about the boss characters; and The Protomen, who created driving rock tracks based in the universe of Mega Man, without using any of the existing themes. I remixed The Megas' track "Metal Dance" and added rap lyrics on the breaks of their song, and it became a very popular track online. Mega Ran was born.

Was I first to write nerdy raps? Absolutely not. As far as rap went, Del, The Funky Homosapien made a track called "Proto Culture" in 2000, which was about how much he enjoyed Sega Dreamcast. The track sampled "Morrigan's Win Theme" from the hit arcade game *Darkstalkers*, which was also a Capcom title. Legendary rapper Kool Keith has been rapping about spaceships and robots for decades. Biz Markie's most popular songs are about how uncool he has been. The Fresh Prince, aka Will Smith, with his squeaky-clean image and witty rhymes, could arguably be called a nerd rapper. Though the Wu-Tang Clan probably wouldn't like it, their obsession with Kung Fu cinema can definitely be categorized as nerdy.

In 2005, a website called Urban Reviews posted a review on my first EP release *Fundamentals*; on the same day, right underneath, they reviewed an album by YTCracker called *NerdRap Entertainment System* in which he rapped nerdy bars over samples from games from *Dig Dug* to *Lode Runner*. The track "Meganerd" touched me the hardest.

Over the signature introduction theme from *Mega Man 3*, YTC dropped the rhymes that would help to influence my next direction in the same way that Chuck D's words did fifteen years earlier.

> This is the life of a meganerd, baby…
> We doin' things and we making it happen, right
> From the Trash 80 to a black Mercedes
> No one can stop us now 'cause we keepin' it nerdy, nice

As a nerd in denial, this was the mantra I didn't know I needed to hear. This guy was proud of the same thing that I got teased for my entire childhood. This album was also the first time I'd heard the term "nerd rap," and I explored to find out more about it. As I finished more of the *Mega Ran* tracks, I wanted to put them online to get feedback, but I was also deathly afraid of people who were used to hearing Random – the conscious Philly emcee who was so not nerdy – hearing this album. How could I show people my new music and new direction without putting off folks who already were fans of my music and movement? A new name was a start.

I watched the careers of two golden era emcees turned new artists to get inspiration for this change: NYOil and MF DOOM. NYOil began his career as Kool Kim of The UMC's, one of the first rap acts signed to Wild Pitch Records in the early 1990s. After moderate success with the singles "Blue Cheese" and "One to Grow On," The UMCs disappeared for a bit, and a mysterious single popped up on the internet in 2007 called "Y'all Should All Get Lynched," a controversial and fiery attack on hip-hop's directional change. Kool Kim had hit the gym, donned some shades, and changed his name to NYOil.

MF DOOM began as Zev Love X, a founding member of hip-hop group KMD, who appeared on the 1989 hit "The Gas Face." From there, KMD's records were highly bootlegged and never widely released due to label politics. Zev Love X decided a name change would be the best way to release music. He added a Doctor Doom mask and became the mysterious man we know as MF DOOM then later just DOOM, releasing solo and collaboration projects that are now considered rap classics, like "Operation Doomsday" and "Madvillainy." I thought if Random would be known for straight-up rap, then an alter-ego could be created for nerd raps.

Mega Man + Random = Mega Ran. Easy math.

I created a new MySpace page as "Mega Ran" and posted my music there. The first thing I posted was the Wood Man-sampled "Grow Up." No one could've predicted the response. It reached ten thousand hits in a month, faster than anything I'd previously placed on the site. I dropped another, which did even better than the first. These songs racked up thousands of plays and encouraged me to continue the project ultimately called *Mega Ran*.

Sampling tunes from the vast library of *Mega Man* games, I created a world in which I had a dream that I woke up inside of the game and had to pick up where the blue bot left off – blasting enemies through dope rap tracks, instead of plasma shooting arm cannons. The *Mega Ran* album was completed and released in June 2007, in time to commemorate *Mega Man*'s twentieth anniversary. I released a free version of the album that contained ten songs. I hoped that people would like it and then be inclined to purchase the full version, which contained sixteen songs. It worked.

The free version racked up fifty-four hundred downloads in a week on a now-defunct file-sharing site called zShare. The day I released the full version, a review of the album popped up on IGN's website, which is currently the fifth most popular video game website in the United States. The review led to more hits and more purchases of the album. I suspect the IGN review and exposure led to the message I received in my MySpace inbox, from Capcom.

The subject line read: "Re: This Mega Man Album."

My heart dropped. *Here we go*, I thought. *They're gonna sue me. I know it. Grand opening, grand closing.*

I'd hoped they would enjoy the fun, clean lyrics, and catchy choruses, but I also feared they would be offended by my sampling of their tracks on each song.[4]

The message wasn't as malicious as I had feared, thankfully:

Hey Man! I'm Chris at Capcom-Unity!
We heard your Mega Man album.
Don't worry, this isn't a cease and desist! We like to highlight

---

[4] Sampling (v): The reuse of a portion or sample of a sound recording in another recording. Samples may comprise rhythm, melody, speech, or other sounds, and are integrated using digital hardware (samplers) or software such as digital audio workstations. Sampling is a foundation of hip-hop music, with producers sampling funk and soul records, particularly drum breaks, which could then be rapped over. The practice has influenced all genres of music and is particularly important to electronic music, hip-hop, and pop. Sampling without permission can infringe copyright.

cool fan art that we find on the internet, and your album is super cool! We'd like to know if you'd be interested in doing an interview on our website?"

Of course, I wanted to. After a cool interview feature on the website, Chris emailed me with an awesome idea, "Hey man. I don't know if you're familiar, but San Diego Comic-Con is coming up. We have a booth there, and since this album is so popular online, how would you like to come to our booth and sign autographs for an hour? It'll be fun."

I was very familiar with Comic-Con, but I'd never been. Since I was a pre-teen, I'd read about the giant conventions in San Diego where Stan Lee and all the writers and artists met fans. I'd dreamed of attending one, but San Diego was so far away from where I used to live. From Phoenix however, I could get to San Diego in five hours, so I told Capcom I'd absolutely want to go. Amazingly I went from never attending a Comic-Con to getting invited as a guest for my very first one. I'd already become the first rapper licensed by a major gaming company, and I was about to become the first rapper ever to play live on the San-Diego Comic-Con floor. Random was making way for Mega Ran. Or, so I thought…

After spending hundreds of dollars to reserve a place to stay in San Diego and driving up after work, Mel aka DJ DN3 and I showed up to the Comic-Con for Saturday, the busiest day of any convention. There were at least forty thousand people there. We had to park about a mile from the convention center, and DJ DN3 pulled his turntable coffin down a long, hilly road, through thousands of con-goers, to get to the convention. We arrived, and I picked up a badge that said "Raheem Jarbo, Capcom USA," so I was feeling official.

When we got to the Capcom booth, the employees told us, "Oh, man, we have been trying to reach you guys all day." This couldn't be good.

"We're here, what's up?" I asked.

"Well, bad news. We had a few other nerdcore guys here the day before, and they kind of ruined it for you. These guys were extremely unprofessional and inappropriate, using foul language, inviting scantily clad dancers on stage, and it was a bad look. The Con threatened to shut our booth down if we did any music today."

"Other nerdcore guys?" I asked. At this time, I hadn't even heard of nerdcore, let alone several guys who did it.

Mel looked at me with a fiery rage that I'd never seen before or since. "You mean I just lugged this thing all the way here, and we're not performing?"

"I'm afraid not, man. I'm so sorry," the Capcom rep said.

To soothe the burn, Capcom allowed us to sit and sign autographs at the booth for an hour, which was fun, but not what we had signed up for at all.

I was so angry that I went home and wrote a scathing post on a site called RhymeTorrents, which served as the Nerdcore message board and home to the artists who called themselves Nerdcore rappers, lambasting unprofessional acts and asking them to take themselves seriously or get out of the way. I was laughed out of the forum.

I was making music, and playing shows every night, trying to make a dent in the young Phoenix hip-hop scene. It was a daunting task to play a show until 2 a.m., wake up at 6 a.m., and still perform my job effectively, but I did it for as long as I could. When I originally took the teaching job in Phoenix under emergency certification rules, which meant that to keep my job, I had to enroll in a graduate program before the end of the school year. Unfortunately, due to a byline of the No Child Left Behind Act, in public school it was not legal for a non-education major to instruct Special Education students. Because I hadn't started a graduate school program towards an education major within the year, Santa Maria was unable to rehire me, and I was left without a job only one year after uprooting my entire life.

I thought about moving back to Philly, but I decided to see where this Arizona journey would take me and applied to a few more schools. I got several calls from charter schools, which are independently owned public schools that have more freedom to hire and conduct classrooms more loosely than traditional schools. Most of the ones I talked to were so in need they were willing to hire me on the spot, so I took the one closest to my house, at South Valley Academy. I learned that charter schools out west were nothing like the ones I saw back east. Most classrooms were housed in buildings that looked like trailers or mobile homes, which seemed to foreshadow they didn't expect to remain around long. There was no schoolyard, no basketball court, no track, no sports teams. They had just the basics, and I do mean the basics.

Meanwhile, I needed to expand and build my music portfolio. I started a podcast with DJ DN3, called *The RandomBeagle Show*. We talked about music, sports, and whatever we could fit into our hour-long format. It was the perfect cover so I could talk about the things I loved, as well as insert our own works into the program when we needed to. As a bonus third perk, being a podcaster helped me to qualify as press, and earn free access to the concerts and events I wanted to see but couldn't otherwise afford.

Around the same time, famed music executive Sha Money, who made his name finding 50 Cent and other famous rappers, made a second home in Phoenix and started an event called the Producers Conference. This event had a very simple, but awesome goal: to connect producers with artists and to serve as a networking opportunity for beatmakers, unlike anything that had been done previously. In any given year, guys like Swizz Beatz, Q-Tip, and more would show up at the conference as speakers.

As a broke, bedroom producer/rapper, I knew I didn't have much of a way to pay the thousand-dollar fee for producers, or even the desire to pay the one-hundred-and-fifty-dollar general admission cost to get in and sit in on panels. This was a job for Press Credentials. We pushed for press access to the conference, but had no luck. We didn't have the numbers, so I had to find another way in.

I decided to hang in the lobby of the Downtown Phoenix hotel where the event was taking place, hoping to catch a producer or rapper who felt like talking, shoot him a copy of my newest mixtape, and try to get a drop or station ID recording for my show. That day I met a bunch of folks who I now consider to be heroes and peers. MURS, Skyzoo, and 9th Wonder were among them, but the most memorable interaction was with an accomplished producer who was familiar with my work. I wouldn't dare mention him, you'll see why.

"You do the *Mega Man* thing right?" he asked. I said yes, and he then said he appreciated how authentic and true to self the Nerdcore movement was. "Not like that other fake cat that does the *Sonic The Hedgehog* thing.... What's his name?"

His friend chimed in, "Charles Hamilton."

"Yeah, that bum."

"I wish somebody would just punch him in the face."

It turned out that someone was listening because that exact thing happened to Hamilton, by a woman that he was egging on in a now-ancient viral video. People edited the video to have *Sonic the Hedgehog*'s rings pop out of Hamilton when he was hit, and because of this and a few other questionable decisions, hip-hop had effectively laughed Hamilton out of the game, unfortunately. Before this, though, the producer wanted him gone in a much more direct way.

"Yo. You should diss that cat," he suggested to me, as I tried to laugh it off. He wanted me to write disrespectful song lyrics towards a man I didn't know. "I'm serious, man. I'll even make the beat. You write a cold diss record, and I'll put you on, bro." This man didn't smile or chuckle. He was for real. At that time, this producer was fresh off producing four tracks for several other underground rap favorites. After 2010, this man's discography reads like a who's who of rap chart-toppers: 50 Cent, Drake, Future, J. Cole and more have rapped on his beats, and he's built a successful empire today. A decision to go in on Hamilton over a banger from him might have paid dividends.

It wasn't the first time I'd been asked to do something musically that didn't align with my personal beliefs and I knew it wouldn't be the last. As an indie rapper without much to show for my years of hustling, I'll admit it was very tempting to take up this gentleman's beef and declare lyrical war on an unsuspecting Charles Hamilton, but I didn't get what Chuck had even done to deserve a blindsiding on the mic. I told him, "Nah, I don't have any beef with that guy. I don't even know him."

"He bit your whole thing, bro! He didn't start doing video game raps until after you."

Did he, though? Charles Hamilton's Sega-sampling mixtape,

"Sonic The Hamilton," dropped in 2008, a year after the *Mega Ran* album, though it's almost impossible to determine whether my album inspired his. We were on two different coasts, around completely different inspirations.

I didn't want to engage Hamilton in a battle when I didn't know him personally, let alone have negative feelings for him. I politely declined the offer, and I haven't seen or heard from the producer since then. He's done alright for himself. Again, Charles Hamilton did as much if not more to K.O. himself from the rap game than I ever could have with a rap song, so I guess all ended how it was supposed to. The man has gone on to a litany of successful endeavors, and I've done okay. What a weird first meeting, though.

2008 could best be described as the beginning of the "blog era" in hip-hop. During this stretch, hip-hop stars were made on rap blogs. 2DopeBoyz, HotNewHipHop, Complex, and many other sites became the ultimate tastemakers, breaking future celebrities like Drake, Lupe Fiasco, Kendrick Lamar, J. Cole, and more. The influence of rap blogs was seen at the top of the business, when the magazine *XXL* launched *The 2009 XXL Freshman 10* issue, where they would pick the ten rappers most likely to become stars. Many rappers were coming directly from blogs at the time. 2009's list is considered one of the best and gave *XXL* credibility as a preeminent tastemaker and predictor of future success. The class included rappers Wale, B.O.B., Kid Cudi, Currensy, Blu, Mickey Factz, and our friend Charles Hamilton.

In 2008, to ride the wave, *Complex* magazine started a competition called the Online Hip-Hop Awards to find the next star. As with all online voting competitions, it got ugly. There was a category of "Rapper on the Come Up" or something like that, and I asked my fans online to vote, even adding an incentive that if I won, I'd work on a new Mega Ran project to commemorate the *Mega Man 9* game that dropped. After a few days, I was in the top five.

I got excited, with a week left in the contest, and continued campaigning. I got to top two within three days, then in first place with forty hours left. I looked the next morning again, and the entire chart looked exactly like *XXL*'s Freshman list. Someone had rigged the system. Wale was in the lead when he had never been on the chart previously. I was nowhere to be found in the top ten. I was upset, but I remained calm. I worked on the *Mega Ran 9* album anyway, and I'm glad I did because it contained my biggest hit since then, which was a little tune called "Splash Woman."

To write and produce "Splash Woman," I went back to my roots. On a winter trip to Philly, I drove sixty miles to Newtown and reconnected with Samik, who I hadn't seen since that day outside Lab Addicts. I asked him if he could work with the "Splash Blue" theme by Ippo Yamada, the theme with the first female boss ever in the *Mega Man* series.

Samik tells the process of my writing the song as "The Nuggets Story." Once he finished the phenomenal beat, I asked him to play it on repeat so I would get in the groove and write out the story. After playing the beat maybe five times, he got hungry and took a trip to a nearby Wendy's for chicken nuggets. I stayed behind and wrote – and Samik insists that in the twenty-five to thirty minutes it took for him to get the nuggets and return, I wrote the "Splash Woman" song. I don't believe it was that fast, but I was in a zone and I do tend to write quickly when I'm inspired. And I certainly was inspired because what came out of it was a love song about meeting that female boss. We thought the song would be a success right away, and we were right. In March 2009 I released *Mega Ran 9*, led by "Splash Woman," which became my biggest hit up to that point. I still end shows with it ten years later.

When I finished that album, I realized it was time to take music seriously. I was struggling at school, and I wanted to try to live my dream. Going to conventions and performing was way too much fun. I began sending my music out to blogs in hopes of getting a featured post and effectively become the next Charles Hamilton.

I got rejected by every one of them. Very few hip-hop people wanted to touch "nerdcore" because of the negative stigma surrounding it. The term nerdcore conjured up images of White middle-class guys who were inspired by Eminem and wrote songs of angst and fire, while working at well-paying jobs and treating the struggle of the nerd as if it were the worst form of persecution next to racism, sexism, and homophobia. On top of that, there were sound quality issues. Most sounded like they were recording their songs on an Xbox headset mic. Being the exception to the rule in nerd rap worked out as far as helping me to gain fans, but when it came to building a rep in the music world, it was like a scarlet letter. Rap outlets would tell me "oh you do that nerd thing," and ignore me. Later they'd say things like "you the nerd thing, but you can really RAP though!" Not sure if that was a compliment.

There was one person willing to work with me, though. I happened to befriend an individual by the name of Kyle Murdock on MySpace, not making the connection that it was the same Kyle "K" Murdock who worked at XM Sirius satellite radio, and made beats for a group called Panacea. I heard their first album *Ink Is My Drink* in 2006 and was hooked on the combination of raw rhymes and spacey beats by Raw Poetic and K-Murdock. I played it for anyone that would listen at the time. One day he posted a bulletin that he was seeking new music to play on his hip-hop mix show, *SubSoniq*. I submitted my two albums, *The Call* and *Mega Ran*, to his mailing address, still not making the connection.

Weeks later, Kyle sent me an email stating that he liked *The Call* and LOVED *Mega Ran*. He mentioned that he made beats and was considering working on a video game-based album. It was then I put it together he was *the* K-Murdock from Panacea. I almost passed out. The same group that Kadeem Hardison and I bonded over, backstage at Rock the Bells. It was the first time I'd ever been approached by someone I was a fan of, telling me that he was a fan of mine.

I was happy to start working on this yet-to-be-named-video game rap project with Kyle, but I told him I'd had a few prior jobs I had to finish up. I had released *Mega Ran 9*, which was extremely successful, but to balance and preserve the hip-hop cred I had worked so hard to build, I released a mixtape called *TeacherRapperHero Vol.1*. I was recording my next project *Patches and Glue*, a more traditional hip-hop album that I put together to counteract and balance the amount of attention that *Mega Ran* received.

I didn't want to be known as a one-trick pony, so the next release had to be different, for me. For the *Patches* record, I'd need classic hip-hop tracks, boom bap, and soulful sounds. Kyle agreed to produce one track for the EP. He did what became "The Beatdown," one of my favorites there. I remember us on the phone, talking about how the album would sound once "The Beatdown" was completed, while I was on a lunch break at my teaching job. Since then, I knew he would remain a part of my projects moving forward.

Kyle came to visit Phoenix once, but I was on the road touring at the time. He recorded an episode of our podcast with DN3, and he and Kyle became friends. I promised him that we would collaborate on a more fleshed out project soon. When we did, we began work on what would become one of my best-received albums, *Forever Famicom*.

Chapter Twelve

FOREVER FAMICOM

Then he met a man, his name was K-Murdock
Played a couple tracks for him and they were hot.

—"Episode III (A New Day)," *Forever Famicom* (2010)

B Y 2008, I'D RELEASED A few projects that had taken off, but they weren't enough. I was still working at a struggling school and fitting in music whenever I could. With me living in Phoenix, and Kyle "K" Murdock residing in Washington, DC, he and I would record in a very interesting manner, through emails. It's the norm now, but the process was complicated in 2008:

MURDOCK emailed RAN mp3 files of beats.

RAN wrote to the beat and recorded.

RAN's ENGINEER zipped up and emailed the vocal files to MURDOCK.

MURDOCK created a first mix of the song.

RAN emailed back some notes on the mix.

MURDOCK put more bells and whistles, or "sauce", on the song for a final version.

RAN approved the mix or suggested more changes.

MURDOCK finally mastered the entire album once all songs were approved.

This meticulous process led to the album taking much longer than average, but with the songs only running through two people, it kept things moving effectively. It took two years from the first beat coming my way to the album's release in June 2010.

Subject-wise, I wanted the album to be more about me than about simply sampling an already-popular video game theme and retelling its plot, so I told a lot of autobiographical stories from my childhood over K's dope beats. Every song was recorded in separate studios because of our distance, but when I had the chance to work in close quarters with Kyle, I jumped on it. We recorded the most personal cut together: "Dream Master."

During a holiday trip to Philly, I borrowed my mother's car and drove two hours to DC to meet with Kyle for the first time and work on music face-to-face instead of over emails and Skype. He played me the track to "Dream Master," and I had the flow, the beginning and ending instantly. It was time to create the rest. I asked Kyle if I could have the room, and I laid down on the floor. The song took me back to childhood, to an innocent time, when so many of the events that brought me to this moment, all the good, bad, and ugly occurred.

As I wrote, I remember shedding tears, wiping them away quickly and sniffling. Kyle would pop into the door asking if I was okay, or offering drinks or snacks as I wrote. The tears were based on the reminders of my not-so-awesome childhood, but also in celebration of my life at that moment. I thought about Christina, I thought about the lunchroom sessions of Marvel cards and narrowly avoiding violence and drugs in high school... about creating *The Call* and struggling to be noticed and it all went inside the song.

Kyle's production managed to get an emotional response from me that music hadn't done up until that point. I knew from that writing session that this would be a special album. I didn't finish "Dream Master" in "Nuggets Story" time, but I still finished it pretty quickly, because the heartfelt storytelling, nostalgic beats, and a great concept that had never been attempted on this scale before gave me hope for this project.

Meanwhile, when I returned back to Phoenix, I had to make it through the school year, which gets easier after Christmas vacation. They say that's when you as a teacher can begin to smile and ease off the gas pedal. I survived the school year at South Valley and made some long-lasting relationships there. It was in year two that things began to fall apart. I knew after the first three back-to-school faculty meetings were held at shoddy Mexican restaurants (where we had to pay for our own lunch) that something was terribly wrong. By the fourth meeting, Principal Hernandez told us she couldn't offer any of us further employment because South Valley was being sold, restructured, and rebuilt. That happened in September, well into a new school year. I was without a job again and had nowhere to turn. For the second time in two years, I considered going back home.

A few week later, I took a job at a third charter school in Phoenix built on an exploration model, which was very similar to that of a Montessori school. Country Gardens Charter School had peer mediators handle fights and student problems. Students would self-teach to groups called Centers. Teachers were more moderators than anything else. I watched other classes run like well-oiled machines, while my classroom ran like a 1972 Dodge Dart. I just couldn't get the hang of the new program.

In the Centers model, a teacher had to set up three group activity stations that the students could work on independently, while the teacher stood in front of the class and lectured to one small group at a time on a new concept, then rotate every 15 minutes. My centers always needed help, leading to me leaving the lecture group constantly to assist, which took everyone off track. It was vastly different from what I had done in the past, and required a level of commitment I just couldn't give at the time, with music beginning to go well for me.

Right before the end of the school year, I was laid off. They were clear to tell me that I was not fired, but I was the result of a mid-semester budget cut, which I'd never heard of. We were always told that after a hundred days of school, all funding is released for the school year, so problem kids can get expelled without them counting against your numbers, and teachers are usually locked in for the year. Confused and depressed, I went outside to my car and noticed a warning from the Phoenix Police Department telling me that to avoid a fine I had to either change my car's tags from PA to AZ, or get an inspection and update my Pennsylvania emissions sticker within thirty days. I wasn't ready to fully commit to Arizona, so I had to go back to Philly. I decided to take a long road trip and turn it into a rap tour.

The "Back to The Future Tour," as I dubbed it, went from Arizona to New Mexico, then to Texas, Nashville, and then would end in Philadelphia with a concert at a venue. Then I could get my car up to speed. My partner in rhyme, Dave Miranda aka "Mr. Miranda," joined me on the trip. We had ten dates booked, throughout the southwest, then a long ride up north from Nashville to Philadelphia to end it.

On the first day of tour, we were shorted pay by a drunken New Mexico show promoter, who had forgotten his arrangement with us and offered us a Green Chile Shot for our trouble. Fun, but not what we came for. I'd say we might have broke even on the road, thanks to merchandise sales – even though in every city the house may have been half full, the people were all extremely enthusiastic. Our best show might have been in Dallas, where we played a raucous house party and met some folks that are still friends of mine to this day.

During that tour, I stopped at a Burger King in Nashville before a show scheduled for that evening. I noticed everyone crowded around the television, which was set to CNN. They were following a story reporting that Michael Jackson, the King of Pop, had died. No one wanted to believe the story, so everyone was searching hard to confirm or deny the report. It turned out to be true. Michael Jackson was dead at fifty years old. I was stunned and paralyzed with grief, but I still had a performance that night. It was the most depressing show of my life. I blocked the entire memory out of my head. I still had to drive the remaining eight hundred miles to Philadelphia. I bought a copy of Michael Jackson's Greatest Hits from a record store and spent most of the drive playing "Man in The Mirror" on repeat and crying.

On the drive, I thought about my most memorable music moments, and they all involved Michael Jackson. A seven-year-old me staying up late to watch the Grammys in 1984 after MJ had won eight awards, and me hoping he would get his ninth, even as the credits rolled. Begging Mom for a "Beat It" leather jacket, then later for a "Thriller" jacket for Christmas. Buying the last copy of "Thriller" on vinyl from our local record store before they sold out. Attempting to emulate the moonwalk for a week straight after *Motown 25* aired. It felt like I'd lost a family member.

Michael Jackson's impact on music and culture were phenomenal. Hard to imagine, but at the height of MJ's popularity, the president of CBS Records had to threaten to pull all other artists' music to get Michael Jackson's "Billie Jean" into rotation on MTV. MJ broke down barriers and transitioned from another face in the R&B crowd to the unquestionable King of Pop. Later in 2009 after Michael's death, his final concert rehearsals were packaged in a film called *This is It*, and it remains the only movie I've ever walked out of without finishing in the theaters. I just couldn't stand to watch Michael in the condition he was, barely himself, giving his last to do what he does best, performing for us. I'm a stickler about not wanting to see things that artists didn't intend to show us. So, after my death, please don't release songs or books that I didn't want released, okay? Thanks.

The same week Michael Jackson died, Willy Northpole, of South Phoenix and a signee of rapper Ludacris, was readying his highly anticipated debut album, *Tha Connect*. In the buildup leading to its release, Willy had appeared on national television in Phoenix sports garb, shot videos in the neighborhood, made several local appearances and had campaigned hard to get the city behind a very strong movement. This was to be the moment Phoenix hip-hop reached the mainstream. Powered by a strong single and Ludacris's multiplatinum buzz, no one doubted that Willy Northpole was about to become a superstar. All he needed were the numbers to cement his place in history.

That was the hard part. While the album sold out in every record store in Phoenix on the first few days, *Tha Connect* was drastically under-shipped everywhere else. I was in Dallas on release day, and Dave and I attempted to purchase the record, and the Best Buy employee had no recollection of the album reaching store shelves. Added to that was the unfortunate timing of releasing the very same week of Michael Jackson's tragic death. Heck, Farrah Fawcett died the same day, and no one even talked about that, so a rapper from Phoenix didn't have a chance. All of MJ's albums shot back onto the charts, while *Tha Connect* underperformed, failing to crack Billboard's Top 200.

In the month after getting let go from a third teaching position, I felt like the universe was telling me it was time to spread my wings and chase a rap career. After watching Willy though, I wasn't sure anymore. I didn't think I had enough momentum yet. The *Mega Ran 9* album was out and doing well, thanks to a Capcom co-sign, but that wasn't paying me. I had a song I really believed in, "Splash Woman," which was gaining traction, but I struggled to make rent every month, even with three roommates. I returned to Phoenix at the end of the summer and accepted a job offer at yet another charter school, Omega Schools, which was my last teaching gig.

That fall, Rocksteady Studios, Eidos Interactive, and Warner Bros. Interactive Entertainment released a game changer for the Xbox 360 and PlayStation 3 systems: *Batman: Arkham Asylum*. Reviewers and players alike loved the game, calling it the greatest comic book video game of all time. *Arkham Asylum* won many "Game of the Year" Awards and was the game that pulled me back into video games after a short hiatus when I had sold all my possessions to move out west.

Since games were back, and an even more expensive hobby than when I'd left them earlier, I needed a steady job to buy consoles again. Right when I thought I was out, they pulled me right back in. Until 2011, Raheem the teacher and gamer ran the roost.

I think the decision to go back to work after the summer off and tour might have slowed me down a bit in the long run, but I made the most of my lost time.

Forever Famicom dropped in summer of 2010 and was an immediate hit. Kyle and I had interviews and write-ups on the biggest hip-hop sites and publications as well as gaming outlets. I wasn't expecting the kind of love we got, but I guess it made sense. K-Murdock's hip hop cred with Panacea combined with my growing gaming clout gave this quirky video game rap project legitimacy that it would not have had otherwise had I worked with someone else. Telling people I knew K-Murdock and had even recorded with him made them respect what we had done so much more. Many people named it their album of the year, and even the C word: *Classic*. Looking back, it's a special album, and I'm super proud of what we've done. Too proud, because when people ask about a follow-up or sequel, I quickly change the subject because I just don't want to toy with something so special.

I took the album to Fat Beats Records in Los Angeles, a staple in underground hip-hop for years. Several years earlier during the release of *The Call*, I'd been turned down at their New York location, so when I handed the LA store clerk a copy from my backpack, I still had the same hopes they would carry my album on their hallowed shelves next to Rakim, Redman, and The RZA, all hip-hop legends I'd looked up to.

The clerk looked at the title and flipped the album over skeptically. He asked me the question I knew was coming, but in the nicest way he could, "So, uh… who's on this record? Like, the beats, the rhymes. Any notable names?"

They were all notable to me, from Schaffer the Darklord and Int80 of Dual Core on "For the Gamers" to Jermiside on "Double Dragons" these were some of the best MCs around, and if they weren't household names, they deserved to be. But I mentioned the producer first. "It's got beats from K-Murdock of Panacea, and…"

"… Word? Panacea on *Rawkus*?" he asked, referring to the record label that launched Talib Kweli, Mos Def, and so many underground hip-hop luminaries. "We love Panacea. Cool, I'll put it in the store. We'll take five copies to start." They sold and they asked for more. We were in business. If the story had ended here, I would have been just as satisfied. This was the first bucket list goal I'd ever actually accomplished. Sadly though, five years later when Fat Beats closed, they were not able to pay out any consignment sales monies.

Even though the record had traveled all over the world, and was loved and enjoyed by people everywhere thanks to the Internet, I was still excited to see my music on a store shelf. I remember as a kid taking my allowance to Sound of Germantown or Funk-O-Mart in Philly, buying a cassette or CD, ripping off the packaging, and reading the liner notes on the bus ride home. I wanted kids and adults to feel what I'd felt back then. Those stores are closed now, and in 2010 one of the only places to get good indie hip-hop was a mom and pop shop like Fat Beats.

Next, Kyle and I, along with Matt Weiss aka Storyville, Larry aka Count, who was our driver who I'd met on my message board and later became great friends with, traveled the southwestern United States over fall break in a way-too-small car, on a small venue and convention tour to promote the album. This was where the term "Bits and Rhymes" was born. A play on the term "beats and rhymes," it would explain to folks what Murdock and I do, creating hip hop that relies heavily on video game technology, which used to be measured in "bits." We slept on floors and played in some of the most unorthodox venues, anywhere we could. There was the small game shop in Phoenix, the comic convention in Dallas at the airport training facility hotel, and the hippie commune in Houston, where I stepped in cat dung during the set. Any place that opened its doors to us, we rocked it.

I had a good amount of success with *Forever Famicom*, but I couldn't help feeling like I had wasted an opportunity to make this my full-time career. I knew the next time I got a chance, I wouldn't waste it. I found a groove as a guy who created good rap songs inspired by video games, and a growing fanbase allowed me to fly all over the country to perform. On one of those trips, I bought a used PSP (PlayStation Portable) on Craigslist and on it was *Final Fantasy VII*, arguably my favorite game of all time. During the flight I played the game from the beginning with headphones on and it brought back so many memories of what a game-changing moment that was in 1997 when I first sold everything to get a PlayStation.

The music and storyline inspired me to begin work on an album that would re-tell the story of the game, but in a fresh new way. I'd put a filter on my voice to be Barret Wallace. I'd use "Cry Of The Planet" to talk about real issues within our real world and the parallels of the game and real life. I came back to Phoenix motivated, and when I told Mel aka DJ DN3 about the news, he had news of his own. He was leaving.

For the last two years, Mel was my roommate, so it was easy to knock on his door, head over and begin a five-hour recording session at the drop of a hat. But things were changing. Mel's girlfriend had recently moved in, and they discussed moving to San Francisco together – a move I was happy about externally, but I was extremely saddened on the inside about I would lose my best friend as well as recording engineer and show DJ. We were living like bachelors, two single men in a huge house on the west side of Phoenix, but once a woman entered the dynamic, it all drastically changed. She would complain about our late-night music sessions, or guests coming to the house on weeknights, or the dishes not getting done. Once Mel told me about the move, I knew I couldn't keep the home, so I'd have to find a new place to live. If the Mega Ran story were to continue, I would have to take on a grueling solo mission.

As I cleaned out my room for the move, I found a business card of a producer named Cisco, aka Lost Perception, who I'd met earlier at a beat battle, and we talked about creating a project together based on *Final Fantasy VII*, which he also loved. I wanted to research fully, so I put seventy hours into the game and once done, began writing for the album, as Lost sent one beat after another.

Without Mel, I didn't have access to recording equipment at all, just an old condenser mic Matt gave me three years prior that collected dust in my closet. I didn't know the first thing about digital recording anymore, last recording at Lab Addicts about seven years prior, and recording technology moves so fast seven years is basically an eternity. I'd recorded on an analog board in PA, but in AZ all I had access to was a half-decent desktop PC, and no money to buy ProTools or other professional recording software. So, I innovated.

I procured some cracked, or pirated software thanks to The Pirate Bay and a few other file-sharing sites, and before I knew it I had a full service version of Cool Edit Pro, which was one of the more basic examples of recording software, but it did the trick. To learn to mix my recordings, I watched YouTube tutorials into the early morning at my new apartment, before I even had a couch. I started recording vocals on Lost's beats in my closet. After three months, the album was almost ready, all it needed was a name.

I'd originally settled on the name "Vinyl Fantasy," because I thought that was catchy – in the way that traditional DJs and producers burrowed through crates of vinyl to find that perfect sample, I was digging through the video game soundtrack for the perfect sonics to match the words of the songs. I was almost set on that name until I posted online the album was done and took a poll of suggested names, and someone in the comments said "Black Materia." I gave it a ton of thought, but I really liked the name. I was swayed.

In *Final Fantasy VII*, The Black Materia is one of the world's oldest and most deadly forms of materia, or magic. There is only one Black Materia, as is the same with the White Materia, its opposite. The person who possesses the Black Materia can use it to cast the spell of Meteor, which is known as the "Ultimate Destructive Magic," powerful enough to destroy the entire world. I wanted this album to stand as the ultimate fan tribute to FF7, it had to feel just as powerful. So, it's kind of important. Also, at the simplest level, I'm Black, so I thought the name was perfect.

Black Materia released on January 31, 2011, which was the same day in 1997 the game released in Japan. The first single, "Aerith," which was based on the most tragic story in the game, came a week before and the critical response was bigger than anything I'd done before it, foreshadowing the future popularity of a highly anticipated project. I released "Avalanche" next, a song about the eco-terrorist organization that serve as the heroes of the story, and the results were about the same. What I did on the release was something I did with *Mega Ran* in 2007; I'd release a piece of the album for free. The first 6 tracks were a free download on my page, and I figured that if people enjoyed those six for free, they would gladly pay ten dollars for the rest of the album. The free version did pretty well. We hit two thousand downloads in the first month. But the true impact of this album wouldn't show for another month.

In late February I got a text while in class, telling me the song "Avalanche" was on the first page of Reddit, a website which represents the top stories on the internet at any given time. I didn't understand the significance at the moment, but I did as the day went on. I received several texts throughout telling me about this awesome placement on Reddit's page. "YOU'VE GONE VIRAL, CHARLIE BROWN!" one of the texts read.

On my break, I went online and found the Reddit post with three hundred-plus comments – all contained positive feedback about the song. When I checked my email, I saw tons of new purchases of the album, and even interview requests from some top websites and magazines from all over the world, including *PlayStation* magazine, which ran a three-page article on me that month.

After the smoke cleared, the YouTube hits for "Avalanche" shot up by one hundred thousand. *Black Materia* was ranked nineteenth on the iTunes Best Sellers list, above releases by Lil' Wayne and Kanye West. I couldn't believe it. I celebrated for a second, but I couldn't help thinking there was more to do. I had to set my phone down and continue planning for the class coming in. I was pretty sure Wayne and Kanye didn't have to work a nine to five job, let alone one that gave as much grief as mine. This was when the idea of making a move towards a full-time music career became more real. It was time to try to change my environment.

CHAPTER THIRTEEN

QUITTING

They ask, "Ran, why'd you quit?"
I say, "It quit me first."
—"Voices," *TeacherRapperHero Vol. 2: Two Weeks'*
Notice (2011)

I'D ALWAYS HAD THE FANTASY of telling off my boss and strutting off a job, George Jefferson style, but Mom taught me better than that. I always give notice. You never know when you might need a recommendation or if a future position will open, so it's important to keep a good rapport. I've held a bunch of jobs in my life, most of them unfulfilling, but each gave me a different perspective on life in the workforce.

During college, I worked at Boston Market one summer. I had the unenviable job of dishwasher, which involved scraping baked-in chicken guts off the rotating spits in the back with an ice scraper and high-powered water hose. Between scraping spits, we had to wash all the serving trays and dishes. It was by far the most disgusting job I've ever worked.

One Friday night was rougher than most. We got slammed hard by a never-ending parade of customers, and I had a mountain of dishes to clean in the back with no help. The new manager screamed and screamed because he had to get up early the next morning to take his kid to college. I, the lowly, slow dishwasher, was keeping him from going home.

His yelling didn't make me speed up; in fact, it might have slowed me down. Eventually, he came over, grabbed some dishes, and started busting suds right along with me. I wondered if he had a breakthrough.

We could have shared a smile, maybe even wiped soap suds off each other while some special value flashed across the screen like TEAMWORK. In truth though, he angrily splashed and washed dishes at breakneck speed because he wanted to leave. That night I learned yelling at people never solves anything. That became very valuable in my teaching career.

We finished at 10:45 p.m., forty minutes after we were supposed to leave. I always tried to work in the suburbs so I wouldn't have to deal with the inner-city element. That meant that I had to catch buses late at night and walk through some unsavory neighborhoods. The twenty-two bus had a very long route; it ran straight to the Willow Grove Mall, a suburban shopping center about fifty minutes from the center of the city, so the bus didn't run very late. If I was waiting for a mall bus after 10 p.m., I was waiting for a miracle. If I was waiting for a mall bus after 11 p.m., I might as well forget it.

I took the time to thank the new manager for helping with the dishes before throwing my jacket on and running for the door to catch the bus. I made it outside just in time to see the rear of the twenty-two bus as it rumbled by. I jogged about a quarter of a block, with desperation in my eyes, but my efforts were futile.

I sat at the bus stop, dejected, and even a little frightened. I had no idea when the next bus would come. As I rubbed my hands together to warm up, cursing myself for taking so long on the dishes, guess who rolled up to the stoplight? It was my manager. He had come to save the day and give me a ride to the bus depot where I could catch another bus and get home at a reasonable hour. Bless that man! At least, that's what I thought as I got up and walked toward his car. I assumed he saw me. Then, the light turned green, and he pulled off as if he'd been shot from a cannon. *VROOOOM!* I think his tires even screeched. Maybe he didn't see me after all... or worse, maybe he did. All this scene needed was for his car to barrel through a puddle and soak me. I got home around 1 a.m. that morning and had to show up the next morning at nine.

The next day, I called in and quit over the phone. I can't blame that manager entirely, but the job just wasn't for me. I enjoyed the food, but at sixteen I just wasn't ready to get humiliated for a few bucks. Maybe it was my cockiness, I don't know. After I quit I got my last check, feeling almost proud of the stupid decision I made. Quitting was my way of trying to make them pay for their treatment of me. My younger self wasn't aware that they'd just find someone else to do my job and go on with their business.

My next job was at a CVS Pharmacy that opened in my neighborhood. Because it was new, and I needed a job, I broke my own rule of not working close to home. It wasn't the mean-spirited bosses who spent all day flirting with customers and employees who delegated the most menial tasks to me that made the job tedious, but the sheer boring nature of the work. It wasn't that terrible though, until the day when things got real.

It was a Tuesday night, and the store was dead not even twenty minutes until quitting time. A woman with a baby came in, grabbed some groceries, and headed for the register. As I started to ring up her purchases, she remembered one more item she needed and went to get it. That wasn't a problem because no one else was in the store, and I was in no rush. She walked away and left the baby in the cart at the front.

Just as she disappeared down the aisle, three masked men came in the store with guns and demanded I empty the register. One climbed over the counter and yelled in my face I should hurry up and not be a hero. I panicked. I pleaded with the man I didn't have any reason to protect the store. I think my words were, "I don't want to die for CVS, I'll have it open."

I pressed the NO SALE button that opens the register. Of course, it failed. The gunman behind me got impatient and hit me on the side of my face with the gun handle. I pressed NO SALE again and again and each time got an annoying "beep" signifying an error. I finally figured out that it wouldn't open because I was in the middle of a sale. The woman with the baby.

Just as I realized what the problem was the woman came running up the aisle screaming, "My baby, my baby!"

Despite the gunmen's warnings to stay back, she grabbed the cart with the child in it and sped out the door. One of the robbers followed her out. The other stayed close to me and demanded that I give him the money as fast as possible.

I heard what sounded like a shot outside the door. I thought the robber must have shot the woman who ran. Next, I heard sirens, signaling police approaching the area. The second robber left the store, with money, and cigarette cartons in hand, and made his getaway.

It turned out that the first man had slipped and fallen while running, and the gun discharged. Once they heard the sirens, the men ran off but were found a few minutes later, hiding on a nearby porch. The police locked them in a paddy wagon and pulled up to the CVS.

They asked me to come outside, look in the back of the wagon, and positively identify the men; I had to look the men who had threatened to kill me twenty minutes earlier in the face and ID them. I couldn't do it. My nerves were racing, and during the robbery, I tried my best not to look directly at the assailants, so as not to provoke them. I couldn't give a definitive yes or no if these were the guys. I didn't want to put an innocent man behind bars, and my memory just wasn't as good as I needed it to be under the circumstances. The officers were extremely upset by my lack of cooperation.

"Look, we know how you guys feel about snitching, but we really need you. Look closely," the officer demanded as we watched our breath sail into the cold night air. He was referring to the "Stop Snitching" movement that had permeated the inner city in the late '90s, boosted by anti-police hip-hop lyrics and oversized white t-shirts with huge STOP signs emblazoned on them with "snitching" written underneath. These were part of a popular trend toward not cooperating with police under any circumstances, as a response to police corruption and violence in the city. I hadn't subscribed to this philosophy, and even if I had, I don't think to point out a person who waved a gun in my face and threatened to kill me for a few hundred dollars would qualify as snitching. But it's kind of complicated.

[5] A victim of a crime who is asked, "Hey, who did this to you?" can't get labeled a snitch for answering the question. If the perpetrator, when asked about his crime, says, "Yeah I did it, but I did with him, him, and her," that's a snitch. Regardless, it's a thin line that I thought hard about whether I'd cross if the situation presented itself.

"I... I don't know," I stammered. "I really didn't get a good look."

The frustrated officers took me to the police station that night and

---

[5] Snitch (n): A person who tells on another person for the purpose of lessening the punishment for their own crime.

showed me pages and pages of suspects. I was absolutely no help. Black face after Black face. Some scowling. Some smiling. All looking right into my eyes. They all looked the same after a while. The officer asked me to give a statement on what happened once, then again to another officer, and then again to a third. After what seemed like three hours at the station, they eventually told me I was free to go. They didn't walk or drive me home. They simply walked me to the door, and pointed me to the bus stop, as if to say, "Thanks for nothing." I was terrified walking the street alone. My mother was at work so she couldn't pick me up, and none of my friends drove.

Luckily, Nate, our store's greeter, saw the whole thing and was able to identify the men. It was his testimony that put the men in jail, as he recounted the night's activities perfectly in sync with what the store's surveillance camera showed. Weeks later, they had us come to court. On that day, as if by some ridiculous act of serendipity, my glasses broke. I had to attend the trial unable to see clearly. There's no way the officers would believe that one.

I later returned to work, but didn't feel comfortable working the register again. Instead, I worked the floor as a greeter and stocker. Eventually, they had a need for someone to work the register. I wasn't ready to fulfill it, so we mutually agreed to part ways. I couldn't hop back on that register, which reminded me of having a gun in my face. It was time to move on.

I quit teaching in a less spectacular, but equally explosive fashion. By early 2011, I was burning the candle on both ends. I moonlighted as a rap artist while teaching middle school classes at Omega School from eight to three every day. I stayed after school at least two hours per day to catch up on the day's grading and prepare for the next day. I toured in the summers and on weekends. I was taking days off here and there to play shows in different cities, flying out on Thursdays or Fridays, and barely making it back to work on lesson plans for Monday. As far as creating, I was on the computer late learning new recording techniques until 2AM, and still going to work at seven every day. It was not the best schedule for someone trying to make a difference in the classroom.

On a January afternoon in 2011 during a weekly staff meeting, a teacher brought to our attention that a student who had graduated the previous year was having difficulty getting accepted to community college. She was told her high school diploma wasn't enough. For community college.

Mr. Michaels answered the query clearly and quickly. "Oh, that's because we're not accredited. We don't give out high school diplomas." My face must've said "WHAT?!" because Mr. Michaels turned to me and said, "Mr. Jarbo, you have a question?"

"Yeah, um... Yeah. So, we teach up to the state's standards, and we don't give kids enough to even get into COMMUNITY COLLEGE?" I may have been a little loud.

Another teacher interjected, "Actually, we don't even teach to the state's standards. We don't teach a foreign language at our school."

Mr. Michaels felt validated by this tidbit. "Yeah, most of our students speak fluent Spanish, so we don't need to offer language courses."

"One problem with that," I interjected. "The student in question is African-American. She is not an ESL (English as a Second Language) student." I felt Mr. Michaels' heated gaze on me, so I turned to the rest of the teachers, hoping to gain their support, and continued. "So, our school does not give our students the tools they need to go to college? They don't even have a chance. Got it." I sat down and tapped my pencil on the table at a rapid one hundred and eighty beats per minute. Silence fell over the room.

I imagined myself as that girl's parent getting the news that, after twelfth grade graduation, my kid couldn't go to college, community college no less, not because of her grades, but because the school did not give her what she needed to be successful. "Maybe she can go to a real high school now," I asked in a lower tone. "Okay, sorry, Mr. D. I'll be quiet now." After that, I had a feeling that my days were numbered. Maybe the success of Black Materia was secretly giving me courage that I didn't have before, because I don't know that I would have acted that boisterous in a staff meeting otherwise.

My mother and father both agreed (for once) that quitting my job for something as unstable as music was a bad idea. I don't think they knew just how unstable my teaching situation was at Omega. They didn't know about the times that our paychecks came back short, and I had to overdraft my account to put gas in my car to make it to work for the week. I didn't tell them, because I didn't want them to worry. Every payday, I was completely broke and depressed. After all I had been through, I didn't have faith in the educational system anymore. I couldn't bring myself to be a part of something I disagreed with so wholeheartedly, when music on the weekends was like heaven.

I remembered my ex telling me I should "get serious" and think about my future. To get a real job and not a hobby. She'd wondered how long I planned to "mess around with this little rap thing." I had a feeling I had a chance to make an impact in a way no one understood. That I might not become a superstar, but was still forging my own path in a new industry, thanks to the Internet. It felt like the beginning of something big. I was about to mess around and change my surroundings. Music was much more than a little thing to me – it had become a major part of my life.

Not long after that day, like clockwork, *Black Materia* gained even more popularity online. Turns out people really enjoyed *Final Fantasy VII*. An album about this game touched a pop-culture zeitgeist I had no idea existed. Venues asked me to play more gigs. I finally decided it was time to start thinking about the next step.

I started planning my exodus from day job life to a career as a full-time musician. Without a record label or manager, I had no idea where to turn. I put extra effort into my current job. I sent more emails than usual about show booking. While working on the way to break the news of my departure to my school and students, I started getting more emails and calls than ever before asking me to come play shows. I was all out of sick days at work, so something had to give.

As the momentum continued to build, and the demand for Mega Ran grew, I had a conversation with my principal Mr. Michaels who told me, "You can't serve two masters." I think he wanted to let me know a time would come where I'd have to make a choice. I was ready to make that choice and leave Omega, and teaching behind.

Mom told me to never quit a job without another lined up, and even then, to never burn a bridge. On a Monday morning in March 2011, I typed a resignation letter and handed it to Mr. Michaels. The letter said that in two weeks, I would step away from my duties to chase a wild music dream. I thanked him for the guidance and work experience he provided. He shook my hand and said he understood and was thankful I let him know in advance. I returned to class and taught my students, same as any other day, but also… not. I wouldn't leave for another two weeks, so I knew I had time to tell the students the full story, over a pizza party or something.

But you know what they say – man plans, God laughs. In this case, it was my principal who got the last laugh. The story I detail briefly in the song "Laughin' At Ya" is this one: My principal arrived at my classroom at the end of the same day. He thought since I was leaving in two weeks it was time to start the inventory and checkout process for employees. We sat after school for three hours and counted every textbook in the classroom and every key I'd had. I didn't understand why he wanted to do this now when I had two more weeks, but I'd get it soon.

After the tedious counting process, Mr. Michaels prepared to leave the room, then stopped short and said, "oh" as if he had just remembered something. He told me "Remember that day last week that you had to call out for, to do a gig someplace?" I nodded. "Yeah, I have to get you to sign a paper, just saying that I talked to you about it and gave you a warning. Just doing my due diligence."

"Okay," I said as I signed the form. "See ya tomorrow."

Mr. M had other plans. "Actually, I have another piece of paper for you."

In the smoothest of magic tricks, Mr. Michaels removed the top sheet of paper, exposing a second sheet: a termination letter. He had decided I didn't need to wait two weeks to get started on my new life, and he let me go, effective immediately.

My heart dropped. That explained the count, the keys, the whole process. I was fired. On the day I tried to resign. It was like the petty end of a relationship gone sour – *you can't quit me, I quit you first*. I didn't have a moment to speak to my students, as they were already gone for the day. No final goodbye, no pizza party. I was out of a job.

"Well, at least you get to get an early start on your new career," he said with a smile as he packed his files. "Best of luck, Mr. Jarbo."

To make the worst day of school even worse, Mr. Michaels let me know as I prepared to leave that report cards were due at the end of the week.

"Sir, with all due respect, I don't work here anymore."

Mr. Michaels had me by the grapes. "Yes, but in order to receive your final paycheck, you have to complete any outstanding paperwork. Please bring those report cards in by Friday, or else."

I was screwed. My perfect plan for quitting required me to get one more paycheck I could save as the nest egg before taking the Nestea plunge. And I couldn't go on a tour, because to get these report cards done, I had to grade an entire milk crate of exams this week, or I don't even get the paycheck I already worked for. I sat in the classroom for another thirty minutes thinking, then came up with the plan.

I was now out of work and without a security blanket – my plans had to change quickly. In an amazing twist of fate, in the same week I got two important phone calls and offers. One was from former Phoenix radio jock-turned-entrepreneur, Karlie Hustle, asking if I was interested in taking over her music business class at Phoenix College a few days a week. It offered decent money, and the opportunity not only to teach adults, but to teach them something they wanted to learn. I found the idea very intriguing. I considered it for a week until I got the second call and offer, which changed my life.

The second call was from mc chris (always stylized as lowercase), a nerd rap pioneer. He was planning a huge 2011 tour to promote his upcoming album *Race Wars*. His fans had voted for me, Random, to open for him. Chris called me and made me the offer of a lifetime, which I gladly accepted. The plan was forty-five dates in fifty-four days, playing thirty minutes a night in front of sold-out crowds. More importantly than the money, I had the potential to make the fans to keep the Mega Ran ship going for another seven years. It was a no-brainer. I thanked Karlie for the opportunity and suggested another friend, who still teaches that music business class.

But there was one issue that needed resolution. Friday came, and report cards were due. I was so anxious and worried I hadn't graded any of the papers I took home. So, I decided to fight petty with petty. I pulled out my trusted black ink pen, and I gave every one of my seventh and eighth grade reading and social studies students the same grade:

An A+. Straight down the line. I gave out A's like Oprah used to give out prizes on her show.

I dropped the report cards off at school and promptly began the first day of the rest of my life. I took that tour with mc chris and saw the country, and I'm glad I did. I made friends and fans that are still with me almost 10 years later. That opportunity has allowed me to open doors for other artists, bringing them on tour, which makes that moment so special. I hope mc chris knows how many musicians he's fed just by offering me that break.

After that long tour, I came home refreshed and ready to get back into the studio. I recorded a Christmas album, with beats by DJ DN3, then began work on what I considered to be my life's work up until that point, *Language Arts*. The plan for the album was a three-part CD, a video game, and a comic book. I couldn't make this project alone, so I needed help. We hit Kickstarter to crowdfund the project, and the final total received from patrons was a whopping 516 percent of the desired goal. Because of this the *Language Arts* albums released without a hitch in 2012.

The game and comic were not as smooth, though. J1 Studios, who designed the comic, made a great first issue, but no other hard copies were created. I promised our backers they'd get a hardback trade of the story, but that never happened. Every time I see the owner of J1, he ensures me it's coming, one day.

The *Mega Ran in Language Arts* video game was a glitchy, difficult, but fun platformer with cool sounds. Sadly, two months after the game hit online, after weeks of promises that they'd port the game to iOS and Android, Chicago studio Lunar Giant decided to remove the game from the online site, and anywhere else it might have turned up. The game and comic were dead two to three months after release, throwing *Language Arts* promo plans into a topspin. I spent most of the Kickstarter money on promoting the album, with enough left to buy a used laptop.

So while you never know what a creative project will end up like, I learned that crowdfunding can help get the hard questions and challenges out of the way early to help you focus on creative endeavors.

One day out of nowhere, I noticed that the Black Materia album, my most successful project, had begun making waves outside of video game spaces. When I began playing the songs out at gigs, I remember a person at a show in Philly asking me if I was still a part of RAHM Nation. I said yes, though our talks had lessened, I always enjoyed being affiliated with a group of like-minded people. The person said to me "Oh, cause you're not on the website anymore, just wondering. This was news to me.

I emailed the webmaster who was also an artist at the label, and asked why Black Materia hadn't been on the site, and his answer was strange. "You should speak to Ohene." When I did, I was chastised for not being a team player. My releases were coming at frantic speeds, and I wasn't informing anyone at the label of my moves. I got upset at the time, but I was guilty as charged. Ohene's words have stuck with me since this call. "You operate like a boss and not an employee. It would behoove you to be your own boss." This motivated me to be a boss, and to make Random Beats LLC a reality as my own production company. Since then I have self-released most of my music with the slogan of "unpredictable sound since 2005." Additionally I've been able to extend a hand to other artists I really enjoy, like SkyBlew and Last Benevolence. I would have never had the heart to make such a move without a person that I admired encouraging me to do so.

CHAPTER FOURTEEN

TRAY

We ain't convicts, just trying to survive, kid.
My kids might have responded
Like Trayvon did.

— "Losses," *RNDM* (2015)

T HE STATE OF FLORIDA v. George Zimmerman was a criminal prosecution of George Zimmerman on the charge of second-degree murder stemming from the shooting of seventeen-year old Trayvon Martin on February 26, 2012. On April 11, 2012, the state charged George Zimmerman with second-degree murder.

After a year of heated debates, discussions, and hot takes by would-be pundits, everyone was positive that Zimmerman, who murdered an unarmed boy on the streets of Florida, would see jail time for the shooting. Nine-one-one calls recorded Zimmerman saying, "f*cking punks, these assholes always get away" after reporting on Martin's presence in his neighborhood, citing a rash of break-ins in the area. After calming Zimmerman down, the operator told him "do not follow," as Zimmerman grabbed his gun and followed Martin. After disobeying the advice, the operator then told him to keep a safe distance.

He did not. Martin with his hoodie on, noticed he was being followed and called a friend, who told him to be careful. Zimmerman approached Tray, asking, "What are you doing here?" and after a scuffle, he shot Trayvon in the chest from close range. Trayvon was conscious ten to fifteen seconds before perishing within the gated community, just blocks from where his family lived.

Not long after this, I was unpacking from one tour and repacking for another, The "Coin Op Crush Tour," which took us from Texas to New York. I was excited at the possibilities that came with late-night drives into new cities with a few of my closest homies, Dominic "DJ Organic," Khin-Tay, Mario "SkyBlew" Farrow, and Chris "EyeQ" Allen. It wasn't until I had finalized the routing for one trip however, that I realized it could turn out as one of the more interesting trips, and not for the best of reasons.

Dom asked me what the tour trail looked like, and I happily read off the list of shows I booked. "Texas, Louisiana, Mississippi, Georgia, Florida, The Carolinas, Virginia…" He stopped me. His next question was a little odd, as his face showed legit concern.

"Are there any White people riding with us on this tour?"

Living most of my life as a large Black male, I have tried to seem as non-threatening as possible. Many Black men end up hurt, jailed, or even killed for their black skin and appearing to those without as scary. With Eric Garner of New York and Alton Sterling of Louisiana in mind, I have always tried not to offend anyone or escalate a situation, knowing how much I would stand out, and that my mere presence might offend or inconvenience people. My strategy came in handy in Langhorne, PA, a suburb of Philadelphia with a population of about sixteen hundred.

Years earlier, in 2006, my first long-term teaching position was at Woods Services, an alternative school in Langhorne. At least 90 percent of the residents of Langhorne were White. The students, high-risk, and behaviorally challenged as children tend to skew toward

African-American or Hispanic. Most lived on campus until they were old enough to live on their own.

Langhorne was full of green trees, huge roads, and clean surroundings. It was nothing like the city I was raised in. I caught the city bus to work every day, then walked the half-mile trail to the school in the woods every morning, which was great exercise.

I realized right away, as the only African-American male teacher there, things were a little different. Most days, my cohorts drove right by me on their way to work, only to say later, "Hey Mr. Jarbo, I thought that was you out there," while I changed from my sweaty t-shirt into a dress shirt to prep for the day. By day ten, it was obvious. They knew it was me out there and none offered me a ride.

On July 13, 2013, the trial of the decade, at least in the eyes of Black America, came to a close. That July afternoon, I had a concert in Seattle at The Vera Project, an all-ages volunteer-run community space focused on education through music and art. Right before I hit the stage that afternoon, I was glued to my phone, refreshing CNN for updates on the trial. The rumor was a verdict would go down on that day.

After sixteen hours of deliberations over the course of two days, the six-person jury rendered a not guilty verdict on all counts. Due to Florida's controversial Stand Your Ground law, they determined Zimmerman's life was in danger, and that he operated in self-defense.

Zimmerman beat the case. He returned home.

Back in Langhorne, while standing on the side of the highway at a stop, waiting for the bus to take me home, I saw a large pickup truck quickly closing in on my location from atop the distant hill. There were two huge flags perched on the back of the truck: one was Old Glory, the traditional American Flag, and the other was the Dixie flag, the Southern Cross, a good old Confederate Flag flapping in the afternoon air.

I didn't fear much until I noticed the erratic swerve that the pickup driver showcased while pulling up toward an African-American woman and me at the bus stop. As the truck closed in, I noticed that there was a younger White child, no more than seventeen, in the bed of the pickup, waving the Rebel flag fiercely with a unshakeable amount of pride. The truck arrived at our bus stop with a screeching halt, and the child in the back looked me straight in my eyes and said words to me that I've never forgotten in the ten plus years since.

"Hey, nigger! The jungle is THAT way!"

Zimmerman was going to walk. I knew it deep inside, and it just hurt me so much I was right.

I felt every emotion. It felt like my Uncle Bobby all over again. Hurt. Angry. I cried in the green room before the set. I deleted the planned set list from my laptop. I didn't even want to perform.

When I hit the stage, I opened with a song I hadn't played in years, a track I love, called "Push." I mainly played that for hip-hop crowds, which this was most certainly not. My opening act was a video game cover band called "The Icarus Kids," based on the NES game. Before I started, I asked for a moment of silence from the majority all-White, all-male crowd. Most did, while some chatter and even laughter ensued. I had the feeling that they didn't know or care that Trayvon's killer had just gone free.

I don't remember the set at all. I played some songs and got some cheers. It might have been the most uninspired forty-five minutes I've ever given to a show in my career. I walked off stage defeated and saddened. The justice system had let me down. I kept thinking to myself, *what if that were me? What if I were walking with a hoodie on and someone thought I looked suspicious and they should protect their neighborhood from me?* I packed my things and prepared to end my night early, forgoing any usual hugs and merchandise sales.

Dom's concern was legit. Driving while Black (DWB) is a very real thing.

With each police pull-over, I readied myself for the worst-case scenario: the police officer shoving his state-issued gun into my cheek and reeling off a string of racial epithets in my direction while telling me Black lives DON'T matter.

Luckily, the extent of my experiences a police car was usually limited to a semi-diet-racist line of questioning about what I do, where I'm from, why I'm on *their* road (there was always a sense of ownership) and how much money one makes from singing rap tunes. One officer even tried to guilt me, letting me know he wished he could make a living traveling to new places instead of, say, stopping people from getting to those new places. In each situation, I tried to cushion the blow telling them about my past as a teacher and that I make video game tunes, but once they heard the word rap, it usually got awkward. Turns out most older men are not fans of rap music and can't fathom that anyone would ever want to pay a person a dollar to hear it.

The pickup driver pointed the opposite direction of the bus route, and cackled, very proud of his joke, which may have been funny to me if I hadn't been in the center of rural Pennsylvania with no escape in sight. I was too stunned to respond, so I just stared.

I suppose the driver was upset that he didn't get the response he desired, so he lifted a sawed-off shotgun from the passenger's seat and pointed it out the window.

"You feelin' froggy, boy?"

I didn't know what else to do. I just froze. I stood stiff as a scarecrow as if my Stacy Adams shoes were stuck to the asphalt. The pickup pulled off, the afternoon air filled with the laughter of these two slack-jawed yokels. As the truck skidded across the asphalt, I just stood and breathed... stunned at what had occurred.

As I packed at the merchandise table after a strenuous set, someone walked up and asked, "Was Trayvon related to you?"

He seemed unaware of how Trayvon's death and injustice could have affected me if he weren't a relative. Trayvon was a seventeen-year-old, standing five foot eleven, one hundred and fifty-eight pounds, in perfect health. He looked like my cousins. He looked like my friends. My students. So yes, he was related to me. But I had a hard time verbalizing that to the man who asked, So I simply said "no, man," and continued packing. But I was hurt. In this environment, I had no shoulder to cry on. No one to console me. No one who even understood. I left the venue dejected. I questioned what I do, and if it ever even mattered. *How relatable am I if others can't relate to me?*

I wasn't just disappointed at the lack of knowledge of what had happened, but I was upset at the lack of empathy displayed in the room that evening. I consider the Seattle scene a fairly socially conscious community, and it shocked me my fans hadn't known what was happening to Black and Brown people – that Trayvon's reality is most Black men's worst nightmare. These people had lived such carefree lives… and actually thought I operated in their world for an hour a day. But, in truth I lived in a completely different world – one where my skin color and size are weapons others can use against me at any given time. It scared me so much. It still does today.

The funny thing about racism is no matter how much you try to ignore it or suppress it, it has a way of smacking you in the face. Most people will say people of color are more obsessed with race than those who are not. That couldn't be further from the truth. The truth is that people of color are reminded of their race more often than people who identify as the majority. We don't even notice we are different most of the time until it directly affects us. I remember traveling to Japan and having small children grab my arm, amazed at my dark complexion. I've seen people of other races cross the street when I approach. Women clutch their purses, raise their windows or hit their car locks in shopping mall parking lots when I walk by. I don't remember that I'm dissimilar until I'm *shown* it, usually in the most jarring way possible.

I have the hardest time balancing what I do as Mega Ran with who I am as Raheem. I get the amazing opportunity to provide an escape to my listeners and concert-goers, with whimsical rhymes about robots and spaceships. I also get to enter spaces where not many African-American males are, and to share my world with people who have no idea of my background or lifestyle. So, the Trayvon moment in Seattle was when I realized that I have to share. I have to be the ENTIRE me everywhere, because perhaps, everyone can become better for it. Since then I decided I'll do my best to show all of me in every creation.

You'll hear me use dialect that I use with my friends on the block, even when I talk about things like video games. I want people to know that they are listening to a Black man when they hear me. The worst thing I hear is, "I don't really see color when I look at you." That means you don't see my experience. So please, if you read this, see my color, just don't judge and define me by it.

CHAPTER FIFTEEN

CARDINAL SINS

Eight years later I thought the remixes would move you,
But I was truly saddened they didn't meet your approval
—"The Meeting" (*RNDM*, 2015)

I N JANUARY 2014, *LA WEEKLY* had put out an article called "Five Rappers Who Will Be Big in 2014." The list included me, and set me on a path to the next level, or so I thought. But by this time, Mega Ran was running on autopilot, for better or worse. After two straight years of successful tours and groundbreaking projects, I had found a formula for success and was lulled into a false sense of security by it. I was playing a convention what almost seemed like weekly, getting paid well to travel, and put up in four-star hotels. I'd gotten so stuck in a routine that I would play literally the same set at every concert. The same seven to ten songs, depending on how long I was asked to play, and I didn't innovate or challenge myself with any of my releases.

I think the downward spiral began in the previous year, when I was asked to play a concert in Phoenix connected to the Phoenix Comic-Con in 2013. As usual, I enlisted Mel to play the show with me. The show was hosted by MURS, one of my favorite rappers, and promoted by Universatile Music, the company who brought Public Enemy to The Blunt Club seven years earlier. With these forces combined, I was extra motivated to put on a great show for a bunch of influential folks who had never seen us before.

During a rehearsal for the show, Mel angrily told me that his job had changed his schedule, and he would now have to work early on Sunday, the day after our show. I felt Mel's pain, but as a person who spent many nights up late writing and performing just to attend work groggily the next morning, I was confident he was up to perform the tasks in question. Mel asked me to request we get moved down the lineup, and out of our current co-headlining spot. This was not an ideal plan in my mind, so I asked him not to reconsider. We were scheduled to go on at 10:30 and I was fine with that. He knew what I knew though – that hip-hop shows tend to run much later than expected.

On the day of the show, a few lineup changes led to us getting moved into the headlining spot. Mel was visibly worried about our show time going after hours, and made sure to inquire between sets if he thought the downtime between acts was too long. He asked me once more to talk to the band before us, The Insects, about moving our set. They were, after all, the listed headlining act on the top of the flier circulated. I agreed to talk to them, and their lead emcee, Brad B, told us he had already told his friends their show time and wouldn't want to move it any further. But to assuage our fears, Brad was willing to shorten The Insects' scheduled thirty-minute set.

As The Insects were onstage rocking out to the packed room, Mel and I were like batters in the on-deck circle, just ready to step in and bring it home. After about twenty minutes of set time, Mel did something I don't think I'd ever seen. He got onstage, manned the adjoining second turntable deck, donned his headphones and began queuing up the songs for our set. I knew that time was of the essence, but I'd never before seen the next DJ hop onstage during the current DJ's set and start scratching. I thought Mel's hastiness was in bad taste, at best.

Then, something happened. I must have looked away from the stage for ten seconds, and in that time, Mel began yelling at DJ Foundation, The Insects' sound provider. Foundation stopped the music. Brad B turned around. Mel looked at him and hurled an insult. A standoff on stage ensued, with one hundred fans watching. I was frozen stiff in shock. Luckily, our host, MURS jumped into action and stepped in between. He grabbed Mel, looked into his eyes and asked him, "What's the problem man?" When he got no response MURS demanded, "Talk to me!"

Mel had a blank look on his face, as if he were in an anger-induced trance. There were no words. I asked him what had happened and he snapped back into DJ mode immediately. "Let's get this set going, man."

We got the set going. I proceeded to play the strangest forty-five-minute set ever, wherein Mel did none of the things we rehearsed—no hype man adlibs, no dance moves, no witty banter. We had discussed an encore fake-out at the end of the set, where I end a song suddenly and leave stage, pretending that the show is over. Our plan was that the crowd would cheer for one more song, then we would return in sixty seconds to end the show properly. I did my part and ended the song and walked off stage. The crowd did their part and cheered, "Mega Ran, Mega Ran, Mega Ran..." so I returned to stage to raucous applause. I asked a question that I knew the answer to: "What do you guys want to hear next?" They all talked over each other, with "Splash Woman" as the song repeated most. I looked back at Mel and said, "Okay DJ DN3, let's give it to 'em..."

When I turned around, Mel was unplugging his turntable and wrapping up cords around his elbow. As I stared with my mouth wide open, eyes squinted with my head turned to the side at a forty-five-degree angle, he snapped the cover onto his DJ case and pulled it off stage. I looked back at the hungry crowd and said, "Well, I guess no encore tonight guys, sorry... Thanks for coming." They sighed in disappointment and just like that, the show ended. Mel scurried out of the back exit, his last words to me being, "I gotta wake up for work tomorrow, man. I'm out."

I won't bore you with the kindergarten level of he-said/she-said argument that followed this episode, but the ending result was that as of that night in 2013, DJ DN3 was out of performing shows with Mega Ran for the foreseeable future. This negatively impacted our friendship more importantly. Our daily phone calls and texts slowed. Our collaborations halted. The next month, Mel told me he was moving out of the apartment we shared. I was without my road dog, and my best friend. I sulked through the year, creating music and playing shows, but I was not myself by any stretch of the imagination.

I still called myself Random, aka Mega Ran in 2014, but my music was all Mega Ran. I was sampling and re-flipping video game soundtracks and making music that while pleasing to fans, was empty and soulless upon reflection. I decided having two names was too much to handle and it was time to move forward, so by the end of the year I dropped Random completely, in more ways than one.

At the beginning of the year, I realized I was nearing a special milestone, or at least I would make it one. February 2014 marked eight years since the release of *The Call*, my seminal album and accomplishment most special to me. I wanted to commemorate it by re-mixing some of the songs and re-releasing it. When I asked DJ DN3 for the original files, Mel told me he hadn't been able to save those 2006 sessions throughout all the moves he had made, so the album couldn't be recovered. The only way to honor it would be to re-record. So, I got an idea.

In the time since that first release, I began calling my music "Chip-Hop," as it was a combination of chiptune and hip-hop music. I decided I would re-record the existing songs from *The Call*, but first, we would re-produce them in an eight-bit chiptune style. It seemed genius at first, using what I'd learned in these eight years to create an eight-bit anniversary edition. Klopfenpop, a talented Washington-based producer, assisted on several tracks. The album sold well, but I remember I couldn't find any press that would talk about or review the project. That happens at times, for various reasons. I ignored that and moved forward.

To drum up some media attention, we did something so strange but that I knew would be successful. Klopfenpop and I collaborated on a cover of the 1990 song "Turtle Power" from the group Partners N Kryme, and made a pretty snazzy 8-bit version. The song received the press postings that I'd hoped the album would, so we put that song on the album as a bonus cut to help it move a few more units. It worked.

Looking back, I wish I had never released *The Call: 8-Bit Anniversary Edition*. It's one of my few regrets as an artist. On top of its title being a mouthful, the album just was completely unnecessary. It probably wasn't the best idea to revisit something so special to me and almost trivialize it by throwing bleeps and bloops under personal tracks I was so proud of like "The Call" "Motivate" and "Raze the Bar." I sold the album on CDs I placed inside the plastic black dust sleeves that came with cartridges for the Nintendo Entertainment System, after I discovered I could buy a box of them for cheap on eBay. Even the cover of the album looked like a scene from *Ninja Gaiden*, with me appearing ready to scale a huge mountain for a boss fight – far from the pensive black and white photograph of myself by the Benjamin Franklin bridge my friend Hope had taken back in 2005. It was a complete pander. Not even a month after the release, I was ashamed of the album and it's probably the only release of mine I don't own a single copy of. I have since removed it from most digital retailers. No one asks me about it, so I know that I did the right thing.

I realize now why I did what I did. While *The Call* remains a seminal piece of history to me, very few of my fans have heard it or recognize songs from it when I perform them live. I wanted supporters of Mega Ran to understand why the album was so special to me, and it would hurt me when they didn't appreciate something that I had worked so hard on. So, in my mind, in an attempt to make things better, I inadvertently committed the cardinal sin of a creative – I dumbed my art down. I made it colorful. I put a shiny bow on it. None of those songs had the heart or soul their original version had. After the last piece of cardinal red vinyl sold, I removed all traces of the album and never spoke of it again.

The release of this album and trying to make sense of a friendship lost sent me into a creative tailspin. I lost motivation to create new and meaningful pieces of art, because I had to keep the lights on. I attempted to make an EP every month of the year, tapping out after just three months. I was fortunate enough to be playing a convention every month, and touring every few months because without that, I may not have been able to make it through this period.

It was during this year a video director, Michael Cardoza, approached me about directing a documentary. I thought this was perfect. Recently, I began playing local shows with a band, The Lo Classics, who were making their name known in town playing concerts. I met up with them a few times and was impressed with their work ethic. They offered to replay some of my existing songs and they sounded like new creations with a live band behind it. I fell in love. Since Michael was filming us, I thought the best possible outcome was to film a weekend-long tour, so I began booking shows in Phoenix, Vegas, Los Angeles, then we would end the tour at a huge concert the next weekend in Seattle.

The tour went extremely well, as we played to large receptive crowds and Mike got great footage. Phoenix and Las Vegas were successful shows but Los Angeles was different. Due to two band members being Seventh Day Adventists, they were not able to perform with us in Los Angeles on Saturday. The band's DJ decided to tempt fate by suggesting we play a full set without a bass player and keyboardist, but with using recorded tracks of their parts that they had played in rehearsal. This was a terrible idea, and led to us starting our set almost an hour later than scheduled. The sold-out crowd had practically left by the time we began playing our bass-less and keyboard-less set. I eventually played on my laptop and we limped through the concert. Again, Los Angeles *proved* to be bad luck for me.

While LA is an unlucky town for Mega Ran, Seattle is where Lady Luck shines brightest. We were invited to play mainstage at PAX (Penny Arcade Expo), which took place at the gorgeous Paramount Theater in downtown Seattle. Every seat in the building was taken, and the PAX staff set up the perfect evening of video game inspired music. The lineup was myself, Big Brigade playing *Mega Man 2*, and *The Protomen*, the Mega Man-inspired rock opera. Right before showtime, Ian, the show's stage manager, came to me and said that he wanted to tell me that one particular person in the crowd was really looking forward to my show: a man named Keiji Inafune.

Inafune-san is known *as* the father of Mega Man. He didn't actually invent the character, but he was arguably the first to draw the character back in 1987. He also worked on *Street Fighter*, *Dead Rising*, and many other successful titles. After many years at Capcom, Inafune had quit just a few months prior, and there were rumbling about his next project being a Mega Man successor. But here he was, at my show, waiting to see and hear me play live. I couldn't believe it. I had to immediately use the bathroom. Before I did, Ian also let me know that we were on in two minutes, and to make him proud. We did. The show was probably the greatest live set I've ever played. The drums were crisp, the keys were bright, the bass was deep, and K-Murdock was there be the perfect player two. Afterwards, Inafune's translator told me he thought my show was "outstanding." I've never forgotten that. I felt like I'd found a bit of myself that was lost the year before. And I had Inafune to thank.

Chapter Sixteen

MIGHTY

You know it's on from the moment you land
Ain't no better place to be than inside Tokyo's Hands
—"Tokyo Hands" (To Japan With Love, 2016)

K EIJI INAFUNE WAS AT PAX 2014 for the same reason I was: to regain something that he had lost… himself. He had just resigned from Capcom, where he had worked for twenty-two years prior, and I had just quit my job as an educator. So much of what he said in his 2010 blog post, titled "Sayonara," resonated with me and probably encouraged my move:

> A manager's work means evaluating your subordinates
> and speaking your dreams. Anyone who can do both
> of those is a manager. I thought that when I came here,
> and I still think that now. People that really know me,
> can see where I'm coming from. I'm not a regular dude.
> It's probably because I'm strange.
>
> I'm leaving Capcom with the intention of starting my life over.

He went on:

> *It would probably be good for me to sit gracefully in
> this seat and become a leading figure in the industry.
> However, I cannot do this. Settling down means death*

for a creator. As long as you are a creator, you cannot settle down... I love Capcom. Probably more than anyone in the world. However, it's not always the case that your hopes are realized. Just as it was with the girlfriend I loved long ago.

Settling down means death for a creator. Those words hit me hard. I printed the page and posted this on my bedroom mirror. Inafune wasn't just moving on because he wanted to start fresh, but he needed to, in order to feel alive again. It was much like I did in 2011. Creating is far more fulfilling than managing, whether in a game development situation or in a classroom.

While conducting a panel at PAX that weekend, Inafune launched a Kickstarter campaign for his new project, which up until then was a total secret: a spiritual successor to *Mega Man* titled *Mighty No. 9*. The project was seeking nine hundred thousand dollars in thirty days, and surpassed that goal before the end of the one-hour panel. The ending total was over four million dollars including PayPal donations. Now the jury is still out on whether or not the game lived up to expectations, but what happened three months after the Kickstarter ended is still unbelievable to me.

I was ending 2014 on a high note, ready for a monster 2015, when I had at least two big album releases planned. I signed my first recording contract since 2008, with Brick Records in Boston, for the release of *Soul Veggies*. Brick was a home of traditional boom-bap hip hop since the late 90s, so I knew I couldn't hand them an album full of video game samples. Matt "Storyville" Weiss and I worked on a fun, throwback record and planned for a February 2015 release, and planned a winter 2014 tour to support it.

While on the road I got an email from Steve Yu of Comcept, asking me if I had kept up with the cast of composers announced from their involvement with *Mighty No. 9*. I had, because it was almost a who's who of *Mega Man* soundtrack musicians, from Manami Matsumae who had composed tracks from *Mega Man 1* and on, to Ippo Yamada, whose "Splash Blue" track from *Mega Man 9* became the foundation my

"Splash Woman" song. I was a proud backer of the project and couldn't wait for it to release.

Then Steve dropped the bomb. He told me that on the explicit order of Keiji Inafune, he wanted to ask me if I was willing to not only join the group of musicians working on the soundtrack, but if I wanted the job to create the ending credits theme of the game. I was in a crowded van but I remember screaming, "OH MY GOD" at the top of my lungs while we drove through the snow-covered Midwest on tour.

It's every musician's dream to compose on a big budget project, but to get the ending credits theme? That was the fantasy of a lifetime. I never thought that would happen to a guy like me. Inafune knew exactly what he wanted, and it was right within my wheelhouse. He wanted me to sample the existing main theme that Manami composed, then turn that into a completely new creation, much like I had done with so many soundtrack themes before that.

I was on the road at the time touring the US with Storyville and Dan "Danimal Cannon" Behrens, both incredible musicians and human beings. We grew so close during that tour and I updated them on every detail of my talks with Comcept, so when we finalized what they wanted, I knew I wanted to involve both of them somehow. Comcept asked me to write and produce a song over nine minutes long. In the world of hip-hop that is an eternity. I had never written a song over five minutes before, so I asked why this unique requirement. Steve told me because the massive number of backers (over seventy thousand) all of which who needed mentioning in the roll of the credits at the end, the total time needed to complete this was nine minutes, or as close as I could get. We had our work cut out for us.

I brought in all the big guns for this one, calling up every producer I had worked with in the past to assist with production. There was one person I was afraid to call: DJ DN3, aka Mel. my estranged best friend of five years. I hadn't made any music with Mel in over a year by this point, and I didn't know what he would think about working with me again. But it wasn't a hard decision to make. Mel had been with me from Day 1, and one small disagreement shouldn't stop us from working together on what was possibly the biggest placement of my career. Once I put my pride aside, I called Mel, and we resumed our friendship like it was never tainted in the first place. We resumed our conversations about sports, video games, and Spike Lee movies just like the old days.

Once all the pieces were in place, we agreed to make an epic ending song that contained four parts. The beginning was a separate piece of the theme song, sampled by DJ DN3, with a rap and chorus from me, cut short and interrupted by a different, more somber piano-led riff that started with a verse from Storyville, defining what being Mighty meant to him. Once he ended his verse, I would begin a new sixteen-bar verse and the bass notes would kick in, leading to the first chorus and then a key change. After this, I would enter a second verse and chorus over some added synths, then after repeating the chorus once more, switching to a guitar solo by Danimal Cannon. After the solo, the chorus would return, followed by recordings from the highest backers from the Kickstarter campaign. I had asked Steve to ask each person to record their name and "mighty number" or backer ID number, then to follow that with the statement "I am Mighty." As I said, epic.

Once the smoke cleared, we ended with a seven minute, ten second song that was truly "Mighty." I started it with the Webster's Dictionary definition of the word mighty, which I thought made so much sense upon further inspection: "Possessing great and impressive power or strength, especially on account of size."

I took the word size to mean not just physical stature, but any other limitation placed upon a person by society: knocks based on looks, on environment or upbringing, even on race. We are mighty.

I turned in the seven-minute track that wasn't quite as long as they initially requested, but was told by Steve the song was well received throughout the office and he or Inafune had no notes on the music once we turned it in. Success! We had completed a song included on what likely was the most anticipated game of 2015. I couldn't have asked for a better roll-out for what was arguably my best solo album release, *RNDM*, dropping in September, the same anticipated month of the release of *Mighty No. 9*.

In the second verse of the song I wrote as if I were Inafune. I studied his "Sayonara" blog post and wrote down what had to be his thoughts, coming from such a "sure thing" at Capcom, betting on himself to start anew with everything to lose and nothing but personal fulfillment and satisfaction to gain.

> Through the fire the turmoil and trouble
> I have climbed to the highest of heights, came through
>   the rubble
> And I didn't have the slightest idea of who to run to.
> The situation's dire, when you livin' on the bubble
> And I love you but I must prosper,
> For prosperity, and my propers
> You monsters are not scaring me,
> Cause I'm mighty, a lion in the jungle.
> Feel the fire and the rumble in my tummy.
> You never taking this from me,
> Cause I'm hungry jack, pancake the landscape
> Running backs, hand off, I'm never coming back.
> Shake it off, hit the scene like a wrecking ball.
> Any problem at all, I'm at your beck and call.
> Heavens fall when I shake it up.
> So unbelievably ill, I couldn't make it up.
> So remember the name,
> It's Mega Ran and Comcept.
> The bomb threat, is real
> And I'm just Mighty.

The timing of the song, the opportunity and the moment seemed completely perfect. It was the comeback I needed to fully rebound from 2014's setbacks… until it wasn't perfect. Comcept announced the game was pushed back due to some last-minute bug fixes, and wouldn't release until 2016. This was the fourth release date change already, and many backers were getting restless. The problem on my side was that I had already counted on "Mighty" appearing as a bonus track on *RNDM*, and the release of *Mighty No. 9* helping to boost my album's profile, so much so it was mentioned in every press release for our album. Comcept was so excited about the completion of the song and at the same time found themselves at the mercy of thousands of upset backers and fans so decided to "leak" the song themselves, presumably to get people excited about what was coming. "World Famous Rapper Mega Ran Will Appear On *Mighty No 9* Soundtrack!" read the post. People were definitely excited.

This was like throwing a rubber squeaking steak to a starving pack of dogs. Once they realized it was not what they wanted, the fans immediately rejected it. YouTube user Haedox, who was also a backer, took to YouTube immediately after the song leaked in a Comcept Kickstarter update, and lambasted the song thoroughly. Other users later uploaded it to their YouTube pages, and "Mighty" became by far my most critically panned song on the internet. Some comments say things like:

"4 million dollars for these struggle bars?!"

"I've gotta rigorously clean out my ears now..."

"Cringy"

"Crap"

"SUCKS"

The song's reception I feel wasn't totally my fault (by the way, I still think the song slaps), but the response to a number of botches during *Mighty No. 9*'s release schedule. Just a few months before the song leak, Comcept released a video trailer to the game that totally missed the mark, where the announcer says you can "make your enemies cry like an anime fan on prom night." Talk about not reading the room. Despite this, it was very difficult to not feel down on myself while reading people trash something that five friends and I poured tons of man-hours into.

I had some friends tell me that they thought the game was a victim of its financial success, because with every reveal of the game, skeptics merely responded "$4 million for THIS?!" and people would immediately join the hate train. It became more fun to dislike it than to attempt to see the good in the game. I think it was doomed from the moment they uttered "Megaman Successor." *Mighty No. 9* is a good game that almost didn't have a chance from the start because of its lofty aspirations. It eventually released in June of 2016 and currently holds a 52% Metacritic score. Plans for a sequel and follow-up projects using the Mighty characters and storylines were scrapped. I assumed

I'd never see or hear from Inafune-san, or even work in the video game industry again.

The song still appeared on my solo album *RNDM* as planned, which released on time in September 2015. Right after the song dropped, I began preparing for a tour to promote my upcoming album. I did interviews around the country; I was never asked about "Mighty," but the fact over seventy-thousand backers got to hear my music is a win to me. I'm still honored Inafune-san choose me for the job and proud of myself and my team for executing it to the best of our ability. I say that Mega Ran's music is an acquired taste – in short if you don't enjoy it, you probably should acquire taste.

On the day that presales for the album *RNDM* opened, I was playing a headlining show in London with Bag of Tricks Cat. It made me extremely nervous travelling out of the country on an eight-hour time difference with an album to promote. While in the green room preparing for the show, I recall recording a video for social media, doing the one thing I hate to do – asking fans to pick up the album from their favorite digital retailer. They listened. The album climbed to #13 on iTunes and went on to feature some of my most popular songs to date like "O.P.", "Your Favorite Song", and "Infinite Lives." The album shot to the top of college radio charts, even passing up albums like *Run the Jewels 2* and Dr. Dre's *Compton*. *RNDM* even made the GRAMMYs shortlist, which isn't as amazing as it seems, but is still really cool. Once the tour ended, I had two huge changes to make. One was to cut my hair, which I had grown the entire year, which was connected to my second, to get married in November. I was able to end 2015 in a very good place both personally and professionally. Next it was time to take the message of this new album around the world that winter.

The first time I toured Japan, it was with Kyle Murdock, and we were lucky. We were an American rapper-producer duo who found inspiration in Japanese games and products, even naming our album *Forever Famicom*. Even with that though, we didn't know any Japanese venues, promoters, or connections. Fortunately, we had other artists to rely on who had been in the market before, and that helped us greatly.

Touring with DJ AAROCK, the rapper Substantial, and his producer Marcus D., we partnered up with a travel agency, so had a translator who helped us get around with ease. Substantial and Marcus D. perform as Bop Alloy, a side project that is extremely successful in Japan. Marcus lives in the country, and Substantial is one of the few American MCs to have collaborated with the late Jun Seba, known as Nujabes, aka the Dilla of Japan, in reference to Dilla, who was highly regarded as one of the most talented hip-hop producers of his era. Being on a bill with those guys gave Kyle and I the credibility that we definitely Benefited from.

We all took separate flights, coming from different origin points, so flying that far without someone to talk to for the first time was quite nerve-wracking. I don't know that I've ever felt a fear quite like landing in a new country without friends, family, or at least a handler, seeing every sign around you in an unfamiliar language and having to handle customs for the first time. When I met the group, all fear and anxiety subsided. Nowadays, as a road weary veteran, I can travel to Japan and most places alone to rock stages without fear. Or at least without as much fear.

Believe it or not though, as much as I love being on stage, the Mega Ran you see bouncing around, and flipping metaphors isn't anything like the Raheem that exists for the rest of the day. I like peace and quiet, and calm activities. Japan is a great place for that because the society is built for efficiency. Japanese residents move throughout society quickly and quietly, seeming to exist only for the purpose of completing a task. Fun is something that Japanese people have to go out of their way to make room for, while Americans find a moment to laugh pretty much every hour on the hour.

When performing in a place where English is not the first language, like Japan, I learned that taking the time to learn some key Japanese phrases will go a long way. When finishing a song, I learned to say *arigatou gozaimasu*, which means, "thank you very much." But I wanted to make sure to make a memory that wouldn't be forgotten. I now do a freestyle trick on stage that is exclusive to Japan, in which I get a friend from the audience who knows English and Japanese, to translate, and then the audience members will hold up items. I'll then make a song up on the spot using those items, then ask the friend to translate in real time. Meanwhile, the DJ plays a beat live and uses two virtual turntables to "juggle" the beat to keep it playing continuously. It's the equivalent of watching a man with feet for hands attempt to juggle while balancing on a unicycle. It's absolute madness. The crowd always loves it, so we've done this every year since.

A year later, I had an opportunity to come back to tour Japan and brought along two friends, Mr. Miranda and Doug Funnie. We were asked to play a few shows around the time of Tokyo Game Show, one of my favorite gaming events. I jumped at the chance. Once our schedule was complete, I reached out to Steve Yu in the oft chance he could help make one more dream come true. Wayne Gretzky (or Michael Scott, depending on who you ask) says "you miss 100% of the shots you don't take," so I was prepared to shoot my shot.

I asked Steve if he could help me organize a meeting with Keiji Inafune, so I could thank him personally for the inspiration and the opportunity just a few months earlier with *Mighty No. 9*. Steve said he would let me know, and within a few weeks, he did. On a day off in Osaka between shows, we got the chance to sit down for an hour with Inafune-san, and in that time, we talked about games, music, influences and driving forces. It was one of the more powerful conversations I'd ever had, and just to be in the same room with someone who was such an inspiration to me was a dream come true. Once we finished, we had Japanese curry with Ippo Yamada and hopped on a train back to Tokyo, full of motivation.

Chapter Seventeen

THE SQUARED CIRCLE

You better get what they got,
Cause we're coming with a crew and you know they
    stay hot.
Tell me what you want to do, cause we just can't stop.
Everybody knows the New… Day Rocks.

— "New Day Raps," *Mat Mania* (2016)

M ARCH 27, 2015, 5:30 P.M. My phone rings. The excited voice on the other end got right down to business. "Hey, so… I know it's in two days, but… do you want to come to Wrestlemania?"

I thought he was joking. But Austin Creed, aka Xavier Woods of the WWE, was not. It took everything in my power to not yell through the phone, "OH HELL YEAH," much like WWE legend Stone Cold Steve Austin would have. "Um… sure," I responded calmly. Wrestlemania was just forty-eight hours away and in San Jose, CA, so I had to make plans fast.

"Oh, and bring a suit," Austin advised. I bought one that day and packed it.

2015 was also the year I reconnected with professional wrestling after a long hiatus, thanks completely to Austin. Many years earlier, in passing he told me about an idea he had about him and three friends forming a team of fun-loving, jovial characters and though they had a rocky start, the group became a huge hit. As "The New Day," Austin and his partners Kofi Kingston and Big E went on to hold the WWE Tag Team Championships on multiple occasions, and their on-screen chemistry is and has always been infectious. Most teams in wrestling usually break up after a year or two, with one of the members going on to super stardom while the others middle in obscurity, but The New Day has remained a unit and as of the date writing this, have the most tag team championship reigns of any active team in pro wrestling.

Whenever our paths would cross on the road, I'd call up Austin and invite him to shows, or he would invite me to wrestling events. Sometimes, as in the case of Wrestlemania, people fly all across the world to attend. This show was extra special, because during the weekend, my favorite wrestler, Macho Man Randy Savage, was getting inducted posthumously into the WWE Hall of Fame. Austin managed to get both of us a sweet blue "Friends and Family" wristband and a white "After Party" band, both of which lead to some phenomenal perks. The first was a bus ride to Levi's Stadium with the rest of the talent's friends and family members, accompanied by a police motorcade by the California Highway Patrol.

We took our seats in the upper deck and enjoyed the show, until Xavier's match began, and an WWE official came to our section and asked for the two of us to come down. Austin's wife and mother took the invitation and sat ringside for a four-way tag team championship match between The New Day, Los Matadores, The Usos, and Tyson Kidd and Cesaro, who retained their titles. After a long match, night fell over the stadium in time for the main event, which saw Seth Rollins sneak in and steal the WWE Championship in what many people call one of the most exciting endings in Wrestlemania history.

Fireworks lit up the night sky as all the friends and family were ushered back to their buses to return to the talent hotel. With the Benefit of police escorts there were no traffic delays. Once there, it was time for phase two. We changed, grabbed our After-Party wristbands and prepared for the nightlife at the hotel's banquet hall.

Once inside the hall, I probably got jitters for the first time in my adult life, outside of a stage performance. I felt like an eleven-year-old at the Spectrum watching Wrestlemania V all over again... except these highly trained professional athletes weren't on the Jumbotron; they were right in front of me. As soon as we walked in, I saw Booker T. Then Mark Henry, then Ric Flair... one legend after another. I couldn't speak. I tried my best not to stare. The only way I could loosen up was with an adult beverage, so I did that. My goodness.

After a few more drinks, I was finally calm enough to interact with folks, and I did it the best way I knew how, through music. I walked to the DJ booth and noticed that the tunes were emanating from the turntables of Peter Rosenberg, Hot 97 personality and probably one of maybe one hundred people in the world who know as much about hip-hop and pro wrestling equally as I do. Peter and I had a good chat about the results of the show, new music he was into and more, and I felt like I had settled into a groove. The person who helped most with this was another friend I'd met through Austin, referee Jason Ayers, who told me, "we all get butterflies, you've just got to get them all to fly in the same direction."

It felt incredible being the least important person in that banquet hall. As an entertainer, I was accustomed to working a room, forced to smile and shake hands with everyone in an attempt to gain an ally. I didn't have to do that here. I could just sit back and take it all in. And I did. I saw people I'd watched since childhood, as they danced, mingled, and partied the night away. I maintained my cool until I met one of my all-time favorites, Bret "Hitman" Hart.

Bret was another character that renewed my interest in wrestling in the 90s, with his feud with Stone Cold Steve Austin an example many revere as one of the best in the history of the federation. Bret also wasn't the biggest or strongest, but always used his wits to pull victory from the jaws of defeat. Austin watched as I began to fanboy a bit about standing so close to Bret, and he doesn't let me live that down very often. I sat next to him and couldn't believe how friendly and welcoming he was to a complete stranger. I'd imagine that people who hear "I love your work" every day of their lives would grow tired of it, but Bret Hart seemed just as engaged with me as he probably was all weekend at autograph signings in town. It just didn't seem real.

I have to thank legendary ring announcer Lilian Garcia for setting the mood and breaking the ice by asking me to take a photo of her with a few wrestlers, so when I asked her to return the favor, she obliged and became my own personal photographer for the night, snapping pictures of me with several wrestlers. After this evening, I can't imagine not becoming a big-time wrestling fanatic again, as I felt like I wanted to know more about the guys and gals I had just met, as well as reacquaint myself with storylines and matches. I was pulled all the way back in.

This interest in wrestling again would help lead to my second major career pivot, one that put me in front of a completely new audience. During a tour, I found out I would visit Houston the same Sunday as the WWE were holding a pay-per-view event called Night of Champions. The show was main-evented by one of my favorite wrestlers of all time: Sting, making a much-anticipated comeback. Sting was embarrassed earlier in the year at Wrestlemania and was returning at age fifty-seven, with a shot at the WWE Championship held by top bad guy Seth Rollins. Earlier on the match card was The New Day, defending their WWE Tag Team titles against another legendary team, The Dudley Boyz. The New Day won the match by disqualification and kept their titles, despite my boy Austin getting put through a table, which looked extremely painful. But no pain would prepare me for what went down during the main event.

Sting suffered a debilitating injury during the match when Seth Rollins performed a turnbuckle powerbomb, a move in which Seth, with a running start, *tosses* his opponent's back and shoulder first into the turnbuckle pads. The move caused Sting's neck to snap back violently, and it was later revealed he had suffered from spinal stenosis, an abnormal narrowing of the spinal canal resulting from pressure on the spinal cord. We watched Sting's final match. As we walked out of the Toyota Center, we saw an ambulance speeding away from the venue with its sirens wailing. "I bet that's Sting," I told a friend. It was. That night and the results made the show tough to watch.

That night at my hotel, I decided to hit record on my iPhone and capture some of my immediate thoughts about the event and what I had seen. Since Wrestlemania, I had experienced wrestling through a completely different lens, as a professional entertainer myself. I released my recording onto the internet and the podcast called *Mat Mania* was born. I named it after the first pro wrestling video game I had ever played, an arcade game by Technos released in 1985. My local pizzeria, Rocky's, had the game and I would dump quarters into it to attempt to win the title and get the honor of inputting my initials on the High Score screen. "RJJ" wasn't cool enough, so I began to input "RAD," that looked sweet. The wrestlers on *Mat Mania* were all completely made-up, but had captured the style of the 80s perfectly with characters like the Mad Max-inspired Insane Warrior, the masked luchador The Pirania, and the wild man Coco Savage, who very closely resembled legendary wrestler Bobo Brazil.

I went from telling my own point of view on wrestling to suddenly becoming a member of the pro wrestling press, which offered me plenty of perks. It was much like when I ran the RandomBeagle show with DN3 years earlier. I got invited to events, got offers to interview wrestlers, and got to get up close and personal with the sport. This offered me a greater appreciation for the artform and the men and women that lay their bodies on the line. I also realized that the effort required to be successful at pro wrestling was much like what was needed for a musician – an iron will. Also, there's no handbook on how to become a success, but success is what you individually make of your opportunities.

By the time the next Wrestlemania rolled around in 2016 in Dallas, I knew I wanted to be there, regardless of how. Over the past twelve months, I somehow became a full-fledged member of the internet wrestling community. People seemed to pay attention to my reactions on matches and storylines. When I realized the people who listened to my podcast had no idea I made music, I decided to merge the two. I prepared an album I also named *Mat Mania*, which served as a dedication project, flipping some of my favorite wrestling themes from the past as well as the present – and I released them every Monday leading up to Wrestlemania in a series that I called "Monday Night Ran." Lynx Kinetic made the beats and I wrote the rhymes. It was catchy, and people seemed to gravitate to it. Top wrestling site Whatculture premiered the tracks every week. The first track was dedicated to Brock Lesnar, and the week of its release, I interviewed with *Sports Illustrated* and *Rolling Stone* about it.

The *Mat Mania* album received five thousand downloads during Wrestlemania week, and I was invited to Dallas by WrestleCon, the largest pro-wrestling convention in the world, and given an opportunity to vend at a table in their expo hall. WrestleCon is exactly what it sounds like: a convention hall full of legendary wrestlers and their fans for a weekend. It was during that week that I also stepped into a wrestling ring for the first time, to play during the intermission of the wacky and unpredictable event called Kaiju Big Battel. In KBB, the wrestlers are dressed up as monsters, robots or aliens, and fight inside a ring full of cardboard "buildings," making the matches resemble the outlandish fight scenes in *Godzilla*. The show was the most entertaining action I had seen in a while.

I knew fans would expect the *Mat Mania* albums to become Wrestlemania weekend traditions, and I was happy to keep it going with sequels. But I refused to number the albums, because I thought the numbers would instantly age the project, so I took a trick from video games and added subtitles to each release. For Orlando, there was *Mat Mania: The Revenge* released in 2017 and *Mat Mania: Battle Royale* in 2018 for New Orleans. The latter release was a group effort, due to the astounding number of wrestling rap songs released in the years past; I wanted to highlight other talented musicians and give them a spot on the album. I recorded four new songs, and the rest of the tracks were by other artists.

In July 2017, I remember washing dishes in my apartment when Austin called me, letting me know that WWE was coming to my hometown of Phoenix. I was excited to get a chance to see my friend in action and hopefully hang out, but he had something different in mind.

"So, we've talked to the writers and we've pitched a crazy idea."

If you know anything about The New Day, this isn't really surprising… but this PARTICULAR idea certainly was. Austin continued. "We've challenged The Uso's to a rap battle that will be hosted by rapper Wale. We want to pre-tape it in a basement… And we wanted to know if we could have you come down and stand with us for the battle."

I said I absolutely was down to do this, as it was the perfect cross-section of all my favorite hobbies, but Austin made sure to let me know the segment wasn't approved yet, and not to get my hopes up. I never do though, because I know how fast things can change in entertainment.

A day later, Austin called me with an update. "... So, they decided to change the plans."

No big deal there. I understood, and told him, "Hey it's fine, hope to catch up with you after the show."

"Uh, no," Austin corrected me. "They want to do the segment INSIDE the ring now, live on TV. Are you okay with coming with us to the ring and doing it?"

Again, this took everything in me to not just yell "NANI???" into the phone like an overworked anime character. Just to confirm, I asked if he was asking if I was all right with: walking a WWE ramp, entering a WWE ring during a live television program, and participating in a rap battle?

Absolutely I was. I gave a resounding yes. This was happening in a few days, and I don't think I slept a wink before the show. When I did doze for a second, I had reoccurring dreams of myself tripping and falling and rolling down the ramp on live television. I just couldn't shake the feeling I would ruin this moment by being clumsy.

I got an email from production confirming the appearance, and when I asked what I would need to wear for the shoot, the producer said, "Whatever you would wear to a rap battle." Okay, sure. Easy enough.

The episode of *SmackDown* aired on the fourth of July, so of course they had plans for some festive dress-up. When I arrived at the venue, I was with five other men; each of them were Arizona-area independent wrestlers, who usually get called on when WWE comes to a town, to play random "extra" roles on television: a security guard, a fake EMT, or this time a group of muscular backups for The New Day and the Usos for their big standoff. After filling out paperwork, a staff member pointed us to a four-foot pile of Independence Day costumes they wanted the guys and I to pick from. By the time it was my turn, the only thing left was an Uncle Sam costume, listed as "One Size Fits Most." I'm not most. I knew this wouldn't fit so I suggested another idea, a New Day tee that I had in the back. The producer approved.

It was on this day I met Wale for the first time, an artist I was a fan of since I'd heard him on The Roots' classic track "Rising Up" in 2008. Wale was a witty, sharp, and poetic MC who always managed to walk the line of skilled rapper with pop commercial appeal and sensibilities. What I do with video game references, he's mastered with sports. He also had been a huge and very vocal wrestling fan for years. He was a huge influence to me and remains such to this day.

When we entered the ring for a dress rehearsal going over our parts and places, I stood in the back, attempting to shrink as I always do, hoping to just stay out of the way and not ruin things. The agent in charge of the scene warned us about which lines of vision to stay out of and how to not to find ourselves directly in the camera's lens, but as soon as he walked away, Xavier said, "stay right off my shoulder, I'm gonna make sure you get some camera time." So I did just that.

After the dress rehearsal, both teams went into the back and worked on their lines, and the New Day even asked me to listen to their practice runs and give feedback on delivery. While I sat and gave pointers, there was a knock on the door, and John Cena entered the room. He was returning that day after a long hiatus, and came into the room to congratulate the boys on all of their success. I made a joke that I thought Cena was coming into the room to tell us he was going to jump into the rap battle with some classic John Cena Thuganomics bars, but John quickly refused. "No, no, not me, my friend... rap is a young man's game – I'm out of that business." The room laughed.

Many people assumed that I "ghostwrote" bars in this battle but alas, I did not. The rumored story is better than the truth – I was merely there to listen. The boys did appreciate my assistance, and even asked me what I'd want for my time. After I'd just had legendary catering and met my childhood heroes, I didn't want a thing and wouldn't dare take it. I asked for the one thing any rapper really ever needs, "Just give me a shout out."

Austin smiled. "Oh, I already got that taken care of."

When the New Day's music hit, myself and the rest of the entourage hopped, skipped, and smiled our way down the aisle to the roar of the crowd. I got so excited, I high fived and fist bumped everyone who reached out on either side. And best of all, I didn't trip and fall.

Pre-battle was fun, but once the battle started, it was war, and the Usos came to win.

The Usos dropped powerful bar after bar. When it was Austin's turn, he held the mic, then turned to me and said the coolest thing possible on live television.

"Mega Ran, can you please hold my trombone?"

I think it was at that moment that my phone exploded, because most of the texts I got said, "I wasn't sure if that was you, but when he said your name? I flipped out."

So did I. It was the best shout out ever and an absolute dream come true.

I wrote some thoughts about my experience backstage on Instagram and before I knew it, I was getting tagged on wrestling rumor sites and my quotes were used to gain inside information on the show and the results. This was when I realized I was a little too close to the business side of the sports entertainment world, and I didn't want to risk endangering the relationship that Austin and I had for a few clicks. So out of respect, I knew I had to make some changes.

After that day I realized that I might be a bit too "insider" to appropriately report on pro wrestling without bias. I just want to enjoy the program and watch it without making harsh criticisms on something I could never do, and to talk trash about guys that I know in real life that are great people. Additionally, while my tour schedule took me away from the recording process, I didn't want to quit another podcast project. I made plans to transition out of the *Mat Mania Podcast*, as we brought on new members: Teek Hall, then Roknowledge, and Neoecks. They helped to keep the show fresh, and now that the show is almost two hundred episodes deep, the brand is strong.

Today my relationship with pro wrestling is complicated at best. I love the feats of athleticism and storylines, but I know far too much about the business of entertainment to fully invest my passion into it like I did as a child. But I have the utmost respect for anyone who can step into that ring and perform at a high level, night in and night out, with no breaks or holidays off, the way these guys do. It's a live-action comic book, played out every single week of the year with no breaks... what's better than that?

CHAPTER EIGHTEEN

BEEF

Heard you only live once, well Imma disagree,
'Cause you can live forever, and forever doesn't cease
— "Infinite Lives," *RNDM* (2015)

TOUR TIME. THOSE ARE MY two favorite words to utter or type, because as a musician we all dream of getting on the road and knocking down stages in strange places, making new friends and fans, hopefully getting paid, and having stories to tell for ages. For all the good I've experienced, I've definitely seen my fair share of terrible times. And no matter how positive I try to stay, it never fails that in the world of music, someone will try to knock you off of your square.

In 2016 the first significant rap beef of my career came from a most unlikely source: the legendary Alex Trebek, host of *Jeopardy*! During a taped broadcast, Alex asked contestant Susan Cole about her hobbies and she said the three words I'd never thought I'd hear on prime-time network television. Voice dripping with cynicism, Trebek announced that Cole was into a type of music that "doesn't sound like fun."

"Nerdcore hip-hop."

Susan explained herself well, I thought. She explained, "It's people who identify as nerdy, rapping about the things they love: video games, science fiction, having a hard time meeting romantic partners," to which Trebek replied, "Losers, in other words."

This set off laughter from the audience and competitors. The twenty-second clip was sent to me hundreds of times via text, email,

Facebook, and Twitter, to the point I had to announce publicly I'd seen it. Gossip blogs began re-posting it, calling Alex's burn "savage" and posting sensational headlines like "Alex Trebek Slams Nerdcore."

I was in Birmingham, Alabama, just finishing up a show, continuing to be tagged in this post when I realized this all-day moment was about to enter hour twenty-five and still had legs. While riding to the hotel I muttered a few lines, and by the time we arrived, I had a few couplets I thought the internet would get a kick out of:

> Alex Trebek you lost a lot of respect.
> I got to check you off the rip for coming outta your neck,
> Talking sideways about nerds, man, you a trip.
> Guess you hadn't heard nerds make up most of viewership.
> Nerdcore is home to some to some serious lyricists.
> I'll break this down in a format you're familiar with.
> This host gets roasted on SNL—yearly,
> Hosts a show for nerds and doesn't know that—clearly.
> No one likes a know-it-all, condescending blowhard.
> Easy to be snarky when you're holding all the note cards.
> Susan got the last laugh, and the cash.
> You're good at any show, you got a lifetime pass.

I recorded myself rapping the lyrics into my cell phone under the dim light of the hotel hallway, and went to bed. When I awoke, the song and video had gone viral, popping up on TMZ and several other news sites. I didn't plan for it to happen, but the attention the verse got led to near-sellout shows for the rest of the tour, and people who attended based on mild curiosity left the venues as bona fide fans. Sometimes it all works out. I still watch Jeopardy every night before bed, so there's no hard feelings.

I try not to dwell on negative experiences on stage too much, but I haven't completely blocked them from memory either, because I feel it's important to keep those in mind for perspective. They all build character. You can't appreciate the good until you've been through the bad. You can rap for five thousand and still have a terrible show, and you can rap for three people and have the best time of your life. And though I may want to pretend that I'm a long way from rapping for small crowds, I'm not. Perspective is so important.

It is extremely important to me that fans coming to a Mega Ran show have the best time possible. Whenever I'm in charge (i.e., when you see my name on the poster the largest), that means I can hopefully make several of the final logistical decisions on that show. If my name is smaller, I'm just support, and I usually have no say.

When I have the decision-making power, I like to ensure that:

1. The show takes place at a safe, relatively clean venue, run by trustworthy people;
2. The quality of the support acts is top notch; and most importantly
3. The show begins and ends at an appropriate time. No one wants to be in a club until 2 a.m. on a work night to see indie hip-hop.

I learned all of these essential tips during a show in Jacksonville on November 30, 2017. It was the only time I ever had a show end early. This was one that, in hindsight, I should've peeped the signs that things could go wrong. The show started late on a Sunday, doors opened at 9 p.m., support acts started at ten (there were at least four of them, not including the two artists I brought with me on tour), and the drinks had flowed for cheap all evening, which had the crowd a little more lit than usual.

The venue was called Nighthawks. I'd worked with this promoter before, and he assured me late shows worked here due to the city's residents' propensity to come out late and stay even later for their music. I started my set around 12:40 a.m., later than I ever had at that point.

I was halfway into my set, doing a skit which I sing the "The Fresh Prince of Bel-Air" theme song. It's a fun bit that gets the whole crowd involved because everyone knows the words. Sounds innocent enough, right? Who knew the cleanest rapper in history could incite violence? It happened on this night.

This time, before I could finish the verse, quicker than you can say, "Yo holmes, smell ya later," I heard a loud crash of glass, and a few screams from the audience. K-Murdock stopped the music, and we heard the promoter of the show screaming bloody murder. His face was a gross mix of blood, glass, and cheap beer.

Turns out a group of women said he was harassing them, and one of them decided to teach him a lesson by blasting him in the face with a full beer mug. The combination of glass cutting his face plus the remaining alcohol in the mug made for a gnarly grip of pain. He screamed, "What the f***!" and "AARGH!" over and over again while running to the bathroom to clean off.

It's probably the only time I've ever used foul language on the stage, as I was so disturbed by the situation. I believe I asked rhetorically, "What kind of bullsh*t is this?" to the crowd of stunned people.

The woman insisted, "Well, he kept bothering us!"

I responded, "You INJURED him!" At the time I questioned if the punishment had fit the crime, but looking back on it, it didn't matter. He shouldn't have been bothering these women, though I'm sure he didn't expect a mug to the... well, mug.

Best lesson I learned: Don't work with scumbags who harass people.

Since the victim (term used loosely here) was also the person organizing the show and paying me, we looked toward him for the next move. He yelled from the bathroom, "SHUT IT DOWN" while plucking glass from his beard. So, it was clear to me that this show was ending early, even though 1 a.m. would hardly constitute an early ending.

I asked the crowd to meet me at the merchandise table for photos and a chance to sell my wares, but the promoter was ready to end the night. "NO MERCH! EVERYBODY OUT... NOW!"

"Well alrighty then," I said from the stage. "Show's over, guys, I'm sorry. I'll be back soon, thanks for coming." We ended the show, and with a towel around his face, the promoter thanked me for coming and issued us some cash for the performance.

Ready to leave, I hesitated, the turned to the promoter and asked, "Were you bothering those women?" He denied it of course, but his tone led me to believe he was a little sore from his advances getting rejected.

"I even bought those yuck-mouthed broads free drinks!" He exclaimed. That was a red flag for me. *What does that have to do with anything?*

I can't help thinking if I had exercised a bit more of the leadership given to me, fully warranted in this regard, this might not have happened. If I'd had my way, we'd have performed earlier and been out of the building before midnight, not stuck on stage at 1 a.m.

Since then I've learned it's worth having the conversation about keeping indie rap shows timely. The age-old idea of "waiting for people to show" is terribly outdated and, quite frankly, lazy. If you tell people you're playing at eight, you shouldn't have to wait until twelve to catch the late coming stragglers. Those folks deserve to miss out.

My worst show was my first show. 2001. We had a venue a few blocks from my house, called Moody's on the Pike, which held a weekly open mic night. I played there with a few friends and rapped the songs on my PlayStation-made beats, about life on our block, Woodstock Street, affectionately known as "The Stock." So, I creatively sampled and interpolated some lines and sections of Prince's hit "Pop Life," and we called it "Stock Life." Genius, right?

We spit our PG-rated bars to the adult contemporary crowd, full of high school vocabulary terms mixed with what we'd learned from the MCs of the day.

The crowd went mild.

Not only is sampling/interpolating Prince without having his pipes one of the most sacrilegious acts one could ever embark upon in Black music, midway through my verse, I heard members of the audience start to make an annoying fire truck-like sound, which got louder and louder, as our surefire hit chorus was coming up. This sound was a reference to *Showtime At The Apollo,* the long-running television talent show, where if a performer got enough boos, then right there on the spot, a dirty, dusty hobo character named Sandman Simms would come out on stage, and literally use his cane to hook you off the stage, then dance a thirty second jig in your place. The siren signaled it was time to Enter Sandman, and not the Metallica album.

The weird thing was that Moody's hadn't adopted the *Showtime At the Apollo* booing ritual, so these people in the back getting the noise started were just doing it for the people who knew. I knew, so I felt it. We ended our song early and never played "Stock Life" again.

Los Angeles, the city of big dreams and even bigger coke habits, is the place I've had my most challenging performances. I don't know why, but there always seems to be an obstacle keeping me from greatness in the city of angels. I love LA, and some of my best friends live there, but it's a place that everyone goes to become a star, so predators are lurking around every corner. It's very easy to get scammed out there.

My first show in LA was a part of an event held by a label full of cats who were part of a dope hip-hop scene. A great night was put together, with cats like Percee P, Dibia$e, Peanut Butter Wolf, and most of Stones Throw Records in attendance. Among their crew members was DJ Haircut, who later took up singing and became the successful musician Mayer Hawthorne. But prior to the superstardom, he was the local DJ of the night, who had one job: let the record play.

However, most house DJs and venue staff, especially in LA, secretly hate their job, especially when they have to watch an artist they've never met get center stage. Much like sound techs at a venue, they are there to facilitate the show and let others shine, but usually have dreams of shining on their own. They have bands, released albums, and would rather do anything else than make you look good. DJ Haircut had Mayer Hawthorne's future on his mind that night and couldn't give a crap about doing his job correctly.

When I got the signal I was on next, I realized I had to follow an impressive set by DJ Houseshoes. Definitely a tough act to follow in this room. I decided to break the ice with my variation of a Dilla joint, "Shoomp." Again, another act of sacrilege, in the same room with people who made music with Dilla and called him a friend, to rap over his beats, probably. I had no idea.

As I was on stage rapping my face off, DJ Haircut behind me prepared to do what they call in the wrestling world "going into business for himself." Haircut was scratching hardcore, so loud he drowned out my lyrics, acting as if he was auditioning for the DMC Awards. What's worse, he started resetting the beat back to its beginning point constantly, rewinding to the point my balance was completely thrown off. My background vocals started coming at me in the wrong place, causing me to fumble over lyrics. I looked like an idiot. Looking back, they might have viewed my rhymes over Dilla beats as a cheap way of pandering to the pro-Detroit crowd in LA. I wasn't. It was a part of my set for every show of that tour.

After a day off to reflect, just two days later Sean Healy organized my next LA show. He's a famous (or infamous) promoter on the west coast, known for making artists do "Pay-to-Play" scams (strategies, techniques, tomato-tomahto) to get gigs. Before the show, he had his people mail me one hundred tickets to Phoenix, six hours away from the show, to encourage me to sell these tickets. I tried online but to no avail.

When I pulled up to the venue, a big man resembling Ving Rhames asked me, "Yo, how many tickets did you sell?"

I said, "None, but here they are right here."

He said back, "You can come in, but you can only play five minutes if you didn't sell anything." As I started to balk, he set me straight. "Yo, usually you don't play *at all* if you don't sell tickets. I'm just being nice because you came from so far."

Worse, although I didn't sell any tickets hand to hand, I saw at least ten people in the room who were there to see me but bought tickets at the door. They watched me play two songs and scram, and I got no credit for those sales.

Here's the problem with the Pay-to-Play model: it counts on presales solely, which is a good way to judge attendance, but doesn't account for some concertgoers who are not able or willing to purchase up front. Another problem with this model (scam, whatever) is that it drastically lowers the quality of the performing acts when you literally say that *anyone* who can get twenty people to give them ten dollars can hop on stage and play. Some artists will just eat the cost, pay the promoter two hundred dollars, and play to whoever is there. Respected headlining acts are punishing their fans just to have people in the room, having them sit through hours of amateur acts.

So, every show that you leave with money in your hand is not a good show. How many folks will return if they had to wait until 1:30 a.m. to watch you play, and sit through twelve terrible bands?

I wish I could say this was my only rough experience in LA, but it wasn't. The last one happened just a few years ago. I played a show there with None Like Joshua on a Wednesday night, packed the club out and sold tons of merch, and at the end of the night, were given two five-dollar bills for Joshua and me to split as our cut from the show's promoter. Ten dollars. That's it. Time to do some math: Tickets sold for twelve dollars in advance, fifteen at the door, about one hundred and fifty people attended, so I just *knew* we'd make a decent payday, but we made a whopping ten dollars. Enough for a Subway foot-long. I won't be returning to AMPLYFI on Melrose any time soon, so I have no shame in dropping their name in this book.

Another time in LA (when I say LA is tough, I mean it): I played a networking event called Mindscape, where people pitch ideas and share short talks about why their idea might be the next big thing. I was scheduled as the entertainment at the intermission portion of the show, a position I don't like, but am familiar with playing, when due to scheduling issues, they moved my performance to the end of the night.

"It'll be awesome, you'll close us out, and everyone will leave on a high note," the organizer said after I'd driven six hours to the show.

When it came time for my performance, the organizer who also served as the event's MC, hit the mic and when I thought was going to introduce us, said the last thing you want to hear right before you're about to hit the stage. "Thanks so much for coming out, guys! See you next Mindscape! Get home safely, peace!"

He sent everyone out of the room just as my first beat played. No mention of my performance, nothing. I was now tasked with playing a completely cold room half empty at best by the time I started, if that. I had to literally wrangle the remaining people and ask them to stay put as I performed. I don't know if I'd have accepted the gig if I had known I was the walk-off music. It was like when The Roots play as *The Tonight Show*'s credits are rolling, even though I'd imagine anyone in that crowd wouldn't think of getting up and leaving while The Roots are rocking.

The most recent terrible series of shows occurred when I allowed myself to lose control of the booking. In 2014 I embarked upon the Fam Fiction Tour with Fresh Kils, Coolzey, and Schaffer the Darklord. It excited me to rap with such a wide range of artists, in what was my first tour coordinated by a booking agent. The tour was part of a "feeling out" process to see if I'd be a good fit for the agent's roster.

The tour was like a musician's version of the show *Survivor*. Imagine four indie musicians, dropped into a car, given a route to cover and very little else... with the goal to keep our wits amidst complete chaos. We were all connected to a google drive sheet with several blanks in significant categories, like net pay and day of show contacts. These were filled in as we travelled by the booking agent. The first show was in my home city of Phoenix, usually a great city for me, and less than fifty people attended. After the show, the coordinator told us that he hadn't heard a final confirmation from the booking group until the day of the show, so that hurt promotions. He also couldn't pay us the originally agreed upon amount. Not a great beginning, but things happen.

We knew things were heading toward disastrous territory when, on the second show of the tour, the local promoter stated he knew nothing of the show until a week before, resulting in a lightly attended ABQ excursion. The pay for the show also mysteriously changed from a guarantee to a door deal on the Google sheet. I think it was clear that the promoter or his assistant changed the deal at the last minute, which was horrible etiquette.[6]

As an experienced touring artist in the US with a critically acclaimed album, K-Murdock and I thought the next natural progression was to move toward touring in other countries. This all began when the London Anime Convention invited me to play as a musical act. I had played conventions all over the US, but to get invited as a guest at one in

---

[6] Door Deal (aka Door Split)(n): An agreement that the performers will receive a portion of the money made from admission prices. This amount is not a guarantee because it is based on the number of patrons who pay at the door. Not what one would prefer, but one might take it in cities or on days where a show's success is uncertain.

another country was an honor I couldn't pass up. We worked on getting to England.

Right around the time of the London Anime Con, I heard of an event going down nearby, the SuperByte Festival in Manchester. A chiptune/lofi-based festival, SuperByte brought out chip musicians with Game Boys, Famicoms, and Mega Drives to play some of the coolest tunes all under one roof. I was the only vocal musician scheduled, which made me a highly anticipated act.

Kyle and I rolled out without much of a plan, staying with friends whenever possible and keeping costs low. By the end of the tour, with most shows going off without a hitch, we were added to a last-minute London show in Brixton, an area known for its tough types. Being from Philadelphia, I was confident I wouldn't see anything out in the UK that I hadn't seen before at home, ten times worse. We'd heard stories of men stabbing folks in dark alleys out there, but nothing affected us. Our biggest threat came in a much more unexpected place.

Our lodging for the evening of the Brixton show was a confused, jumbled last minute cluster of an idea. Running low on funds, we opted not to get a hotel for the final night of the tour and rely on the kindness of fans (read: strangers). One fellow suggested a friend's pad in Brixton, and when the show ended around 2 a.m., we took a taxi to the location. As we approach, I called the man, but there was no answer. Once outside, we called the friend of a friend again, who still didn't answer the phone. After a five-minute wait, we called again... no answer.

We waited outside for twenty minutes in cold weather, knowing not a soul, thinking the worst until suddenly a drowsy figure emerged and opened the front door. "Oh, hey, you must be the blokes my mate told me about," a groggy voice muttered. "Come on in."

We enter the rugged cobblestone home, exhausted and ready to pass out. The man said, "Okay, not a lot of space here, so you guys should sleep in the kitchen. It's the only place with heat, so that'll do ya."

I looked around and noticed what looked like last night's meal still on the stove, with dirty plates on the table and in the sink, the floor covered with a thick soot-like dirt covering, and unidentified stains everywhere I looked. A black light in this room would have surely turned up some repulsive results.

I picked a small chair against the wall in the kitchen as my resting place for the night, using a second chair for my feet, and Kyle, with no other options in sight, decided to sleep under the kitchen table. That's correct, under the kitchen table. The cleanliness of this place was dreadful, but out of options we had to make the most of it.

After four hours of the worst sleep imaginable, we awakened to the sound of a different roommate making coffee. We groggily arose, ready to start the day in any place other than here and resume our UK tour. Ready to leave without a shower, I looked at Kyle's face, and his eye looked like he'd been in a sparring match with Mike Tyson. "Yo K, what's up with your eye, man?"

Kyle looked in the mirror and noticed his left eye completely red. He had a strange infection, no doubt caused by our suspect sleeping conditions. We postponed our train ride to the next city so that he could take a trip to a local urgent care facility. They got him some antibiotics, and he was fine within a few hours, much quicker and easier than I dared hope.

I wish that was the toughest part of that UK tour, but it wasn't nearly. Our last tour stop was in Cardiff, Wales, a three-hour train ride from Manchester, our home base. Our supporters there affectionately call it "Mega Ran-Chester" when we play gigs there. Manchester is probably my favorite place to play outside the US. The shows are always phenomenal, and it's such a lovely music town. We were late as usual, scuttling down the busy streets to the train station to catch our ride to Wales, and what always happens to me in clutch situations happened at this moment.

I had to go to the bathroom.

Kyle had already walked through the turnstile, and I ran for the public toilets with eight minutes before our train, telling him, "I'll be right back." I had every intention of making it back in three. One problem though, the toilets at Manchester Station required a coin for entry, which I did not have. I ran into a coffee shop and quickly made change with a purchase, then ran to the restroom to handle my business. When I stepped out, my train was pulling off.

I jogged to the turnstile, but the rail attendant stopped me. "Train's gone, mate" he said. I didn't have cell phone service in the UK, to save money, and I didn't see Kyle anywhere. He was on the train. I waited an hour for the next train, pissed at myself for not waiting to use the toilet on the train. Our point of contact, James, was supposed to meet us at the Cardiff station and he knew when our train would arrive. I hoped everyone would wait for me.

I hopped on the next train and quickly purchased Wi-Fi to communicate with Kyle throughout the three-hour trip, but he didn't respond. James did not either. I was certain that I'd lost contact with the team and would have to end the tour, disappointed I had made it to the final show of the run and then lost it all. Luckily when I arrived, Kyle and James were there at the station waiting, and the Cardiff show wound up being one of my favorites of the entire European run.

After making it through the UK, it was time to take it to the motherland... Japan. Traveling to Europe is a fun challenge, but no place has ever stimulated my palate as much as Japan.

At the time of writing this chapter, I've been to Japan eight times in the past seven years, and each time has been more enlightening than the last. If I haven't overstated enough in interviews and my music, I'm so very inspired by Japan and its culture, probably more so than any other place in the world. It's the place that created so much of my fondest inspirations, from gaming to anime, even fashion and music, so it's like a homecoming every time I return. I call Japan my *mecca*, my homeland. It's so crucial to everything that I am personally and professionally.

So even though there is a language barrier, I've found that if I met my audience halfway, it made for a most memorable time. I'm thankful for Kyle willing to try so many new things on stage with me. It has made us both better in the long run.

CHAPTER NINETEEN

LOVE

Ain't nothing like a hip-hop chick
One I can just chill and talk hip-hop with
Love, laugh live life, yo you get my drift.
   —"Hip-hop Chick," *Language Arts, Vol. 2* (2012)

I MET MY WIFE, RACHEL THROUGH a mutual love of two of my favorite things – food and hip-hop. In 2007, after making the move to Phoenix and re-launching a teaching and rapping career in the Grand Canyon state, I managed to play a few shows in the city and began getting my footing on the scene, but I missed home. Nothing beat the sights, sounds, and tastes of Philadelphia.

One day, on my Myspace page, I posted a blog that read:

WHAT A MISTEAK.

I'm beginning to really like it here in AZ, but the food just isn't the same. What I want more than anything is a cheesesteak. I went to a sports bar here and ordered a "Philly Style cheesesteak" expecting a small piece of home, and got the wateriest, disgusting, poor excuse for a cheesesteak this side of the Atlantic or Pacific. I'll never make that mistake again. I'll just learn to do without and save my steak urges for when I get back out to Philly this winter. But if you live in AZ, please don't order a Philly steak. That's a poor representation of us. – Random

This post got a few comments, mostly from Philly native friends of mine who knew my pain, and some who even volunteered to eat a cheesesteak in my honor. How noble of them. But there was one comment by a woman named "Raquel," who said she knew of a great steak spot in Phoenix that had gotten rave reviews, even from Philly steak enthusiasts. Couldn't be.

Raquel, who told me later that her real name was Rachel, was talking about Scottsdale's Philadelphia Sandwich Company. I went there (without her, I was too cowardly to see if she wanted to join me) and enjoyed it. But before I ate, I asked the employees if they were from Philly. They responded with South Jersey, and that was good enough for me. New Jersey is a state so small, its culture is built on the large cities it borders. North Jersey is a smaller New York, and South Jersey is an extension of Philly – in style, slang, and steak preparation. It was legit.

I messaged Rachel to tell her I'd enjoyed the grub and thanked her for the suggestion. She and I met again at a show of mine later that year, when I was asked to open for one of my favorite rappers, Common.

I hadn't known it then, but Common was her favorite rapper too because he hailed from Chicago, which was close to where she was born and raised. I posted that I was playing the show and had a few tickets for the event to sell. The promoter gave these to me to make a few bucks. Rachel messaged me asking for tickets, and we agreed to meet up at another performance of mine that week to make the transaction.

That performance was for my early birthday party as well as a show for my new album, *The 8th Day*, which released on 8/8/08. There was cake, rap, and good times. Rachel showed up with her friend, looking HOT, but respectable. I sat at a high-top table while the two of them cracked jokes and talked about hip-hop, life, and more. I felt like we hit it off well, but I was still playing the field and finding my footing in the scene.

Our first official date was dinner and a DJ Quik concert in town. I set up the dinner and Rachel suggested a concert. She knew a member of Quik's band who got us into the show and even backstage – what a first date stunt move. We had a blast. When I got into her car at the end of the night, I noticed a lanyard for Rock the Bells – the huge concert series held in Northern and Southern California every summer back then. I had been to one previously, so I knew from that point forward she was a *real* hip-hop head.

Rock the Bells shows were typically composed of honest, hard-working, and organically built hip-hop acts. It was considered a true school event, holding firm to the classic hip-hop values of "love, peace, unity, and having fun." The last RTB event happened in 2007 (check that), but before then it was on the top of my bucket list as a place I'd love to play live. It was the only place you could have seen Snoop Dogg, Wu-Tang Clan, and Lauryn Hill all at once.

After three or four more dates, Rachel and I made it official. She drove to Laveen where I lived on work nights, over thirty minutes each way, so we could hang out. I remember the day I told her those three words for the first time very clearly. After a tumultuous year at Country Gardens Charter School, I got laid off. I struggled to fit in and adapt to their loose disciplinary system and unconventional teaching methods, but my efforts were in vain. At the end of the day one Friday, the principal popped into my classroom to tell me I was let go – budget cuts were cited as the reason.

I called Rachel and told her the news. She said, "I'll be right there." I'd never lost a job before. I'd also never had anyone drop everything they were doing to console me in a time of need. I was overcome with emotion. She helped me remove all my items from the classroom, and even offered to rough up the principal for me. I really believe she would have. It was a sweet ending to an emotional day.

We drove to my house and unpacked the car. I looked her in the eyes, fighting back my own tears, and said, "I love you." Luckily, she responded in kind, or that would have made for an awkward situation (and a much shorter chapter).

Once laid off and collecting unemployment, I decided to use the time to continue building my music career. I called in every favor I could and joined my friend Dave Miranda for the "Back to The Future Tour." We drove my Kia from Arizona all the way to Philadelphia. It was the first tour I'd ever been on, self-booked, no hype man, no driver, no agent, just me Dave and a mic.

Most shows were tiny, either in makeshift music venues with suspect sound equipment, or bars and taverns where the regulars couldn't care less about the performers on stage. This tour was small, but the enthusiasm was there. Making little to no pay, at best we rapped to anywhere from twenty-five to thirty-five hyper fans. On other occasions, we performed for the other acts on the bill and the sound tech. Regardless, we made the most of this and had a great time seeing the country.

When Rachel found out Dave had to fly home early to return to work on Monday, she organized a vacation trip to Lexington, Kentucky to see a friend, and stayed there until I was done with the tour, so she could help drive back to Phoenix with me. We got a lot of bonding done over that time.

After five years of countless concerts and adventures together (enough to fill another three books by itself), I decided to propose the best way I knew how – interpretative dance. Nah. You know me, rapping is what I do. The story began at a concert, so it only made sense for music to be involved at the next level. I planned an on-stage proposal.

MAGfest had requested I play in Washington DC, which was a yearly event that attracts over fifteen hundred people to a huge hotel for concerts and games on a cold January weekend. It was the perfect place to propose. I told the staff the plan and bought the ring the day before I left for tour. I stood at the counter of Kay Jewelers, comparing notes to email conversations we'd had in the months and years prior about her ideal ring. Just as I found a ring that closely matched one of her favorites, my phone rang. It wasn't my (hopeful) wife-to-be, but a very popular video game magazine wanting to do an interview with me right then and there. I couldn't say no, so I conducted this interview while making one of the most important decisions of my life; I shared that fact, which made for an engaging and honest interview. This all happened two hours before I caught a flight to DC.

The moment you buy an engagement ring is one of the most stressful times of your life, other than the act of getting married. You know you're making a life-changing decision and you want the rock to be just right; she's gonna have to wear this for a while. For me, that was the only time cold feet entered the equation. I spent the entire flight to DC awake and questioning if it was the right time, place, way, and/or person. I thought about every loose end in my life that hadn't been tied up… every frog I'd kissed until then, and every childhood dream about my future. In my mind's eye, I pictured Rachel right there next to me. I knew she was the one.

The plan was simple: Perform a freestyle, then bring her on stage and rap the proposal to her while getting on one knee. Amazing stuff. I thought it might even go viral. I expected to see her shortly after I got there, but due to plane delays and the insane Washington, DC traffic, she arrived thirty minutes before my performance. She told me, with disappointment in her voice, that she was exhausted and asked if she could miss the performance. There was no way I could allow that to happen so I told her that she couldn't miss it. I tried to think of any reason to dissuade her from leaving without letting the cat out of the bag. I think I did well with the excuse I came up with. She finally caved to my incessant nagging and agreed to attend.

Then I thought of another issue. I needed to know where she was during the set. She could stand anywhere in the crowd, and I wouldn't know. I needed her up front. To allay my concerns, I had a member of the MAGFest staff come to the room, get her, and bring her to the stage.

There's always a small level of nervousness before performing. It's said that the day you stop feeling it, is the day you should stop performing. Whether five or five thousand are waiting, the moment when someone tells me "You're on in ten minutes" produces a nervousness that overcomes me. I usually have to go to the bathroom immediately. TMI? Before that show, I got butterflies like never before, except these were more like drunk pterodactyls. When Rachel arrived backstage about thirty seconds before the show started, my friend Matt a.k.a. Storyville almost gave away the surprise when he expressed how happy he was to see Rachel, who he'd seen countless times before. Matt jumped in the air screaming "Rachel!" and hugged her.

Showtime.

The curtain rose, and I did my thing. The set went well enough, then I started the freestyle section backed by a band known as BitForce. Halfway through it, I walked to the back and escorted Rachel onstage for the conclusion and the big finale. I hadn't rehearsed that moment, I just trusted my gut, leaped with my heart, and let my instincts and rapping skill guide me through it. It was all a blur at the time, but thanks to watching it back on YouTube I even know the words:

> Rachel, my dear,
> I need you to spend the next hundred years,
> With me, and uh, never ever quit me.
> Through the ups and the downs, do you get me?
> When it gets rough you can carry me,
> Rachel Denise Walker, will you marry me?

I dropped to one knee and proposed in front of about five thousand eager fans, with even more watching online. She was a bit mad at me for having her onstage after such a tiring day, but I was just so happy she made it. In the end though, the plan worked to perfection – she said yes.

I got the ugly cry out of her.

On November 7, 2015 I married my best friend.

Chapter Twenty

READY TO LIVE

I ain't afraid of death,
I just don't want to be there when it happens.
—"Old Enough" (Extra Credit, 2017)

2017 STARTED LIKE MANY OTHER years had, with me on stage. I was playing a concert at MAGFest in Washington, DC, when a new idea popped in my head for an album project I'd always wanted to do. I had done tribute projects to games I had loved, TV shows and wrestlers, but none to the musicians who had influenced me. Someone at the merchandise table happened to mention that March of 2017 would mark twenty years since the tragic death of The Notorious B.I.G., one of my favorite rappers ever. Over the years since he passed, I'd heard of rappers reusing lines of Biggie, even remaking his tracks, but never a full dedication mixtape, and that's what I wanted to do. I called up my friend Fresh Kils, producer of "A Poet," told him the plan and we got to work after DC on what would be my B.I.G. tribute album.

The best thing about seeking out the way to pay homage to Biggie's output was that tracking down the source material wasn't hard. Almost every song in his discography contained a sample from an older song. While my mom saw that as a detriment, I thought it was spectacular. I assumed that re-sampling a sample wouldn't be very difficult, but the challenge would be in making these tracks sound similar enough for the listener to recognize, but different enough so that people wouldn't think the project was a cheap cash-in.

One of my college professors praised Biggie's storytelling ability, calling him a modern-day griot, a word used for a member of a class of traveling poets, musicians, and storytellers who maintain a tradition of oral history in parts of West Africa. To make his point he cited B.I.G.'s song "Got a Story to Tell," in which Biggie tells the unbelievably clever tale of a secret rendezvous with the girlfriend of a player from the New York Knicks basketball club, which is interrupted when the player comes home earlier than expected ("Maybe it was rained out or something," Biggie explains in the skit—impossible since basketball games are never cancelled due to rain). Biggie gets the brilliant idea to pretend he was robbing the home, and that's how he makes it out without incident. His myriad of lies at the end of the song while attempting to explain it to his friends just makes the story even more hilarious. I knew that I had to recreate that song for the mixtape, and I did by talking about the most unbelievable day in my life: November 8th, 2016.

In the middle of yet another tour, MC Lars and I were in a minivan, traveling through the American Midwest, on the way to a show in Minneapolis at the world famous First Avenue venue, connected to the 7th Street Entry, where the late great Prince got his start and filmed the classic "Purple Rain." We were the opening acts on mc chris's tour, which was going extremely well. As we drove, we saw TRUMP 2016 and MAKE AMERICA GREAT AGAIN signs on every billboard, in front of every home, and on every store along the way. We laughed, thinking "Oh, these poor souls. How could anyone believe in Donald Trump?"

We had stopped off a few days prior to drop off our absentee ballots, making our votes count. We were proudly with Hillary, much like we thought the rest of America was. When we pulled up to the show, Lars and I discussed how we were not going to make any mention of the election today, just that we hoped everyone voted. We did not. After my set, I went next door to grab a bite to eat, and there was a television on in the restaurant, tuned to the local news. The anchorman stated that the race was too close to call in many states, while in the Midwest, Donald Trump held a steady lead over the favorite, Hillary Clinton. We were about to get an upset.

I came back to the venue in time to join Lars on stage for a few songs that we would play from our forthcoming album, *The Dewey Decibel System*.

Between songs, Lars asked on the mic, "Should we check the results right now?"

I shook my head and mouthed, "No."

We played our songs and had a blast as we always did, making sure to not make another reference to the results of the 2016 presidential election. After the show, we drove to the hotel, silently. I didn't sleep a wink that night. It might be the first time I remember crying after an election. I simply couldn't believe it.

The next morning, I woke up with a text from a friend that read, "As the most positive person I know, please tell me that we're not doomed right now."

I read the text three times and didn't know how to respond. I tried to gather my thoughts and nothing came together for me. I wanted to tell my fans and supporters that things were going to be okay, that Trump's idea for America wouldn't become a reality. But I could not. Politics had always felt like a battle between the lesser of two evils, but this time it felt like the greatest of all evils had won. Lars and I tried to talk through this on the ride to our next city, but we both wound up crying by the end of the conversation. I wrote a really long Facebook post that in essence said the one positive I could pull from a Trump victory was that in times of crisis, art usually becomes bolder and more dynamic. If this trend holds up, the Trump administration will bring forth a groundswell and return of conscious, socio-politically focused art – and in turn, music will improve.

I would start with myself, and my version of "Got a Story to Tell." In it, I tried to maintain a tongue-in-cheek approach on such a traumatic moment by painting it as something that was so unreal, that surely all of us were dreaming.

> Thankfully it's almost a wrap.
> Worst campaigns in history; they both fall flat.
> First Ave., we on, cool as a fan, mics in hand,
> Know they won't elect that man,
> But they can and they will though.
> I'm trying to chill though,
> Even though these results

Are looking kinda ill yo.
I keep singing all the songs I wrote,
Thinkin' 'bout all the homies that I know don't vote,
And how I hustled from the road to get my absentee
    ballot in.
No doubt in my mind, this cat won't win...

This was a scary song to write. Prior to this, I hadn't taken my thoughts on politics to music. It wasn't because they weren't important to me, but I feared I was ill-equipped to deal with the eventual debate that songs like this would land me in. After I released the video, the first few YouTube commenters got the response I'd expected out of the way quickly.

"Stick to raps about video games. You have no idea what you're talking about."

"You idolize a gangster like The Notorious B.I.G., but ridicule a self-made success story like Trump? Stick to the nerd raps."

"You might wanna keep rapping about Mega Man and shut up about politics."

Many people want musicians to just shut up and sing, or stick to the music, not taking into consideration that we are also citizens, who walk these streets, pay taxes, and have a right to speak up on the way things are. These same people conveniently forget that for as long as we have existed, music has played a major part in the political fabric of our culture, and cultures around the world. Protest songs have played an essential part of music for centuries and will continue to do so. James Baldwin has so many great quotes, but one of my favorites is, "Artists are here to disturb the peace."

This release in 2017 inadvertently put me on a path to becoming a person I never imaging becoming – one who uses his platform to speak up about injustice, no matter how uncomfortable it was. I asked myself: *What is the point of having a following, no matter how small, if you don't do your best to make sure they hear the truth?*

I was ready to live to the fullest, despite how it might rub others the wrong way. I'm in a privileged position blessed with the opportunity to perform for crowds, though most of these were for a majority white, male audiences. It's the perfect opportunity to seize a teachable moment and use that time on stage to educate as well as entertain. Whereas in 2013 I couldn't verbalize how Trayvon's death shook me, I had found my voice and was ready to disturb the peace.

On my next release, *Extra Credit*, I revisited one of my favorite books of all time, *To Kill A Mockingbird*, to retell a story of discrimination I had known too well. The first time I'd read Harper Lee's book I was in the fifth grade, and even then, the story sank into me and never let go for many years. I just couldn't understand how a person could stand guilty in the court of public opinion before trial, despite evidence to the contrary. It was an early wake up call to the inner workings of the justice system in America. We shot a video to a song called "Airplane Mode," and in it, while just hanging out with friends, I was arrested for no reason and was transported in the back of a police car. That scene wasn't just for dramatic effect; it was and is a reality for Black and Brown people. And though my interaction with the police ended peacefully in the video, that certainly isn't the case all the time.

Sometimes as an artist you really have to remain careful about creating a self-fulfilling prophecy. Life has a way of imitating art sometimes. DWB (Driving While Black) is a very real thing, and the numbers don't lie. African-Americans are pulled over on average three times more than any other race, and are ten times as likely to die at the hands of police. It's not paranoia – it's fact.

After spending five years as a touring performer, driving up and down America's highways and byways, I always ran a loose ship. I was lucky enough to never have faced an arrest, suffered the fear of getting pulled over, or received any type of traffic violation or warning until recently. Yet on the *Extra Credit* tour, I was pulled over while out on the road *five* times.

There was the time during February in upstate New York, where, despite greeted by the nicest Highway Patrol officer, who commended me on my signaling before lane changing, pulled me over because I hadn't given enough time and warning between the signal and the actual lane change.

There was the time in March outside Tulsa, where I was pulled over for driving in the fast lane too long.

There was the time during April in Arkansas, where I was pulled over for well, you know, I don't even know why I was pulled over there.

There was also the time during May in Omaha when I was pulled over for tailgating the car in front of me and not giving the proper amount of space.

There was the time during June in North Carolina, where I was pulled over for speeding in an area with no posted speed limit signs.

There was the time a few years ago in Missouri when my tour mate was profiled and followed out of a Walmart to the parking lot, leading to us getting surrounded by squad cars.

These all sound like legitimate offenses, right? Well, here's the kicker. On none of these occasions was anyone charged or arrested.

However, on each of these occasions, I was asked to step out of the vehicle, if I had any weapons or drugs on me, and patted down and searched. And, in a new development, something I had never seen before, in real life or the movies occurred. If we were on the highway, in the last few instances, while my paperwork was processed, they "asked" me to sit inside the officer's vehicle, in the passenger's seat. That's correct. I've been inside of a police vehicle three times now, and just once was a video shoot.

A new protocol, perhaps? Not sure. But there I was, in a police vehicle, out of range from my friends (who were attempting to film on their phones), and behind the officer's dashboard camera, if there was one, with nothing but my word against his to detail the events of whatever might have happened next.

I imagined the worst of the worst-case scenarios. A scuffle. A chokehold. Or worse, a gunshot. But no matter what, I maintain despite the scary in-betweens of life on the road, there's nothing more satisfying or inspiring than getting to see new places. Just make sure you obey the rules of the road when you do. And say a prayer.

CHAPTER TWENTY ONE

A NEW RECORD

Might not leave my kids with wealth,
But I can leave a legacy and records that are felt
—"Family," *Mega Ran Com: Mission* (2014)

E VEN THE GREAT STAN LEE, a builder of universes, who passed away
while I was in the process of writing this book, struggled with his
place in the world, despite forging a legendary path. Lee stated:

> I used to be embarrassed because I was just a comic
> book writer while other people were building bridges
> and going on to medical careers. And then I began to
> realize: entertainment is one of the most important
> things in people's lives. Without it, they might go off
> the deep end. I feel that if you're able to entertain, you're
> doing a good thing.

The best part about being who I am now is anywhere I go, from
comic-cons to anime cons to festivals, even at the grimiest hip-hop-
centered shows, I get to talk video games, comic books, or pro wrestling
with any of the show-goers because they know exactly where I stand
on my love for nerdy things. Even people I would never have expected
to get it, get it. I opened a show for the great Sean Price (RIP) and, as I
was figuring out the next track to play, a man in the front row rocking
a Phillies cap and hoodie said, "Yo, play the *Mega Man* jawn!"

I couldn't believe it. I asked, "You down with *Mega Man*?" He nodded in agreement. The raucous Philly crowd roared in approval.

So, I played the *Mega Man* jawn. Again, and again. Year after year. Club after club, con after con. Will people get tired of the *Mega Man* rapper? Is that all that I am? Who knows?

Here's what I do know; even if there's nothing else, I want the world to know me as the guy who wasn't afraid to talk about what he knew and loved, who gave his work the love and care it deserved while bringing smiles to people's faces. I want history to know me as the guy who made a way out of a no way situation and showed others the path to independent success.

People ask me, "Why *Mega Man*?" It's as easy as "Why NOT *Mega Man*?" but also a complex answer. I love the music in the Mega Man games, and that's apparent. There are so many iconic tunes on those games I can connect to key moments in my childhood, and even adulthood. When I released the *Mega Ran* album in 2007, it wasn't to get rich or go viral – it was a love letter to something that had raised me for so long, and taught me to appreciate video game soundtracks. I feel so blessed others in the world feel the same way.

The second time I traveled to Japan, my friend Jeriaska arranged concerts with several accomplished composers in the video game scene, and we combined their sounds with mine to create the *Mega Ran Japan Remix* album and a documentary Blu-ray. These folks weren't just good musicians, they'd worked on classic game titles, from Streets of Rage 2 to Ape Escape and many more. The songs, while not my most popular, are among some of my favorites. During that trip, I got to speak with each remixer about what made *Mega Man* so important to them – they all had similar stories about the Blue Bomber. It wasn't just me. I wasn't the only one. I needed to know I wasn't as weird as I thought I was all these years ago. Like that crowd in Philly, musicians a world away had just as strong a connection to *Mega Man*'s music as I did.

Over the years, I've made so many *Mega Man* tracks that I got an email from the Guinness Book of Records this year asking me exactly how many *Mega Man* rap tracks I've made. I counted one hundred and thirty, which he called to tell me was a record… by a long shot. Guinness then made me an offer I couldn't refuse.

The reps at Guinness emailed me with a comment I often get: "If you're ever in London, you should come by!"

I responded with an unexpected, "Well actually, I'll be in London in three months!" Was I really visiting London then? No, not exactly. But I also wasn't going to miss out on an opportunity to appear in the pages of the Guinness Book of World Records. I called my friends in the UK, and within three months had arranged a short tour of the country. With the contacts I had accrued on my last few tours, things came together easily enough. I left a day off at the beginning and end of the tour in London for possible Guinness-related activities.

The crew at Guinness, elated at the news, planned out my day once my flight was booked. They sent a car to pick me up from the airport, like I imagine celebrities get. During this hour-long ride, a scene similar to *This Is Your Life* played in my head. My entire professional career flashed before my eyes. Playstation-made beats. Burned CDs. Four-track recorders. Breakups. Getting booed at Moody's. The freestyle in the park. I could hear my friends, my wife, even my mother asking me, "Did you ever imagine it could come THIS far?" I did not. I was across the world, getting picked up and driven to receive a Guinness World Record. It felt like a dream. I'd done something beyond even my wildest imagination. Young Raheem (and Scott) would feel so proud. I cried in the backseat of the cab.

Once I arrived, they had a sign up that said "Welcome, Mega Ran!" which sent the waterworks back into full blast. "All this for me?" I asked.

The staff then directed me to the on-site shower where I could get refreshed. They also had a meal prepared for me at the office, and we began a photo shoot. After capturing pictures, we went live on the Guinness World Records Facebook page and discussed the record. I played songs to an audience of thirty thousand via live stream. I got the chance to talk to the world about how a video game changed my life thirty years earlier. I still have a copy of the Mega Man issue of *Nintendo Power* that started it all. To say that this experience was surreal is a massive understatement.

The day after our meeting, my tourmate Sammus arrived, and we went to the movies to see *Black Panther* in South London. I remember the hype levels for the movie as off the charts in the US, with people of color feeling elated to see themselves represented on screen in such an extravagant production. I had no idea how that would translate to England. It did though, and in ways far beyond what I could have imagined.

The theater was full of dark-skinned people of African descent, dressed in traditional African garb. They were just as affected by the representation on screen as Americans were, and it was beautiful. I heard an older couple behind me sniffling by the end of the movie and saying things like, "I never thought I'd see this on a big screen." What was just another Marvel blockbuster to some became a landmark cultural event for Black people all over the world. I think seeing it in another country really helped to bring it home for me. For the second day in a row, I cried like a baby.

There I was, an African-American male, who found success in hip-hop music, much like many others had, but far differently. I attempted to carve a path where none was before, almost accidentally and I still live every day traveling into uncharted territory with no map, no key, and no guide, determined to keep making the first footprints in a world where none existed. I'm like Lewis and Clark if they were nice on the mic.

I managed to accomplish something that I never even knew possible in a sub-genre of music that is still fighting to become relevant and understood every day. I don't need riches or to win Grammy Awards (I wouldn't turn one down though), but all I've ever wanted, I've gotten, ten times over. I could think of the let-downs and situations that never panned out, but there are so many more that turned out better than I could have imagined, so I would rather dwell on those.

A few months later, Guinness mailed me an official plaque as well as a copy of the 2018 Guinness World Record book with my picture and a full-page article inside. I cried tears of joy as my wife and I framed the plaque and hung it on my office wall. I can't even call an event like this a bucket list moment; because I never dreamed it would be possible in a million years. There aren't a ton of success stories in Philadelphia, and even if another great thing never happens, I'm confident in the fact that I feel like a success every day.

When I say I've lost almost as much as I've gained on this journey, I mean it. No number of accolades can make up for the heartbreak that disappointment can bring. Friends have abandoned me. I've missed family funerals, weddings, and other important things for tours and shows that may not have even paid off. I've played the show of my life, been adored by hundreds as I walked off stage, only to receive a pat on the back for my efforts; and I've had to sleep in my car for the night because I couldn't afford lodging. I've had people come to me after shows and tell me they were suicidal and that my energy or something I'd said on stage made them want to live again. I've had people tattoo my lyrics onto their skin. My inbox is full of incredible stories from fans about how a song has gotten them through a rough moment. I put all of those into a folder that I labeled MOTIVATION, and I read it whenever I have a moment when I'm down.

The experiences I've had the opportunity to take part in have proved absolutely worth it, and I'd do it again in a heartbeat if I had the opportunity. I've made lifelong friendships through music, and the sacrifices I've made have led to a life story worth telling. I'm extremely thankful for it all, the good and the bad.

I have a loving wife and a mother to care for, a career to keep afloat, and a few thousand fans that accompany me every step of the way, through every triumph and every slip-up. For those things, I'm truly thankful and blessed.

You know, I heard those words so much about having to work twice as hard to get what I want out of life, that I finally learned how to apply it.

And as for a snappy, catchy, witty way to end this book, I'll leave you with one more of my own quotes: "The best part of the story comes at the end… and that part hasn't been written yet."

Thank you for reading!

Peace and Love!
Raheem

First Trip to Japan, 2011

First Trip to Paris, Fall 2012

Little Mega Ran with Santa, 1980

MAGFest with Bitforce, K-Murdock, Kadesh
Flow, CMF, EyeQ, Jan 2018

Mega Ran and Dad, June 2018

Mega Ran and friends at _The Call_ release party Feb 2006

Mega Ran and Ippo Yamada, composer of _Splash Blue_ which became _Splash Woman._ 2016

Mega Ran and Keiji Inafune, Fall 2016

Mega Ran and K-Murdock at The Smithsonian, 2017

Mega Ran and Momma Ran in Philadelphia, 2014

Mega Ran Freestyle, Orlando FL, 2012

Mega Ran Gets A Guinness World Record, Feb 2018

mega ran in studio 2004

Mega Ran in the ring at WWE Smackdown, July 4, 2017

Mega Ran with Transformers, Christmas 1985

Mega Ran, DN3 and Common, September

Mega Ran, EyeQ. Kadesh Flow and Shubzilla,
Anime Expo 2016, Los Angeles

On The Way To Prom, Fall 1995

Penn State Graduation, Fall 2000

Rachel and Raheem at their Engagement Party, 2015

Raheem and Rachel at their wedding, Nov 2015

Raheem at Christmas, 1982

Ran and mom at his 6th grade graduation, Fall 1989

Random in the Church, 2004. Photo by Hope McDowell

Still Shot From The _Fly_ Music Video Shoot, 2008